MORE MURDER IN THE FOURTH CORNER

TRUE STORIES OF WHATCOM & SKAGIT COUNTIES' EARLIEST HOMICIDES

1st edition.

Chuckanut Editions
Village Books
1200 11th St
Bellingham WA 98225
360-671-2626

research and writing by T. A. Warger
cover design by Vladimir Verano
page design by Brendan Clark

ISBN 9780989289160

LCCN 2015953540

Printed in Bellingham WA, USA.

also by T. A. Warger

books

Mount Baker (with John D'Onofrio)

Murder in the Fourth Corner

documentary films

The Mountain Runners (with Brian Young)

Shipyard (with David Lowrance)

Foreword

In *Murder in the Fourth Corner*, local historian and author Todd Warger chronicled thirteen actual and suspected murders that occurred in Whatcom County from 1880 to 1933. As the county's current sheriff, I was fascinated to learn of the tenacity and commitment my predecessors and other law enforcement officials had in seeking justice for victims and their families. While investigative techniques may have advanced over the years, the basic effective elements of good police work remain constant.

Murder in the Fourth Corner brought vivid reality to the lives of the victims and their families and superbly provided a glimpse into the history and geography of Whatcom County in an earlier era. The tragedy and sorrow that devastated families generations ago does not differ much from those suffered today.

In *More Murder in the Fourth Corner*, Mr. Warger continues the work he started in *Murder in the Fourth Corner* as he reports on eleven murders in Whatcom and Skagit counties.

— *Bill Elfo, Whatcom County Sheriff, 2015*

Author's Note

In a continuance to *Murder in the Fourth Corner*, you now hold in your hands *More Murder in the Fourth Corner*. These new pages contain, once again, a collection of true stories revealing the more unsavory side of our local history. New gruesome murders have been resurrected for your reading pleasure, many long forgotten. Not for a lack of grisly murders and other such slayings in Bellingham and Whatcom County, I have decided to also unearth the heinous crimes of our southern neighbor, Skagit County.

For those of you who have not read *Murder in the Fourth Corner*, I will reiterate that the stories you are about to read are true. I have written them as accurately as the historical record has recorded them and embellish no further. I have no malicious intentions in opening old family wounds. If a post-Great Depression-era story is told I presume local connections have dwindled to nonexistence. The stories within are set against a backdrop of the times of settlement and the Great Depression.

Many cities, towns, villages, hamlets, districts and counties across the United States have their own skeletons that they'd prefer to keep in the closet. Whatcom and Skagit counties are no different. We have had our fair share of heinous criminal acts, murders, slayings, lynching, serial killings, human trafficking, white slavery, and immigrant smuggling, all of which existed just a short time ago, and unfortunately still operates to this day. In Whatcom and Skagit Counties, there were turbulent racial divides and labor riots involving Chinese, Japanese, Sikh and other ethnic groups. Various clashes with the indigenous Coast Salish peoples erupted into unlawful murder. There were recorded cases of vigilantism, where those involved sought quick and illegal justice by their own hand. Clashes involving the dark underworlds of prostitution, prohibition, and the Ku Klux Klan existed amongst us here as well.

For how long can our closet doors restrain the weight of this history? It is our history, like it or not! I want to reveal a portion of it.

— *T. A. Warger, Bellingham, WA, 2015*

Acknowledgments

To all those people who contributed in making this book possible, I thank you sincerely for all your efforts.

I am fortunate and humbled to have had story contributions from Nooksack historian Jim Berg, and Seattle resident Daryl McClary, with whom I am honored to be acquainted.

There are so many people to whom I owe a debt of gratitude for their help:

To Courtney Olsen, my editor, you are magnificent!

Sierra Ellingson and Brian Young, many thanks for redesigning the maps for this edition.

Heather Britain, Kirstie Massey and Katie Johnson at the Whatcom Superior Court, thank you for helping me retrieve court records.

Alison Costanza, Washington State Archives Northwest Regional Branch, and Ruth Steele, Center for the Pacific Northwest Studies, thanks for years of help.

Maggie Cogswell, research assistant at the Washington State Archives in Olympia, many thanks for pulling boxes, upon boxes of prisoner records.

Jeff Jewell, Whatcom Museum photo archivist and historian, thanks for your commitment and suggestions.

Elaine Walker at the Anacortes Museum archives, thanks for your help.

Laura Nelson Jacoby, many thanks for sharing your grandfather Galen Biery's photo collection.

Rachel Mehl and Kim Cunningham, thanks for letting me write about your family tragedy.

Renee Sherrer, thanks for your editing, support and patience.

Roman Stadtler, thanks for your editing and long time friendship.

Vladimir Verano, thanks for another great cover design.

Dean Kahn, thanks for your input on this project.

Brendan Clark, Chuck and Dee Robinson, and all the wonderful people at Village Books, thanks for your help with this project.

In memory of the victims written about in *Murder in the Fourth Corner* and *More Murder in the Fourth Corner*. May they not be forgotten.

Ada "Borssee" Wilson
Addie Roper
Agnes Janson
Christine "Nicholson" Lavine
Clara "Newell" Gaultier
David Shively
Dominica "Mario" Guisseppe
Dorothy McGuire
Elsie "Marjorie Dale "Worstell
Ernest Grimm
Floyd Grimm
Frederick Dames
Fred Helms
Freeman
Gertrude McGuire
Hermit Smith
Hugh Boyd
Jack Green
James Bell
James Logan
J. Horton Thurston
John Erickson
Joseph Dixon
Josephine Thomson
Louie Sam
Martin Orner
Michael Padden
Odia Brisco
Orpha "Wilder" McGuire
Pete Hannesson
Ralph Shoemaker
Sam Thompson
Young Shee Wah

La vengeance est un mets que l'on doit manger froid.
(Revenge is a dish that should be eaten cold.)
        — *Charles Maurice de Talleyrand- Périgord (1754–1838)*

For the thing I greatly feared has come upon me. And what I dread has happened to me,
I am not at ease, nor am I quiet; I have no rest, for trouble comes.

        — *Job 3:25.26*

Table of Contents

Part I
Whatcom

Chapter 1
Ghastly Dealings in Blaine

As the murder scene was depicted in the *Seattle Sunday Times* magazine section, September 22, 1907.

The Fiendish Act

On Saturday night, January 19, 1907, the city of Blaine was still in the freezing "grip of the Snow King." For the past week, temperatures held firm in the 20s, with snow falling throughout Puget Sound. Nearly a foot covered the ground along Washington Avenue. Further to the north, in Vancouver,

B.C., seven inches of snow had fallen on top of the previous nights' seven, and the city's streetcar service was immobilized until a snowplow could clear the tracks. In other places, deep snowdrifts were impossible to remove as the howling wind quickly rebuilt them. Many of the telephone and telegraph lines were broken or down. Police ordered merchants to clear their sidewalks. New Westminster fought to keep the rail lines free from drifts with hired emergency work gangs, and trains coming in from the east were delayed on the tracks.

That same week, Seattle was reporting layers of snowfall from previous storms and temperatures ranging in the 20s. The immediate worry was the reduction of coal supplies as the trains were running low themselves, sitting idle on the tracks, unable to move. Newspapers were calling for impending relief. It was projected that a thaw was coming in the next thirty-six hours and temperatures were expected to rise as rain moved in from off the Pacific coast.

It was that particular Saturday evening when James Marcuse, owner of the City of Paris dry goods store located on Washington Avenue, decided to close his business early due to the weather. No one had entered his shop in hours. Marcuse told his employee, Serinda Adeline (Addie) Roper, it was time to lock-up. Addie had worked at the City of Paris for four years, specializing as a dressmaker, and running most of Marcuse's business.

After locking the front door, Marcuse opened the cash-drawer and pulled out Addie's week's worth of wages, a total of $15.00, and handed it to her. Addie removed a chamois bag from her blouse and placed her pay within. It wasn't the first time Marcuse scolded her for keeping her savings on her person; he suspected it made her vulnerable to thugs. Addie had an adverse distrust of banks, which may have come from the economic collapse of the 1890s. Many had lost their shirt in the financial panic and collapse of banks during the Depression.

Leaving the warm store sometime before 9 o'clock that evening, Addie walked straight into a cold driving wind coming off of Semiahmoo Bay. She headed for the Wolten Brother's Grocery Store, owned by German brothers, William and Paul, to purchase a few needed items. As she was the only customer in the store at the time, her order was filled quickly. Paul, the eldest, fetched Addie's items off the shelves, while she conversed with William.

The Wolten Brother's Grocery Store was Addie's last known stop on her way home. Circa: 1900s. Whatcom GenWeb.

Paying, she pulled a wad of bills from her purse. William shook his head, scolding Addie for carrying that much money. He offered to hold her earnings in his store safe over night, where she could retrieve it the following day when it was light out. He proposed that since it was Saturday night, rough crowds would be on the street, hitting the saloons. The boys were over from the fisheries at Semiahmoo Spit spending their pay on drinks and girls down in the restricted district and a boatload of men had landed earlier from Point Roberts, which always led to an increase in torments about town.

Addie Roper took no heed to the warning. She was known as a force to be reckoned with, and a fearlessly independent woman who could hold her own in a battle with men. She had never married, nor was she ever known to court, and was a great supporter of the temperance movement. She lived directly across from the disreputable Reception Saloon. Those leaving heavy with drink respected her property and stayed quiet around her home. In return, Addie didn't fuss with her neighbors. She had been a resident of Blaine for many years and proudly held the love, admiration and respect of the city.

Perhaps to give the Wolten brothers peace of mind, Addie revealed that she was on her way to drop some fresh fruit off to a sick friend, and would be headed straight home thereafter. Reentering the cold January night, she went about her errands. She wanted to get home early, as the cold temperatures meant it would take longer to heat her home before turning in. Leaving Washington Avenue and turning onto G Street, she carried her umbrella in one hand and packages from Wolten's in the other. Approaching her house, Addie would have heard the wild hoopla coming from the Reception Saloon on the right side of the street. At that point in her journey she would have passed the skeletal trees of the apple orchard, which ran up close to the left side of her house.

A photograph taken of G Street from F Street, in January 1907. To the right, note the Reception Saloon, a façade building behind two poles. Behind the rooftop building (bakery) on the extreme right would have been the location of the Roper home. Bellingham Herald March 16, 1907.

The same view as it appears today, taken in 2015. Whatcom Fitness (in the foreground), was the location of Addie Roper's home. Photo taken by the author.

Down within the orchard, Roy Wren, Oscar McDonald, Irving Hoff and Thomas Stevenson were having a great time throwing snowballs at each other. Addie asked the boys if they were having fun. Arms full, she walked around to her back door where she entered her small mudroom before going into her home. What happened next is conjecture, but is considered the best scenario of the events leading up to Addie Roper's death. For the next twenty to thirty minutes she and an invader would be locked in an intensively violent and brutal struggle.

Addie set her packages on the kitchen table, and placed her open umbrella near a wood fire floor heater to dry. The house had no electricity, and she would have had to remove one of her gloves to light a kerosene lamp. The intruder must have been silently waiting, allowing her time to move deeper into the home, away from the doors and windows. It would appear that she stepped into her bedroom, where the intruder, wearing a red bandana handkerchief over his lower face as a mask, awaited her arrival. What was the intruder's motive? She was suspected to have had money hidden on her, or somewhere on the premises – so it could have been robbery. Were there other intentions? Murder may not have been the objective, as the

21

intruder wasn't prepared; everything that would be used to murder Addie would be pulled from her own home.

Addie may or may not have noticed the intruder before he assaulted her. Having the immediate advantage, he came out of the shadows and struck a heavy blow to incapacitate her. With blood streaming down the side of her face, she recovered and began to fight back. He must have been surprised by her recovery, unaware of her fortitude. The red bandana mask covering his face could have been pulled away, revealing his identity, and then it was, perhaps, that Addie recognized her assailant. He too may have been surprised for a moment, at being recognized, at her will to live, for she fought hard enough to scratch his face with her nails, causing blood to draw upon his cheek. Her defensive assault infuriated the intruder, who in turn hit Addie hard enough to unbalance her, and she fell backwards, striking the back of her head against a sewing machine. The intruder lifted Addie from the floor and flung her onto her bed. She continued to fight him off as he tore into her blouse. It was rumored that she had sewn some of her wealth into the layers of her clothing, and whether he was attempting to locate the wealth, or to unclothe her is unknown. Addie continued to fight, and whether in fighting or protecting her bounty, she tore a piece of lace fabric from her own garments and clutched it tight in a fist.

Infuriated, the intruder had had enough of the wrangling. Did he find her riches? Of that we can't be sure, as it was unknown just how much she had; soon enough, an assessment of her property would be impossible.

The intruder came to the decision that Addie had to die, but he wasn't finished with her yet. She was alleged to be a 37 year-old virgin, and if he knew of her, it was likely he knew this. He pulled her dress up and unbuckled his belt. She must have been screaming; the intruder noted a foot-long rod of some sort nearby, and picked it up. He struck her several times with it to quash her cries. Pulling the red bandana from around his neck, he shoved it down her throat, using the stick as a ramrod to thrust it deeper.

After violently raping Addie, he rose from her limp body, and pulled her dress and petticoats back down to cover her.

The intruder found a small hatchet used for splitting kindling in the corner of the room. Addie must have passed out from the gag and assault, as no defensive wounds were discovered when the hatchet split her skull. The first swing glanced off the side of her head, severing an ear. It was followed by more accurate strikes. The intruder looked upon his handiwork, threw the bedding over her corpse, and doused the bedroom floor with a can of kerosene. After igniting a blaze, the intruder slipped out of the house into the snowy winter's night.

Just after 10 o'clock that evening, the fire alarm at Blaine City Hall sounded, calling in the volunteer fire brigade. Arriving in record time, the men quickly gathered their fire-fighting equipment and ran the short distance over from H to G Street. Fortunately, the city had just purchased a new hose-cart, and the older one was still in service, thus doubling their power. The volunteer force arrived in time to save the house, although the room where the fire started was fairly gutted. The young Roy Wren, who had been one of the kids throwing snowballs in the orchard, ran up to Fire Chief, Frank O'Dell, and proclaimed that Miss Roper was in the house. O'Dell sent runners out to check her work place, only to find it closed. O'Dell's heart sank thinking of her inside the now embalmed bedroom. As the house smoldered, the fire chief and Constable George Wellington investigated the ruins. The interior was still hot and smoking, forcing the men to place wet handkerchiefs over their mouths to breathe. The odor of kerosene was strong, indicating its use as an accelerant. The men noted a mound on the bed. Upon investigation, O'Dell could smell the distinctive stench of burnt flesh. He knew it well enough, a cross between a sweet copper metal and burnt barbecued pork. He realized they had either a tragedy or a crime on their hands. Wellington and O'Dell ceased their sifting of the ruins, deciding to alert the county sheriff and coroner.

The Blaine Fire Hall had just received a new hose cart and fortunately retained their older one. Circa: 1900s. Courtesy of Jim Doidge.

For most of the night, the fire brigade watched for flare-ups in the smoldering home. Whatcom County Sheriff, Andrew Williams and Sheriff's Deputy, Thomas DeHaven, made their way to Blaine by train. Just before dawn, the house was cool enough to enter safely. It was only by sheer luck that the firemen were able to keep the house standing. O'Dell entered the structure, making sure the floor and ceiling were well secured. Seeing nothing unusual in the front room, they worked their way toward the bedroom, where it was evident the fire had started. Remarkably, the floor was still firm. On one side of the room stood an iron bed with a mound of charred blankets, a quilt and sheets.

"There's something under those covers, DeHaven," Williams commented. "Do you smell coal-oil?" Williams conjectured that perhaps the kerosene lamp was the cause for the smell. DeHaven nodded doubtfully at the suggestion.[1]

Williams indicated that the men should back out of the dwelling. "We need to post guards and await the coroner to arrive before we go further,"

[1] Thirty-two years later, in 1939 while in retirement, Deputy Sheriff DeHaven documented the opening moments of the case for "True Detective Mysteries." Quotes have been pulled from this documentation.

24

he said. It wasn't just the fumes of kerosene he could smell; agreeing with O'Dell's's assessment, he too smelled burning flesh.

Addie Roper's house, miraculously saved from total destruction by the Blaine fire department, located only a street away. Courtesy of Dean Kahn.

The remnants of Addie Roper's home on G Street. Bellingham Reveille.

A few hours later, 56 year-old coroner and physician Henry Thompson arrived from Bellingham. The men reentered the room and approached the burnt bundle on the bed. Thompson grabbed the blankets and yanked them back. Williams' worst suspicions were confirmed. The half-charred corpse of Addie Roper lied on her back staring in horror toward the ceiling. Her head was split and her face bloodied, cut and bruised. Thompson waved off the odor of burnt flesh and moved in closer. Although a great deal of the body was blackened, much of the shoulders and head were intact; her long hair was singed away. Thompson made a double take. Looking closer still, he noticed that Addie's mouth was awkwardly open and that her throat was bulging. Her face was a purplish-black, but that wasn't unusual under the conditions. The coroner looked into her mouth and jerked back, looking toward Williams. "There's a gag stuffed in her mouth…it looks like a red bandana handkerchief. And smell that kerosene! Williams, this is murder followed by arson."

Shortly after the fire was extinguished, Constable William Allen "Doan" Dell made his way to the Blaine train depot where the midnight "Owl" train was preparing its departure south toward Mount Vernon in Skagit County. Dell was intent on arresting 23 year-old Raymond Lange,[2] on suspicion of being involved in the murder. Why Dell had this suspicion is unclear. Lange and his business partner, Harry Watts, were taking the train to Mount Vernon to secure funds for a business venture. Dell knew both men, but arrested only Lange, leaving Watts to continue the journey.

---

2   Sometimes documented as "Lang."

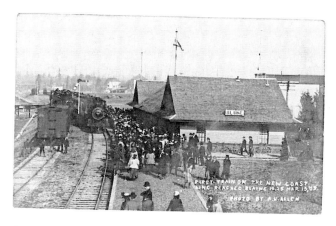

Blaine Railroad Depot, 1909. Constable "Doan" Dell arrested Raymond Lange at the Depot the night of the murder, as he was about to board the "Owl Train" for Mount Vernon. Courtesy of Jim Doidge.

RAYMOND LANGE.
Held as a suspect.

A drawing of suspect Raymond Lange appearing in the Bellingham Herald on January 23, 1907.

Inquest

"Murder of the foulest character, followed by arson has stirred the population of Blaine to the highest pitch of excitement," exclaimed the *Bellingham Herald* on Monday, January 21, 1907:

"The crime is one of the most gruesome and ghastly ever committed in the Northwest," stated Coroner Thompson. "The murderer did his work with horrifying completeness. After cruelly beating the woman over the head, a gag was thrust down her throat. This alone, without the severe head trauma would have caused death by strangulation. To add further horror to the ghoulish deed, the villain or villains, poured kerosene over the prostrate form of the dead woman and set the building afire. Try as he would, the person responsible for the brutal murder could not cover up the fact that the woman had been attacked in a manner that would cause the most case-hardened brigand to shudder."

News of the murder circulated from Canada to San Francisco. Bellingham Herald Headline of January 22, 1907.

Sunday morning, Thompson, with the assistance of Blaine physicians, Drs. Alexander and A. Sutherland, performed an autopsy. The work was performed where the body lay, for fear of disturbing the fragile condition of the remains. It was determined that five blows had been dealt to the skull. There were two wounds to the back of the head at the base. Two wounds were found on the left side of the head, the first at the top of the skull, severing the left ear, another against the jaw, and a blow to the right side of the head. Both doctors stated that the impact of each blow was enough to cause unconsciousness, but not necessarily death. A sharp instrument did the work, presumably the hatchet head found near the body. Though a sharp instrument made the wounds in front, Dr. Sutherland noted a blunt object had inflicted the wounds to the back of her skull.

"A right-handed person delivered the severe wounds found on the left side of the head," remarked Dr. Sutherland. "It is apparent that the woman was facing the murderer while he was delivering his blows."

The most gruesome discovery was the gag found wedged deep inside Addie's throat. It was a red bandana handkerchief with an array of apple blossoms along the edges. Upon removal, they saw it was heavily stained with blood. So tight was the gag that considerable force had to be used to extract it. The doctors assumed something had to have rammed the gag deeper.

A coroner's inquest was held at Blaine City Hall; the jury was sworn in at 4:55 am. They remained in session until 10 o'clock that morning. Thompson led the six-man panel[3] through the crime scene before convening.

The charred remains were lying at the foot of the bedstead, facing upward, where the victim had either fallen as a result of the blows, or was thrown down by the murderer. Her arms were held in a defensive position, as if to ward off the attacker. The left hand gripped a piece of garment, but the hand and the cloth within its clutch were so badly burned that identification

---

3 Chairman James F. Laytham, John H. Dahl, John Penno, D. C. Senter, A. W. Burley and Donald Montfort.

was impossible. The right hand still retained her glove, which, though badly scorched, had preserved enough of her prints to render identification. Two rings were found on the fingers of her right hand, but no trace could be found of a large diamond ring, which Addie was known to have worn on her left.

The position of the body would indicate that after the blows had been delivered, she had struggled with the murderer. It was also held by some of the jury that the bed quilt had been thrown over her head to muffle her cries.

Strong fumes of kerosene still lingered inside the house and on Addie's clothing, which was saturated in an oily substance, indicating that fuel had been poured around the room and over her body in an attempted to torch the home. Somehow, not all of her clothing had been burned. During the night, witnesses observed that the odor of burning oil could be detected from over a block away.

On the inquest stand, in the presence of the coroner's jury, Dr. Sutherland testified that there was no doubt in his mind that Addie Roper had been murdered. Evidence showed that "the blows on the head were directed by a person with intent to render the woman unconscious," and because "the murderer had set fire to the building to cover up the crime," asserted Dr. Sutherland.

Witness James Marcuse, owner of the City of Paris, said that Addie had left the store at about 9 o'clock that evening. He paid her regular salary of $15.00 for the week's work, and he was of the opinion that she had carried considerable more money on her than just the week's worth. Neither Addie's purse, nor her wages, known to have been in her possession while shopping during the evening, were found. Marcuse identified a watch and chain found on the woman's body, as well as the two rings and a stickpin, as markers of Addie's identity.

Witness William Max Wolten testified that Addie Roper was in their store around 9:30 pm, and that he sold her some candy, crackers and fruit. "She was exceptionally jolly," said Wolten. He said he noticed that she carried a considerable amount of money, and suggested that she place it in the store safe, with the opportunity to retrieve it the next day. "She replied that she could take care of it all right."

Witness Paul Wolten corroborated his brother's story, stating that Addie left the store for her home around 9:35 pm, and that no other patrons had been inside at the time. It was after 10 pm when he heard the fire alarm.

Raymond Lange was led from his cell to the inquiry by Deputy Sheriff DeHaven under a barrage of hisses and boos from a large mob gathered in front of city hall. Many snarling remarks were shouted advocating a lynching. Handcuffed and trembling under the gaze of the large crowd, Lange was taunted as he was led inside and seated before the jury. He was "rigorously examined" by the coroner.

Regardless of the pressure placed upon him, Lange answered questions in a vivid and straightforward manner, and was believed to be most convincing. He relayed that he had only arrived in Blaine the Tuesday before, and had been working odd jobs since his arrival. When he wasn't working he would stay at the Reception Saloon, recounting that on the evening of the fire he was in the saloon when someone opened the front door, and he noticed the smell of kerosene. Lange ran to the door and saw smoke issuing from what was Miss Roper's home. He said he yelled "Fire!" and that Clarence Manning, Bud Hess, and himself ran to the house. The front door was locked, so he and Hess broke it in, only to be engulfed by smoke. They didn't think there was anything they could do, so they left.

The questioning continued; the coroner imposed that if Lange were new in town, happened to be in the saloon at the time of the fire, and was the first on the scene, why was it then that he was on a train headed out of town just a few hours later? Lange claimed that he and Harry Watts had been talking about opening a café counter in the back of the Reception Saloon. The train to Mount Vernon was planned, he asserted, to talk with people who Watts knew, regarding money for the venture. The saloon owner Clarence Manning and the bartender Dewey Snavely backed Lange's claim that the two were in fact planning to rent a portion of the saloon for such a purpose.

Lange said that he, along with Watts, intended to leave on the 5:20 pm train, but that the plan had fallen through. Later, however, they met at the depot prior to the arrival of the midnight "Owl" train, which was where Blaine Constable[4] William Allen "Doan" Dell arrested Lange as he was about to board the train. It was then that Lange gave his ticket to Watts, who had not yet purchased one. The fact that Watts did not buy a ticket, and expected to pay his fare to the conductor, was held to be a "queer" act if it were fact that they had been planning the trip.

It was at this point in questioning that Lange posited his belief that Harry Watts and another person knew something of the Roper affair. Lange reiterated the statement by saying, "I have an opinion that they know something of the case." How Lange came to this conclusion, we do not know, but the coroner's authority over the inquest gave Thompson the power to issue an arrest warrant for Watts. Constable William Dell was ordered by Sheriff Williams to travel to Mount Vernon and bring Watts back to Blaine.

Lange realized the seriousness of the position he was in, but maintained his story in such a straightforward and unfaltering manner as to convince the jury that he was not guilty of the crime for which he was charged. However, he was ordered to be held without bond as a material witness until the case was solved. Unfortunately for Lange, being brought to court proffered an investigation into his past and he was found to be a wanted man by the U. S. Army for desertion from Fort Assiniboine, Montana.

Questioning of other witnesses continued, and next up was Clarence Manning, who was one of the first persons to arrive at the fire. He conceded

4   "Constable" and "city sheriff" were interchangeable titles in the early 1900s, and William Dell appears in writings using both titles. He was relegated to night watchman, which was considered the lowest usage of the position.

to breaking open the front and back doors to see if anyone was in the house, crying out "Is there anybody in there?" to which there was no response. He stated positively that he could smell coal oil. As for Lange, Manning confirmed his alibi, agreeing that he was indeed in the saloon at the time upon which the fire must have been started and that Lange was one of the men who accompanied him to the burning house.

After a string of witnesses were questioned, it was the consensus of the inquest jury that Addie was murdered for her money. Close friends confirmed that she had an aversion to banks, and preferred to keep her money in her own possession. She was thrifty and frugal, but was known to be giving to others. Her expenses were light, as she had no rent, inheriting the house from her father. She had a preserving disposition, and this, with her ideas of banking institutions, which was well known to all classes of people in her community, was cited as the leading cause of the attack and subsequent murder. It was presumed that she made a desperate attempt to drive the invader away; the severe blows to the head rendered her unconscious, in addition to the gag in her mouth, and that she had been killed to cover the crime.

At 10 o'clock in the morning the room was cleared of spectators, and the jury rendered a verdict as follows:

> *We the undersigned find Raymond LANGE not guilty. We bind Raymond LANGE over to be used as a witness. We find the deceased came to her death by a sharp instrument in the hands of some unknown person and by strangulation and the building set on fire with gasoline or kerosene. Miss Addie ROPER was most foully murdered in her home and her body set on fire by means of kerosene on the 19th of January 1907 about 10 o'clock; five wounds were discovered on the skull, a red ___ handkerchief was forced into her mouth, the house was completely gutted by fire and the body burned in a horrible way...a most brutal and fiendish murder was committed.*

(Signed) James F. Laytham, forman, C. John H. Dahl, D. C. Senter, John Penno, A. W. Burley, Donald Montfort

"Doan" Dell

After the verdict was read into the record, Sheriff Williams, on Thompson's orders, called for Blaine Constable William Allen "Doan" Dell. The Constable was ordered to proceed at once on the next train for Mount Vernon and return Watts to Blaine for questioning. Williams figured Dell was the last to see Watts and would be familiar with what he was wearing since he had seen him when he had arrested Lange at the depot.

William Allen "Doan" Dell was a hard looking individual, whose features were not a bit pleasing to the eye. He had a dark complexion, which matched his disposition. His steely cold gray eyes were terrifyingly hypnotic and piercing, only enhanced by his dark bushy eyebrows and cropped brown hair. He had a jagged scar on the back of his left hand, a wide cut scar on his right chin, and a deep pit scar on his left temple. Dell was no giant in stature, standing just above five-foot-six in height and weighing 150 pounds. He may have had a slight limp from a broken ankle he had suffered some years back.

Dell was known to drink hard and was feared by the women "inmates" of the waterfront's restricted district for his incalculable temperament. He worked when and wherever he was inclined; occasionally employed at the Jenkins Lumber Mill Co., in Blaine, or the Acme Shingle Mill. At some point he was hired on as a Constable for Blaine.

Dell was born in Ontario, Canada in 1860, the eldest of four siblings. He was generally known by his nickname, "Doan,"[5] as it was his mother's maiden name (Catherine Jane Doan). He made it through seventh grade before leaving to work. He owned a farm, and eventually married Maggie Jane

---

5   Sometimes "Doane" or "Dolman."

Wilson[6] in 1885 in 10th Conc-of-Flos, Wyebridge, Ontario. The couple would eventually have three daughters.[7] Little is known of Maggie, other than that she passed away January 9, 1931 in Seattle, WA.

We know less of Dell's life other than that he had typhoid fever when he was young, and served in the Canadian Volunteer Army. His mother died of stomach cancer in 1892, and his father, Ephraim, died in 1905 of dropsy, also known as edema. Little is know of his brothers, Albert and John, who either died early, or fell out of touch with Dell.

During the afternoon of Sunday, January 20th, Constable "Doan" Dell boarded the train and headed south to Mount Vernon.

HARRY WATTS
Suspected Murderer of Addie Roper

Drawing of Harry Watts. Bellingham Herald.

---

6   Also, recorded as "Rosanna Margaret Wilson."

7   Pauline, Frieda and Edna. All would eventually take the last name, "Frick," presuming Maggie remarried.

Investigation

Miss Addie Roper at 37 years old. Addie was reputedly beloved by all in the small border town of Blaine, Washington. Bellingham Herald, September 12, 1907.

Addie Roper was 37 years old at the time of her tragic death. She had been a resident of Blaine for twenty-five years, and was considered the "Golden Girl" of the city, which was primarily due to the wide breadth of civic activities she tirelessly pursued. Unwilling to give up on her municipal pursuits, and ever the independent woman, Addie never showed interest in courtship or marriage. "Miss Roper," said the *Blaine Journal*, on January 25, "was loving, gentle and kind, a true friend of the poor, the sick and the needy. ... Blaine has lost one of the choicest women and the memory of her beautiful life will have an abiding influence over the lives of others."

Addie was born in Missouri, in August 1869. Her father, Robert Henry from Trigg, Kentucky already had seven children from a previous marriage. Addie's mother, Margaret Kirkpatrick, would bear him eleven more. It was sometime in 1883 that Robert moved most of his family to Blaine, where they settled on Semiahmoo. Shortly thereafter he purchased a house in town on G Street, and the family divided. A portion of the family moved onto a farm across the Canadian border, in White Rock, four of her brothers took residence on the outskirts of Blaine, and three of her sisters relocated to Seattle and Port Townsend.

By 1889, when Addie was 20, her father died and her mother moved to White Rock. Addie was left the house in Blaine, which was paid off. The following year she was making a living as a professional dressmaker.

The inhabitants of Blaine were enraged by the violent nature of the crime in their community. They were desperate to know if the man who had committed the murder was among them. Rumors were rampant; a lynching was the only conclusion they found worthy, and they wanted it immediately. The pressure to find the murderer was surely heaviest on the sheriff and his staff.

Right after the coroners' inquest, Sheriff Andrew Williams began his investigation, accompanied by his trusted deputy, Thomas DeHaven. Williams collected the small axe head and bloodied handkerchief bandana as evidence. The two men looked over the crime scene in daylight for further clues before souvenir seekers descended upon the house. Even in the cold January air, the embers were still warm. Making their way through the charred debris they reentered what was left of Addie's bedroom. The two lawmen sifted through the burnt bedding and discovered a foot-long handle or stick of some kind lying on the bed, which had gone untouched by the fire. Thinking that its locality was odd, they held it as evidence.

With Harry Watts, their primary suspect, actively pursued by Constable Dell, the lawmen walked down to the waterfront where the restricted "red-light" district was located on pilings over the tidal flats, to inquire about Watt's lodgings and possible alibi. The Baudy House, which was four or five blocks from Addie Roper's home and halfway down the city wharf, was one of the so-called "sporting resorts" in the district. The "Madam" or "Mistress" of the establishment, Mildred Neilson, claimed that Watts was at her place playing cards when the fire alarm sounded, and was sure that others would vouch for his alibi, as there were many women in the Baudy House that night. Perhaps Rae Brown, who it was known Watts was sweet on, could back the claim.

One particular working girl, Rita Calvert[8] confirmed that Watts was definitely there the evening of the fire. Mildred Neilson spoke up, claiming, "Harry Watts is too much of a baby to commit a crime of that kind." Asked as to her opinion of who was capable of the crime, Neilson, in a sarcastic tone responded, "Oh, some of the 'Four Hundred gang,' some of the goody, goody people, who likely knew that the girl had money, and probably were detected and had to do the deed to shield themselves."

DeHaven persevered, inquiring if there was any common knowledge regarding Addie Roper in the district. He discovered from the "inmates" that it was generally known that she didn't trust banks and that she had plenty of money in her house. If shopkeepers to the inmates at the Baudy House knew of Roper's private banking practices, it was surely possible that the murderer did as well. DeHaven would claim he used a fine-toothed comb on the waterfront, but to his chagrin, found nothing that resembled a clue as to who the murderer or murderers might be. "As is usual in such cases and among such characters, no one knew anything; they had heard nothing."

After questioning the inhabitants of the Baudy House, the officers went over to the Reception Saloon to speak with Dewey Snavely, the bartender, who said he was willing to give them an interview.

Snavely said he was on duty from 5 o'clock Saturday afternoon until 6 o'clock Sunday morning. He knew Watts well enough to know that he was looking for some startup money for a café in the saloon, and that Watts

8   Calvert was born in Michigan, 1885. Her father was Canadian and her mother, from Spain. The 1910 census lists her living at 611 1/2 Sixth St., 3rd Precinct, in Seattle's Ward 1. Living with her at the address were 43 females and one male, (all 18-35 years old) all with no occupation.

said he was going to Mount Vernon to see a friend for a loan. Snavely told DeHaven that Watts didn't have the nerve to kill a woman. "I do not believe he had anything to do with it," he said.

Dewey Snavely offered the sheriff and his deputy one new clue; he remembered seeing a mysterious man wearing a black slouched hat, with a red-whiskered, stubby-length beard, not once, but twice that night. The first time he came in asking for matches, and he didn't buy a drink. He walked out front and seemed to be looking across at the Roper home. Snavely said he hadn't seen the fellow before, and hadn't since. The lawmen, seemingly, took no notice of Snavely's suspicions.

Sheriff Williams met with reporters, affirming their position on the case, acknowledging that they were aware of the rumors afloat, and assuring that many were groundless and the result of over-imagination. Afterward, he continued interviewing potential witnesses, while DeHaven decided to sift through the burned house once more.

By mid-afternoon the men rendezvoused to compare notes. Williams asked DeHaven if he had any theories, to which he had none. The sheriffs' deputy claimed he "had heard thousands of rumors and suspicions, but tangible evidence, he had none." They began to speculate. It was Williams' belief that the murderer knew Addie Roper and that he had worn the bandana over his face with the intent to rob her unrecognized, but that it had all gone wrong. He proposed that she must have removed it from the robber's face, and in recognizing him, he made the brash choice to gag and kill her, thinking that a fire would incinerate the body and all evidence against him.

Williams posited that rumors claiming Addie "kept a wad of bills in her corset," and that some interviewees also claimed they knew for a fact that she had $20 gold coins sewn into her corset, made it likely that the embroidery found in her left hand was from her own clothing. Why? The hand was also clutching a safety pin with which the money was likely pinned into the corset. Williams surmised that while Addie was fighting off her assailant, she must have torn the garment as a means of protecting her money.

"I think," said Williams, "she was hit when she entered the house, and then, half-conscious, was dragged into the bedroom…robbery was the motive." He feared that the people of Blaine would go into frenzy if someone weren't apprehended soon; he was also afraid that the frenzy and abounding rumors would lead to someone lynching an innocent person, which was the last thing they needed. But the city craved a culprit. As it was, the city police force was rounding up all strangers on the streets who could not give a good account of themselves during the time of the fire, and hauling them to jail.

Matters were not improving when Williams received a call from Dell in Mount Vernon, who hadn't found any leads on the whereabouts of Watts.

Williams recalled the name "Rae Brown," the woman who came up during questioning in the restricted district, and who Watts was sweet on. Brown appeared to be the person in question whom Watts was seeking to secure money for his café business. It was almost certain that she was a house-Madam of her own "sporting resort" in Skagit County, noted to be most attractive; a slim-figured woman with golden blond hair. Williams ordered Deputy DeHaven to take the train to Mount Vernon and find Rae Brown, as that was probably where he'd find Harry Watts.

Disembarking from the train, Thomas DeHaven made a courtesy call on Skagit County Sheriff Charles T. Harmon to notify him he was in their district. There, he found "Doan" Dell kicked back in one of their office chairs, chewing tobacco and chatting it up with deputies Ed Wells and Charles Stevenson. Dell had given the Skagit lawmen a full description of the Roper murder, at one point even declaring, "And the fiend used a stick this long, to beat the girl with and forced a gag into her mouth with it," holding up his hands to indicate the stick's length. The remark came as a surprise to DeHaven. First, although a stick had been discovered, no importance had been given to it. Secondly, only Sheriff Williams and he were present when it was found. Third, up until then they hadn't thought of it as another weapon in the case, rather, just the tool to push the rag in deeper. DeHaven, deep in thought, decided to bookmark the slip until he could confer with his boss.

DeHaven asked the Skagit County sheriff about the whereabouts of Rae Brown, and was given directions. Shortly thereafter, Watts was apprehended without resistance, confirming Williams' belief that once you found her, you'd find him. "You've got nothing on me, DeHaven," said Watts when arrested. Deputy Sheriff DeHaven sized him up. Watts was twenty-six years old, five foot ten inches in height, had an athletic build, and weighed 174-pounds. He was immaculate when it came to his appearance, keeping his brown hair neatly trimmed above the ears and well combed. He took great pride in his mustache, which he wore in the French curl style. He would use a curling iron and dye it various colors.

The distinguished Harry Watts sporting his manicured mustache. Watts enjoyed waxing and dying his mustache to keep up with the latest Paris trends. Bellingham Herald, January 22, 1907.

"Watts in the manner of his kind, was something of a dandy. He walked along with me to the train with a jaunty and untroubled air, his neat and natty appearance entirely unruffled. Nor did his nonchalance desert him when he arrived in Blaine where I placed him in jail alongside Raymond Lange."

Harry Watts' background is scanty at best. Watts was born in Dakota Territory, today's Marshal County, South Dakota, in 1881.[9] His parents, John A. and Laura (Coleman) were from Indiana, having married in Cass in 1879. John was a blacksmith, and could take his trade anywhere. They had a son and two daughters while living in the Territory before relocating to Seattle in 1900.[10] Sometime around the move to Seattle, Harry broke away from the family, moving to Dearborn, Indiana before coming to Anacortes, Washington and eventually, Blaine.

Watts claimed to have worked nine years as an engineer and four as an electrician. Before coming to Blaine, he was employed in the fish canneries in Anacortes. It was during this time that he may have become acquainted with Rae Brown.

Word spread like wildfire that Harry Watts, implicated in Addie Roper's death, was now in the city jail. It didn't take long for a highly charged, resentful mob to surround the jail, threatening violence if the prisoner wasn't released to them. Jail guard was doubled, but there was little the jailers could do if the crowd were to force the small building. Despite the uproar, many within the community believed Watts was innocent; that he had been thrown to the wolves in exchange for the public's need for a culprit. Some claimed he was an all-for-show dandy, and certainly no criminal mastermind. Eventually, the community came to the conclusion that such a dandy couldn't have killed Addie and the hysteria over Watts ended. The citizens pressed on, demanding that the real killer be found.

9   Some documents claim that at some point the family lived in Bonnerville, Ransom County, North Dakota in 1880. Watts, at times, refers to being born there as well.

10   Harry would eventually have three brothers and three sisters.

The next day, Tuesday the 22nd, Sheriff Williams and Deputy DeHaven escorted both Watts and Lange to the county jail in Bellingham to be held. The *Bellingham Herald* said the new prisoner "walked with a jaunty air, although he bore the expression of a worried man…and apparently is very precise as to his personal appearance." The *Herald* also took note that Watts lived with the "inmates" of the waterfront, abandoning his wife, Mamie, and his two infant daughters. As he was being frisked, Watts jested with police that he couldn't wait to be free as soon as the confusion was cleared up. The police understood Watts to be nonchalant and would subject him to a "rigid sweating process in the hopes that something would drop."

While authorities were pursuing their investigation, Addie Roper was laid to rest on Tuesday, January 22, 1907. Blaine's citizens were in mourning. The people of the small community were at a loss by the senseless act, and fearful that the murderer might still be walking amongst them. At 10 o'clock that morning, the Methodist Church was filled to capacity for the service. A sermon was delivered by Reverend Sheafe, and was said to be "masterly addressed" and inspiring. Several hundred more mourners endured the frigid January temperatures outside the church, to pay their respects. Businesses and schools closed their doors as a sign of respect. It was later described that a "large concourse of friends and sympathizers of the deceased followed the remains to the cemetery, the funeral cortege being one of the longest in the history of Whatcom county." The Good Templar (Fraternal Order for Temperance) and the Ladies of Maccabees Lodge, both of which Addie was an active member, turned out. Addie was especially active with temperance work, and the movement was well represented that morning, all dressed in heavy black layers.

After the funeral, a throng of citizen's decided it was high time to "purge [the] city completely of any undesirable persons caught loitering about the saloons and red-light district." A mob descended upon Blaine City Hall, shouting for Mayor William Dawson to clean the streets of transients.

Dawson was browbeaten into complying. Arrests were rashly made of any stranger caught in the open; most were driven from the city limits. Sheriff Williams feared law and order was in danger of unraveling. The more re-strained citizens complained to Williams that, "lynch law is about to prevail and that a howling mob is wandering aimlessly about the city" looking for retribution. In the *Blaine Journal*, January 25th, an editorial stated, "While quiet had characterized their actions, the spirit of mob law has only needed posi-tive evidence of guilt to fan it into action."

The following week madness was rampant in Blaine. Dewey Snavely's suspicious mystery man from the saloon, the one who wore the black slouched hat with the red whiskered beard, soon materialized. The mystery man, whose name was never reported, showed up at the door of a Mrs. Eddy, near the tiny Whatcom community of Lawrence on Wednesday, January 23rd. The man, bearing Snavely's description, demanded that she let him inside to stay the night. Mrs. Eddy, alone with her children, was terrified and refused. The man replied, "Damn you, I will stay, whether you want me to or not," and forced his way in. Mrs. Eddy remained calm enough to gather the children into the kitchen under the ruse of preparing supper for the little ones. Away from the stranger she whispered for the children to follow her outside the back door and to run fast toward the neighbors.

In no time, several armed men arrived at the Eddy home. The in-truder saw the small posse with guns in hand, and ran toward the woodline. After the Eddy family's escape, the stranger had filled a sack full of food, but had cast it aside as he ran.

Meanwhile, both Watts and Lange sat in their respective cells, main-taining their innocence. Williams noted that in all the "sweating" put upon the men during their interrogations, Lange's story never wavered and Watts continued with his alibi of playing a card game at the "Cat House" when the fire occurred. The men were shown the red bandana; Watts sneered, declar-ing that he used nothing but the finest white linen. Snavely, the bartender and Manning, the first on the scene of the fire arrived in Bellingham and maintained that the prisoners were innocent of any wrongdoing, vouching again for their alibis. They offered that Lange was nothing more than an "unsophisticated Texas tenderfoot."

By Friday the 25th, the men around Lawrence were still scouring the woods for the strange man. They told the *Bellingham Herald* that it made little difference if he was implicated with the Roper affair or not, they would take no chances with "such characters who attempt to terrorize women who are left alone at their homes."

In response, newspapers outside the community reported, "True, the minds of citizens of that city are wrought to a high pitch, but there is dignity, decorum and the good citizens of Blaine, law abiding as they are, propose to let the law take its course." The city took the death of Addie Roper to heart, but it cast a pall of gloom and all were desperate to incarcerate the villain or villains responsible. The sheriff's office and the Blaine police department lived in dread that such a "necktie party" might occur, ending the life of some innocent victim. Newspapers tried to stay on the case with official updates from authorities, but little information was available. They assured restless readers that "clews [sic] are being followed with sphinx-like silence, but little of the findings are being made public." The most noted update was the posting of a $1,000 reward for information leading to an arrest and conviction of the culprits.

Watts' Attorney, Jacob J. Noethe filed an application for a writ of habeas corpus in Whatcom County Superior Court on Harry Watts' behalf. The application was based on the statement that his client was being held prisoner without being charged with a crime. Judge Jeremiah Neterer denied the writ, forcing Noethe to file an appeal with the state Supreme Court.

Vigilance Committee

By January 31st, fear and conspiracy ballooned to include adjacent communities. Seattle detectives had their eye on a likely suspect of suspicious nature who was, without a doubt in their mind, an accomplice in the Roper murder. The man in question had deposited $500 into a new account, one-third being British-Canadian currency. The teller had been following the events in Blaine and made the assumption that with Addie Roper being so close to the Canadian border, she would be in possession of large amounts of foreign money. "The depositor seemed very nervous and fumbled with his cash," said the teller. Bank officials claimed that the large deposit, Canadian bills and the man's nervousness indicated that he was guilty of something. Seattle detectives notified Sheriff Williams that they intended to shadow the suspect.

Washington Avenue, the city's main thoroughfare. Circa: 1900s. Courtesy of Bill Becht, Horseshoe Coins & Antiques, Blaine, WA

After Addie's funeral, soaring emotion continued in momentum. Individuals dissatisfied with progress in the case formed a citizen's committee stating Sheriff Williams wasn't doing enough to solve it. Anger was fanning the flames of discontent and people demanded answers that Williams could not provide. Blaine City Attorney, George B. Westcott, was given chairmanship of the group, and immediately caused friction with the sheriff by calling on Canadian authorities to help in the investigation.

Westcott enlisted famed Canadian detective William H. Welsh in the event that the culprits crossed the border into British Canada. Welsh was the real life Canadian counterpart to Arthur Conan Doyle's Sherlock Holmes, noted for solving the murder of three men in Yukon Territory in 1902. In true dogged fashion, Welsh pursued his man, Edward LaBelle, from the Yukon through Seattle and California until apprehending LaBelle in Nevada. Bound in irons, the killer was taken back to the Yukon where he was tried and hanged. Welsh's foot pursuit took only four months and he was celebrated for his tenacity.

Welsh, now General Superintendent of the Canadian Detective Bureau in Toronto, took the train westward to Vancouver, where he engaged Detective Arthur B. Spain to assist him. Welch wasted no time analyzing the crime site, talking to authorities and questioning locals. He read through the coroner's inquest report and the stories reported in local papers. After his investigation, Welch provided his findings to Westcott. He was one of the first to assert that it would require at least two persons to subdue and kill Addie Roper, proposing that she had been hit over the head with a heavy instrument, perhaps the butt end of the hatchet found in the room. He asked, "Is it possible that one man could hold the axe and blanket and at the same time do the job of striking the woman? Doesn't it look as if one man had the axe or whatever instrument may have been used, and the other fellow smothered her with the blanket?" Welsh's scenario ran in the local newspaper,

"The two blows on the back of her head are believed to have been delivered in rapid succession, which caused her to fall backward on the floor. The next idea is that the fiends hurriedly crammed the red bandana handkerchief into her mouth, which no doubt was taken from the pocket of one of the murderers. Possibly the woman regained consciousness and opened her eyes, after which the men probably struck her two more blows on the left side of the head, fracturing the skull near the left temple and another blow struck on the head, severing the ear."

Continuing his version of the evening, Welsh suggested that Addie Roper had entered her home by way of the front door, not the rear, as was previously suggested, speculating that her first inclination would have been to set her umbrella near the heater in the front room to dry. Welch, retracing her steps, knew she had shopped and would be carrying packages. He suspected that her next move would have been to enter the back room to lay her bundles down and to remove her wet outer-layer of clothing. At this point, with her back turned, the men would have struck. Welsh speculated that, "to prevent an outcry, such criminals of that kind, are said to immediately reach in their pocket to get a handkerchief to be used as a gag...Lest she opened her eyes and recognized the persons in the room they would likely throw a blanket over her face." Welsh brought forward two conclusions: Addie Roper was murdered by more than one person, and the blanket was used to stifle her cries and, or, dissuade her from seeing the culprits' faces.

The investigation became of great contention for Sheriff Williams, who considered the Canadians out of their jurisdiction; they would have been of use had the killer or killers crossed the boundary line, but Williams saw the unwanted intrusion as Westcott's affair, and shrugged it off. That was until Westcott took it upon himself to run the investigation. Westcott called

Williams into his temporary office, along with two other Blaine citizens. After a few moments the detectives arrived.

> "Westcott then told me that he had dilatory in getting evidence, and that he had hired two detectives to come and take charge of the investigation and he wanted me to stay in Blaine to give authority to arrest any person that the detectives might desire. I promptly told Mr. Westcott that I would not do so. They could have all the detectives there and they could report to me or the county attorney, as they saw fit."

Williams was further alarmed that Westcott, who was also the attorney for the Blaine restricted district, had no intention of providing any information regarding his own investigation in the Roper case. Westcott threatened to have the citizens of Blaine descend upon Bellingham to force Williams to release Watts and Lange to the custody of the Canadian detectives for questioning, the likes of which never happened. Detective Welch did go to the county courthouse to interview Harry Watts but Williams, who was unable to be present, denied the request. Williams claimed, "It was too important a matter to trust these things to utter strangers." He followed by stating, "Westcott has taken in the matter and the slurs he has thrown toward me sets me to thinking whether he has an objective back of all this…"

The Williams-Welch-Westcott discord would play out in local newspapers for nearly a week, with neither side caving, enhancing the drama of the Roper case. By Monday, February 4th, matters came to a head. The *Bellingham Herald* reported, "Despite all the smoke that has arisen by reason of irresponsible statements of a biased evening and morning press, Williams agreed to amicable arrangements for a Welch-Watts interview." The questioning took place at the county attorney's office with no one present but the two men. After Watts was "subjected to a withering cross-fire of rigid catechism for an hour," Welch emerged from the interrogation without "one whit of information." He told the *Herald* that Watts simply listened to his line of questioning and offered up little. Welch was stumped by Watts' non-cooperation.

Westcott's citizens committee proceeded to "knock all the sheriff's theories into a cocked hat," questioning his moves, quarreling with city officials, and vociferously demanding that someone be arrested. Even the *Bellingham Herald* started making light of Sheriff Williams. In an editorial highlighting the public's concerns, it was reported that half a dozen "somebodies" were rounded up, arrested, and were "eating two meals a day at the expense of the county, and to the profit of the sheriff."

A notoriously veracious Bellingham paper, the *Reveille*, reported, "indignant citizens varied their pleasantries with threats to lynch peaceful townsmen toward whom some Sherlock Holmes had said suspicion pointed." The jesting continued when the editorial swung blows against the sheriff's deputies, who were said to have felt sorry for their chief, and were urged to work harder. In desperation, the deputies tried thinking outside of the box; an idea materialized. They found a man in town who acted as a medium through which spirits informed him where to find stolen goods. To the embarrassment of the authorities, the deputies were said to have fallen over one another in their rush to consult the unnamed mystic.

The red bandana was handed over to the mystic. The deputies were mesmerized as he, with the bandana in his hand, went into a deep trance. He found a spirit who was present and who had witnessed the murder in detail. The spirit told the mystic to look for "Jack," as he was the murderer; a man of medium build, light complexion, with a light mustache. He would have a deep scar scored on the right side of his head and another across the right hand, or it could be that his fingers were missing, the mystic couldn't be sure. Lastly, it was a relative they should set focus upon. As was confirmed in the *Herald*, it was later said the deputies had all they needed to capture the villain.

Further in jest, editorial's mentioned the involvement of other mediums; one woman claimed to converse with a spirit who knew about the Roper tragedy through the knocking of a table. According to the *Herald*,

> "The table, a heavy dining affair, got upon its hind legs and waltzed across the room and commenced to chase the half-frightened delver…backing him into the corner, the table jabbed him in the home of the gin-fizz. The delver protested." And, "The table withed [sic] to talk to the deliver, the medium declared, and the table refused to be quiet until he had taken a strange hold of it. Then the rapping commenced, as did the true story of the murder. It was a tall, heavy, dark, oldish [sic] man who committed the crime. He was no way connected to the family. He had escaped across to Vancouver Island, and was to be found in Ladysmith spending the treasure of which he had despoiled Miss Roper." The article concluded, "The final question was asked. Would Sheriff Williams succeed in catching the murderer? The answer came in 'short, sharp, slangy raps.'" And seemed to say, "The sheriff Pshaw, that mutt couldn't catch a cold."

On Tuesday February 5th, Sheriff Williams and Deputy DeHaven made a surprise arrest of William Allen "Doan" Dell, Blaine's own Constable, on suspicion of complicity in the murder of Addie Roper. The two had Dell under suspicion since DeHaven told the Sheriff of the Mount Vernon "stick incident," where he had heard Dell reveal details that had been unavailable at the time. DeHaven noted that if it weren't for Dell's revelation of the use of the stick, its significance would have likely gone unnoticed in their investigation at the time.

Dell was formally a Blaine Constable, whom for some unknown reason was fired and only recently reinstated. He had a bad reputation, and possessed few friends. Dell was the complete opposite of Watts by way of character. Dell was older, at 45, with a head of heavily disheveled dark hair and an unkempt mustache. He chewed tobacco incessantly. He was uncouth, illiterate, and had an all-out mean disposition.

Williams had been suspicious of Dell all along, wondering why he would have apprehended Lange at the train depot the night of the murder, but would let Harry Watts go, and just why was it that, when ordered to apprehend Watts in Mount Vernon, Dell claimed that he was nowhere to be found, but DeHaven had found him within an hour? Under questioning, Dell provided several different accounts for his whereabouts at the time of the murder and fire, but could find no one to substantiate his alibi. First, he claimed to have been walking his beat, and then helping in fighting the fire. More noticeably, Dell had no explanation for reports of his having had fresh scratches on his face the night of the murder, scratches which were presently scabbed over.

The following day, Whatcom County Deputy Prosecutor, George Livesey, a 24 year-old American born in England, obtained a court order, authorizing Coroner Thompson to exhume Addie's remains for a second inquest. Sheriff Williams believed Addie Roper had been sexually assaulted, which would expand the motive for the crime. Blaine's Mayor Dawson was also being pressed for a second postmortem, which he agreed needed to be done. The results were inconclusive, but the inquest jury recommended William Allen Dell held for further investigation. Dell was rigorously questioned, giving an account of his patrol up to 9 pm the night of the murder, but was extremely vague as to his whereabouts and timeline thereafter. He expressed no sign of emotion or sympathy when viewing Addie's charred remains at the inquest. The jury was unsatisfied with his answers and suspicious of his conduct during the proceedings.

The Road to Trial

On Wednesday, March 27, attorney James B. Abrams, court appointed counsel for William Dell, filed an application for a writ of habeas corpus
in Superior Court demanding his client's release if he was not going to be
charged with a crime. Whatcom County Prosecutor Virgil Peringer in return,
filed a complaint with Judge Jeremiah Neterer, charging Dell with first degree
murder and asked for a preliminary hearing to be held in Blaine.

A few weeks later, Harry Watts' writ of habeas corpus was granted
by the state Supreme Court, but in response to Watss' release, Peringer presented an arrest warrant charging Watts with first degree murder in Blaine
shortly thereafter. Watts was held once more, and taken away with Dell for
a preliminary hearing in Blaine, which kept them both in custody under the
persistence and wit of Peringer.

On Wednesday, May 1st, the two men were brought before a pre-
liminary hearing presided over by Justices John F. Kean, Edwin M. Day and
Hamline B. Williams. Dell was ordered bound over to the Superior Court
for trial with a $5,000 bond. According to Deputy Sheriff DeHaven, he and
Williams were surprised by the unanimous decision of the Justices to release
Watts. Thomas DeHaven claimed, "I was not convinced of Watts' innocence.
Neither was Sheriff Williams. In consequence of my doubts and suspicions,
I spent my spare time that entire summer riding around the county horse-
back, with the red bandana…endeavoring to find some one who could iden-
tify it." DeHaven canvassed every public and private laundry from Blaine to
Bellingham.

As the summer dragged on, the citizens of Blaine became increasingly perturbed with the lack of movement on the case. Finally, on August 1st,
Information was filed in Whatcom County Superior Court by the prosecution charging William Allen "Doan" Dell with murder in the first degree. On

August 8th, Dell was taken before Judge Neterer and entered a plea of "not guilty."

As DeHaven's pursuit for a lead on the ownership of the red bandana came to a dead end, Sheriff Williams suggested looking around Mount Vernon, speculating that if Watts favored Rae Brown's company, perhaps she would know. Acting on the advice, DeHaven headed south. The landlady at the house Brown lived in suggested seeking out a Mrs. Bessie B. Stuart who did Watts' laundry when he was in town. Mrs. Stuart recognized the bandana right away as Watts', having washed it many times. She noted the apple-blossom design pattern. On the strength of this new information, Williams met with prosecutor Peringer and ordered an arrest warrant drawn.

Virgil Peringer had a warrant written out for Watts some time prior, but had decided not to act upon it until he had enough evidence for the arrest to stick. Williams let it be known that a witness by the name of Mrs. Maud Briner had come forward claiming that Watts acted as lookout on the night of Addie Roper's murder. Thirty-nine year old Mrs. Mollie B. Allen had also told Williams that she saw a man resembling Watts sneaking about the Roper home the night of the murder from her upstairs window. Allen lived just a few hundred feet away. She claimed he ran away just before the fire alarm, and then she saw a second man run out of the house, but could not make out his features. This was some of the information Williams held back from the public. It was enough to question Watts further, but less than needed to act upon, until now. Watts would be charged with conspiracy in the murder of Addie Roper.

On Thursday, September 5th, Watts and Rae Brown were boarding a train coach for Seattle when Skagit County Sheriff, Charles T. Harmon walked up, calling, "Mr. Watts?" Watts turned to acknowledge his name, and was surprised to find himself under arrest, with cuffs slapped on his wrists. Brown, equally surprised, was taken in for questioning. It wasn't long before she confessed to withholding information, which prompted the *Bellingham*

Herald to headline their September 6th edition with, "Woman May Solve Murder Mystery: Rae Brown Makes Damaging Statements." Watts was immediately turned over to Deputy Sheriff DeHaven in Mount Vernon. Rae Brown was an unexpected catch for the authorities, to whom Watts was believed to have been too candid with regarding details involving Addie Roper. Williams wanted Brown separated from Watts and held as a material witness. With Harmon's endorsement, Brown was held in Mount Vernon.

That same day, Sheriff Williams and Prosecutor Peringer refused to allow William Dell's attorney, James Abrams to visit his client, even though they had no legal grounds to do so. Abrams filed a complaint, and when the *Herald* heard of the story, they sought contact with him for a quote. Abrams was said to have only smiled, while Williams wanted no interference while Watts was under arrest.

Harry Watts was placed in dark isolation at the Whatcom County jail in the hopes of pressuring him to talk, but he remained silent, unwilling to divulge anything to authorities. Mamie, his wife, had divorce proceedings moving against him, and kept his children away, which didn't seem to affect him in the slightest.

As for Dell, the sheriff was "sweating" him ever harder; scaring him with news that Watts was about to give him up. Dell had been on the verge of breaking several times. The sheriff and his deputies figured that if they stayed on him continuously he would break down before trial. The same pressure was administered on Watts. The fact that Rae Brown was also being grilled weighed heavily upon his mind; if she broke it would be of little use for him to remain silent.

It is a complete mystery why Watts stayed around when he had the chance to flee. There seemed no other reason than his infatuation for Rae Brown. Watts held only twelve dollars on his person when arrested. If he had shared in the robbery loot, no riches were found on him.

The following day, Abrams filed an affidavit demanding that the Superior Court provide him more time to prepare for trial, as the state had issued seventeen new subpoenas[11] while he wasn't allowed to even see his own client. The state declined the motion, stating that the defense would have sufficient time to interview the new witnesses. Prosecutor Peringer declared that the state was not barring counsel from seeing his client, Dell. It was true that a temporary restriction was placed on visitors while Watts was being arrested, but the restriction wasn't limited or aimed directly toward Abrams and Dell. Also that day Attorney Jacob J. Noethe was appointed to represent Harry Watts.

On September 8th and 9th, the attorneys began examining potential jurors. Progress was slow with both the state and defense producing long lists of questions, which took up nearly an hour per each person interviewed. A *Herald* reporter at the selection process described the procedure,

> "On one side of the table, before Judge Neterer, sits the defendant Doan Dell, and his attorneys Abrams & Moore, while directly behind them is Deputy Sheriff Peter Miller, who has charge of the prisoner. Dell appears to take the whole proceeding calmly, and while he shows considerable interest, he displays no nervousness. Across the table are County Attorney Virgil Peringer, Deputy County Attorney George Livesey, and with them are J. H. Roper, brother of the murdered girl, his wife, Sarah, and child, and two sisters of the woman Dell is accused of slaying, Amanda and Frances Roper."

11   Witnesses: Mollie B. Allen, Charles Harmon, J. F. Beard, Archie Corfee, Bessie B. Stuart, Marie Allen, Ellen Brown alias Rae Brown, H. B. Allen, Flossie Allen-Stevenson, Glen Buray, G. H. Calclich, John Kean, Rita Calvert, Mrs. A. C. Abbott, W. M. Walton, Thomas Simon and Ben Thompson.

Although the selection moved slowly, little disagreement was made between the state and defense in the formation of a mutually agreeable jury. The main contention by Abrams was that no Blaine residents were to be in the selection.[12]

Harry Watts was still held in solitary confinement, showing no sign of losing his nerve or breaking down. Word from Mount Vernon indicated that Rae Brown had resolved to remain silent.

The Trial of William Allen "Doan" Dell

The trial of William Allen "Doan" Dell started at 9 am, on Wednesday, September 11, 1907 in an overcrowded courtroom presided over by Whatcom County Superior Court Judge, Jeremiah Neterer.

The trial of William Dell. Addie's sisters, Frances and Arimanta are seen to the right. The Bellingham Herald, September 16, 1907 described the photo as a "Flashlight picture of crowded courtroom during process of Dell trial Saturday afternoon."

---

12   Jury: W. A. Schenck, shingle weaver, city; Harvey Canfield, rancher, Sumas; A. H. Pierce, clerk, city; W. L. McCoombes, rancher, Sumas; A. W. Frost, rancher, Nooksack; P. A. Clark, rancher, Lynden; E. W. Swanson, merchant, Ferndale; W. J. Van Houghton, motorman, city; James Clayton, rancher, Ferndale; W. F. Gwynn, manager, White City, Silver Beach; P. W. Pierce, collector, city and John N. Nygren, farmer, Ten Mile.

Whatcom County Prosecutor Peringer and Deputy Prosecutor George Livesey represented the state. Peringer stood before the jury box and delivered his opening address.

"By circumstantial evidence we will make clear to you, gentleman of the jury, that William Allen Dell, or Doan Dell, as he is also known, conspired with Harry Watts to kill Miss Addie Roper at Blaine, on the night of January 19. The state will attempt to convince you that Dell and Watts did slay Miss Roper, as alleged in the Information filed against them.[13] The state will put on the stand a witness (Mrs. Robinson) who overheard Dell say to Watts on the evening before the murder, 'Not tonight; tomorrow night. I tell you.' The state will put another witness on the stand who heard Dell say a few months before the crime, 'If I ever get the job of marshal back I will ruin Miss Roper, and I understand she has plenty of money. A little coal oil and a match will cover up many things.' The state will show that Dell had only been reinstated as a marshal a few days before the crime," he continued. "The state will further show that Harry Watts needed money to start up a restaurant he had been talking of. A witness will be produced who will testify that Watts stated that he got a piece of money out of the crime. The state will further show that the handkerchief used as a gag on the dead girl belonged to Harry Watts. Witnesses will be placed on the stand to testify as to the actions of Dell after the murder had been discovered. How he refused to arrest Harry Watts after the crime had been committed, and instead placed under arrest Raymond Lange.

---

13   Dell and Watts were tried separately, but it was impossible to keep either out of the trial of the other.

How he went to Mount Vernon later to search for Watts, and instead of going to Sheriff Harmon's office, stayed around town until he learned that Harmon had heard him making inquires concerning Watts. We will place Sheriff Harmon and his deputies on the stand to tell how Dell told of the murder and explained that the gag had been forced down the girl's throat with a stick that long (indicating with his hands). At that time Dell was nervous and we think we can convince you that at the time Dell was giving evidence that he himself alone knew. Furthermore, the state will have witnesses testify as to how Dell tried to have certain persons who knew him and who saw him on the night of the fire, kept silent, and how he tried to intimidate Mrs. Briner and her son, Reliance, and further, Mrs. Allen will state that she saw Watts running away from the Roper house just before the fire alarm was turned in. The state will depend wholly upon circumstantial evidence, but we are confident that we can produce enough evidence to convince you that William Allen Dell and Harry Watts are guilty of one of the most atrocious murders ever committed in Whatcom County."

Attorney James Abrams sat opposite with his law-partner, James F. Moore, for the defense of Dell. Abrams rose and gave a short statement to the jury, restating that the evidence was circumstantial. Abrams moved that the state be compelled to affirm whether it would attempt to prove death by choking or blows upon the head. The motion was overruled.

The first witness called to the stand was Paul Wolten, proprietor of Wolten's Grocery Store, who was familiar with the surrounding location of the crime. Wolten described on a map for the jury Addie's route from her work place to his grocery store and then to her home. He said that he was

59

present during the fire and helped tend to the flames; he did not see Dell at the fire as Dell had previously claimed to Sheriff Williams. Abrams declined to cross-examine.

Frank O'Dell, chief of the Blaine volunteer fire brigade, was next on the stand. O'Dell hadn't seen Dell at the fire either, and confirmed smelling kerosene. From his experience on the fire brigade, it was his opinion that the fire was deliberately set. On cross examination, he was questioned whether or not he could be sure if Dell had been on scene or not. O'Dell admitted he was not looking for Dell that night, as he was more concerned with fighting the fire.

C. C. Troy, proprietor of the Racket Store, testified that he was well acquainted with both Dell and Miss Roper. Troy said as soon as he smelled smoke he went to the Recreation Saloon searching for the source. By the time he exited the saloon he saw the house in flames and the fire alarm sounding. He did not see Dell. With Troy's testimony the court recessed at noon.

The highlight of the afternoon session came when Dr. Sutherland gave testimony that he believed Addie Roper had been "criminally assaulted" (raped). The accusation that a woman of such beloved stature may have been violated left the courtroom aghast and infuriated. Abrams quickly objected, stating criminal assault was not a charge on the original Information against his client. The court was adjourned for the day, and Judge Neterer took the matter under advisement.

When court resumed the following day, Neterer handed down his decision from the following day regarding criminal assault. The state regarded it as a material point, insomuch as rape may establish a foundation for a motive for the crime. Abrams quickly objected on the grounds that Information filed by the state mentioned no such crime was alleged. Neterer overruled the motion, but offered that he would make allowances for information regarding the assault if it proved murder.

Abrams attempted to exclude the charred remains of the handkerchief and axe as evidence, on the grounds that no foundation had been laid. Neterer sustained the motion for the bandana, but the axe was allowed. Then, changing his mind, he decided to allow the handkerchief, contingent upon what Deputy Sheriff DeHaven had to say about it.

Throughout the trial witnesses bantered back and forth as to who saw Dell, and where and when he was seen. The *Bellingham Herald* bylined a column on Friday the thirteenth, "Suspicious Movements and Contradictory Statements of Dell Related to Jury…" Confusion was abounding. Fireman Louis Johnson, for instance, testified seeing Dell ringing the fire bell and helping drag the hose cart to the fire, but had not seen him after. On cross, Abrams tried reminding Johnson of Dell running back for more hose at the fire barn. Johnson could not remember this. Another volunteer fire fighter, Charles Johnson, was asked whether Dell ran to retrieve more hose. Charles Johnson stated he could not remember that, as he didn't see the accused at the fire in the first place.

Charles Johnson stated that he and Bert Jones, a volunteer, were appointed as guards to watch over the house after the fire was out. They were forbidden to allow any entrance into the house until the arrival of the coroner the following morning. Bill Tierney, who also stood guard, testified that it wasn't until after the fire was out that he saw Dell. He recalled seeing Dell standing across the street, and that he called to him, "Is that you Bill?" Upon which Tierney replied, "Yes." "What do you think of this?" asked Dell. "It looks like a holdup to me." At this point Dell jolted back a bit, almost in shock and said, "For Christ's sake, don't start anything like that."

Tierney followed Dell to the train depot to arrest Lange and had seen Harry Watts head for Mount Vernon. "Lange seemed mystified," Tierney finished.

Blaine Constable Edward James Tolford testified to seeing Dell in front of city hall after the murder, and that Dell had offered him treats from a paper bag. He recalled noticing that Dell had fresh red, claw-like scratches across his face. He didn't mention how he came by them, but told Tolford he'd prefer not to talk too much as his mouth hurt. Other witnesses would testify to seeing fresh scratches on Dell's face the day after the murder as well.

John H. Penno, a 35 year-old English Blaine barber, who was present as a juror at the first and second inquest with Dell, was asked by the prosecution to repeat what Dell had initially stated.

Abrams leapt from his chair to object, as "no foundation had been laid for such evidence" and "that the records for the body were the best evidence." The court overruled the objection.

William Dell, claimed Penno, was patrolling his usual beat on Washington Avenue, "visiting various saloons; he went north to E Street, returned and looked after a fire he was to care for, then went over and got his laundry, which he took to his room. Then he returned to Washington Avenue and was near Scott's Saloon when the fire alarm sounded, talking to Kenny Lindsey." When asked about the timeframe, he conferred that it was near 9 o'clock that he had seen him. Kenny Lindsey backed the story of standing in front of Scott's Saloon with Dell, and Johanna Goodman confirmed that Dell had picked up his laundry, but that it had been after 10 o'clock that evening when he did.

Another of the second inquest jurors, George B. Montfort took the stand and stated that Dell had told two different stories concerning his patrol on the night of the murder. On the one, Dell offered that he went north on Washington, turned on E Street, crossed over, and came back. Then, later, he said he continued on to Fourth, and along Fourth to Eighth, then back to Washington Avenue. It was clear William Dell was foggy on his whereabouts the night of the murder.

Young master Roy Wren, one of the boys throwing snowballs in the orchard, took the stand. Wren repeated how he and his friends had seen Miss Roper come home carrying bundles and her umbrella. Later, Wren bumped into Dell, who told him to keep quiet. Wren reported feeling confused, as he had no idea what Dell could be referring to. The other boys, Oscar McDonald, Irving Hoff and Thomas Stevenson all took the stand, backing Roy Wren's story.

Mrs. Maud Briner and her nine year old son, Reliance, swore positively that twenty minutes prior to the fire they saw a man of Dell's description running through the apple orchard from the direction of the Roper home. Later, she claimed, Dell came to her home threatening them to keep their mouths shut.

Moving towards details regarding the rape, Dr. Grey, an examiner at the second inquest testified that he found what appeared to be traces of "criminal assault," but that the body was damaged enough that he could not be certain. This testimony strengthened the state's theory of another motive and added to their circumstantial evidence.

Blaine lighthouse keeper, Norval S. Douglas, a 47 year-old family man with grown children, followed Dr. Grey on the stand. He recalled that about a year prior he and Dell had been standing on the street when Miss Roper happened by. A remark was passed regarding Roper where Dell stated, "If I ever get my job back as night watchman... if I ever get as good a chance as I had a year ago, I'll ruin her...I understand she also carries a large sum of money." To which Douglas responded, "You would have to knock her in the head first." "O, well a little coal oil and a match would cover up many things," remarked Dell. The accumulating witness' testimony was proving to be quite damaging for William Dell.

Later on in the trial, a young man named Eddie Larson told a similar story concerning Dell that had happened a few weeks before the murder. "One day, while passing the City of Paris store with Dell...(he) told me that he would like to ruin the girl,"[14] recalled Larson. The state found the

---

14   Larson's quote may have been reworded for newspaper readership. In a September 14th affidavit signed by Larson and Attorney George Livesay for the prosecution, the actual statement was that, "Addie Roper had never had a piece and I would like to break her in." "Breaking her in" would have implied to have intercourse with her, a detail too graphic to reveal in the paper.

testimony important as it showed Dell had been consistent in his desire to overtake Addie Roper.

Next on the stand was Deputy Sheriff Edward Wells of Skagit County. Wells recounted conversations with Dell when Sheriff Williams had sent him to Mount Vernon to retrieve Watts. Talking about the murder, Wells recalled that Dell shared how Addie Roper's body was found, declaring that the gag was forced down the girl's throat with a stick the length of his outstretched arms. This evidence had not yet been revealed to anyone outside of Wells and Sheriff Williams. Prosecutor Peringer pointed out how self-incriminating the slipped statement was.

Raymond Lange took the stand. The publicity surrounding the Roper case had led to his arrest for desertion from the army. He was transported under guard as a federal prisoner from Fort Lawton. It was said his testimony "dropped a bomb into the defense." While being held in a Blaine jail cell, Dell, after arresting him, came calling the next day.

When Dell questioned Lange he offered, "If you will tell me all you know about the murder, I will set you free," but Lange had nothing to say. Later, Dell came back to Lange and tried to make a deal with him; Dell promised Lange that if Lange confirmed seeing Dell, in the Reception Saloon five minutes before the fire, he would set him free. Lange refused and promised nothing. He felt that Dell, who he considered a friend, had set him up.

During cross, in a sharp tone, Abrams asked, "Did you believe him? Didn't you think he would have kept you in jail, and don't you think now he would have held you if you had told him anything?"

"No, sir," said Lange, "I think he would have turned me out."

"Why?" asked Abrams.

"For a good many reasons since I have learned certain things in connection with the case," responded Lange, intimating Dell's own self-incriminating comments made when he came to visit him in the cell.

With great anticipation from the courtroom, Arthur B. Spain took the stand. Spain briefed the court how he was one of two detectives to be engaged by the Citizen's Committee of Blaine to work the case, and that he had had trouble engaging with Sheriff Williams and his men in their efforts. When they were finally able to interview William Dell, they took a great deal of notes. He intimated that perhaps Dell had felt safe with him or that in their status as Canadian detectives (for perhaps he thought they lacked jurisdiction and that anything they obtained could not be used as evidence in a US court of law), he spoke with them, though not in great detail.

Spain had asked Dell if he had written down his side of the story, as a smart man should record it so as not to have his words used against himself later on. Dell claimed that he hadn't and suggested that the two detectives talk to the four boys throwing snowballs in the orchard, as he saw them playing around 8:30 that evening and believed that they would prove he wasn't in Addie's home at the time. Spain asked Dell where he was at 8:30 that evening, if not near the scene of the crime and, again, Dell claimed he was near the apple orchard.

The detective said that Dell became evasive when asked where he was between 9 and 9:30. "Somewhere about the town," he said. "At this point Dell lost his temper," said Spain. He told Detective Welsh, "I know what you fellows are after. You are trying to muddle me up." Dell was assured that wasn't the case, that they only wanted the facts. Then Spain said he tried an all-together different tactic on Dell. He asked, "Now, Dell, you're a bright man, give us your theory in the matter." Spain told him that he was a man of law, that he knew the people here, as he and Welsh did not. "Surely, you had time to think this through if you were being setup," remarked Spain.

Spain recalled that Dell looked flattered, likely because it was the first time in the case that someone had regarded his "professional expertise." Peringer asked Spain to recite the theory Dell put forward during the interview, upon which Abrams objected. Judge Neterer overruled. All the while, Dell sat chewing tobacco, listening intently.

The story, as narrated by Spain, went as follows:

"Well," Dell said, with a quizzical look on his face, "I think robbery was the motive, and that it was done by one or possibly two persons. I think one man entered the house before Miss Roper came home and concealed himself in there. When she entered she started to pull off one glove, then lighted a lamp after setting down her parcels on the table. It is likely that she then picked up the lamp and started into the next room. It is then likely that she was struck the first blow. It evidently did not knock her senseless, and in all probability she either turned and recognized her assailant, or showed fight, and pulled whatever disguise he had on, so that she knew who he was. He then possibly struck her the second time and she fell back against the sewing machine, causing the wound on the back of her head. The murderer then completed his work, and after gagging her, robbed her of her money, possibly with the assistance of a second man, who might have entered or who may have remained outside as lookout, picked up the lamp and dashed it down on her body, starting the fire."

As he was listening to Dell, Spain recalled acknowledging, "Very good, its practically the same theory I myself worked out." Then Spain told the court, "I next asked the defendant what he thought was used to deliver the blows." Dell proposed an axe or a gun, and how a revolver could have inflicted the wounds.

On the morning of Monday, September 16th, the state rested its case. In all, fifty-eight witnesses were put to stand, weaving a web of circumstantial evidence that placed William Allen Dell in a very precarious position. The supposed climactic testimonies of Harry Watts and Rae Brown never came to fruition, which was disappointing for those in attendance or following the trial.[15] Watts invoked his right against self-incrimination.

Deputy Prosecuting Attorney Livesey delivered the closing remarks for the state. For two hours Livesey recapped the testimony heard in the courtroom. He explained to the jury the definition of "reasonable doubt," and the differences between murder in the first and second degrees, and manslaughter. He claimed that the defenses' case was very weak, and that not one material piece of evidence proved to support their client. He asked them to remember the unexplained scratches on Dell's face, and how he had no memory of how he received them. Livesey pointed out that Abrams was so unsure of his case that he refused to place his client on the stand in his own defense. Closing, Livesey summarized the evidence presented by the state, and explained the meaning of "circumstantial." Prosecutor Peringer would save his words for last.

James Abrams asked that Judge Neterer remove the jury, as he had motions to make, to which Neterer complied. Abrams requested that the court instruct the jury to bring in a verdict of "not guilty" and to discharge the defendant upon the grounds that there was insufficient evidence to implicate his client, and that the state had failed to prove its case. Judge Neterer denied the motion, knowing that it was made in order to complete the record for an appeal to the Supreme Court if convicted.

Abrams asked if the court would allow him two days to organize his defense, but was refused. Judge Neterer granted him until morning to prepare his case, thereby adjourning for the day. On Tuesday, September 17th, Abrams' associate, James F. Moore made the opening remarks for the

---

15   Rae Brown would make the news again on January 24, 1908, when a jealous prostitute by the name of "French" Louise, shot Paul Miller, who held a fancy for her.

defense, first sympathizing with the grieving family seated in the courtroom. Next, facing the jury, he said it was up to them to sort through the cold hard facts of the case and evidence presented before them. He said that at this time they "had no right to have formed any opinions as to the guilt or innocence of the prisoner, and that if any are entertained they should be banished."

"The state has attempted to show conspiracy…has put up the best defense for Dell and…has proven an alibi." Moore encouraged the jury to recall their witness, Kenny Lindsey, who vouched for Dell being in front of Scott's Saloon, and asked them to remember that Dell was said to have been on patrol at the time. Moore spoke further on the witnesses, of Mrs. Maud Briner, who though she might have seen a man of Dell's description running out of the orchard near the Roper home around 9:30 pm, but that she couldn't be sure, and was therefore unreliable. Moore wanted them to take note that Addie hadn't arrived at her home until about 10 pm, so Maud's description wouldn't have fit within the timeline, having seen the someone running prior to Addie's arrival home, and thus, Dell could not have been there. Moore pointed out that the prosecution's own witnesses could not agree whether Dell helped the fire fighters put the fire out or not. More pointedly, Moore concluded that with all of the people Dell had contact with after the fire, no one mentioned having smelled kerosene on him.

All the while William Dell sat unmoved, "calmly chewing a larger quid of tobacco…showing no signs of nervousness and it seemed as though a flinat [sic] smile flitted across his face when attorney Moore said that the state had made the best defense for Dell, and that the prosecution had fixed his alibi."

Attorney Abrams finished the closing, reiterating some of what Moore said, attempting to ridicule and shred the remarks and theories of the state's case against his client. Abrams attacked Peringer's lack of questioning of Sheriff Williams and Deputy DeHaven on the stand, stating that in reality, they had little to offer in the circumstantial trial. Abrams declared, "…apparently (they) did not think much of the case against Dell…"

Peringer followed Abrams with a final rebuttal, disputing the lag in the timeframe. Perhaps for shock value, Peringer claimed that the killer attempted to burn Miss Roper's body slowly, "bit by bit, when the flames got beyond their control," reinstating that it was William Dell who laid in wait as Addie Roper entered her home, and that it was he who struck her down, continuing that the handkerchief was used as a facemask, and that Addie had pulled it off while Dell assaulted her. The *Herald* would later point out that in his closing statements, Peringer's voice cracked and could no longer continue. In all, the defense was able to seat twenty witnesses on the stand, which cast reasonable doubt on the states circumstantial case.

Deliberation

On the afternoon of Thursday, September 19th, Judge Jeremiah Neterer gave the twelve-man jury their instructions before retiring for deliberation. They were to regard the case of rape in Instruction Number 32: "The state has failed to prove that the crime of rape…has been committed… you can not consider this question for any purpose whatsoever in connection with the crime of murder," as well as Number 33: "…the defendant is not charged in the Information in this case with the crime of rape upon the person of Addie Roper and that you can only consider the question of rape in connection with all the other facts…tending to show him guilty of murder…" And, finally, Instruction Number 34: "…you can not find the defendant guilty upon the ground of bad character, upon the ground of suspicion, nor because the greater weight of the evidence may tend to show the defendant guilty…"

After twenty minutes of deliberation, the jury returned with a question for the court - they wished to visit the crime scene. Neterer denied the request on the notion that by allowing them access to the crime scene, evidence would be introduced after the jury had already gone into deliberation. Twenty-three hours later Neterer called the jury out and asked if there was anything the court could do that would help them in reaching a decision, upon which the jury asked if the court's instructions could be reread.

Behind closed doors, the internal debate was heated. The first ballot had opened three camps: four for murder in the first, four for murder in the second and four opposing acquittal and in compliance with whatever the other two camps should decide. The situation remained unvaried even after six more ballots. After hours of debate, the four in the more extreme camp of murder in the first degree had swung the four holdouts and convinced one other juror from the second degree camp over to their side, which moved the vote 9-3. The next ballot mixed it up even more; one of the three in opposition stood for second degree, while the other two voted for acquittal. In another ballot, the vote swung back to where they had started, at which point arguments ensued that those holding out for second degree murder were not going to hang a man on circumstantial evidence. Finally, the men came to the agreement that they would all get what they wanted if Dell were put away for life.

After thirty-two hours in deliberation the twelve men came to a decision. The verdict was read, finding William Allen Dell guilty of murder in the second degree with the potential to receive life imprisonment. Judge Neterer sentenced William Allen Dell to life at the state penitentiary in Walla Walla on October 9, 1907. In response, Dell pleaded, "Your Honor, I was tried by a prejudiced court and jury. I am not guilty of the crime charged." Judge Neterer replied, "I assure you that you were not tried by a prejudiced court, and I am confident you were not found guilty by a prejudiced jury."

The prisoner was remanded to the custody of the sheriff. After receiving the verdict, Dell seemed unshaken. Deputy Miller escorted him out. It wasn't until then, out of sight, that Dell sank to the floor and Miller was forced to half-carry him back to his cell. Dell turned to Miller and said, "Gee, they handed me a bunch."

Harry Watts on Trial

While "Doan" Dell was on trial, Harry Watts waited in confinement for his turn in the courtroom. One could imagine Watts' eventual deterioration during his incarceration, lengthy as it was, but he managed to maintain his innocence and seemed to show no sign of concern. Even after he found out the verdict against Dell, Watts laid on his bunk and shrugged, telling those surrounding that it had nothing to do with him. Meanwhile, on Tuesday, October 8th, Virgil Peringer filed Information in Superior Court formally charging Watts with first degree murder. A few weeks later, on October 22nd, Watts received a summons from his wife of seven years, Mamie, for divorce. She filed it in King County claiming non-support and desertion. It had been five years since she had seen her husband.

Counsel for the defense, Jacob Noethe, immediately filed affidavits in an attempt to prove to the court that prejudice against Watts existed, and asked for a change of venue. Noethe claimed his client's name was dragged through the mud in Dell's trial, which wouldn't allow for a fair venue or impartial treatment. Judge Neterer rejected his request.

By December 5th, after a time consuming selection where potential jurors were asked such long-winded questions that it was hard to gather enough of them who weren't bewildered, a jury[16] was finalized. When Watts entered the courtroom he was described by the *Herald* to look "as debonair as ever, and his confinement in the county jail has not altered his appearance to any noticeable extent."

16   Jury for Watts included W. E. Kale, Roeder, farmer; W. T. Follis, Meridian, logger; C. O. Mulder, Lynden, carpenter; E. A. DeGolier, Everson, mill owner; Marcus Tuttle, Lummi Island, farmer; George W. Smith, VanWyck, farmer; Albert Matz, Ferndale, rancher; A. A. Rogers, Bellingham, contractor; W. H. Carpenter, Woodlawn, logger; Frank Honey, Rome, rancher; G. Frank Moody, Bellingham, merchant.

The trial of Harry Watts began on the freezing winter's morning of Friday, December 6, 1907. It had been nearly a year since Addie Roper's murder; her black charred house would remain standing in Blaine until the trials were over with.

As it had been with William "Doan" Dell's trial, the courtroom was packed with community spectators, Judge Neterer presiding, and prosecutors Peringer and Livesey represented the state. Jacob Noethe, counsel for the defense, was the only new player. Peringer's opening remarks were similar to that which he had delivered in Dell's trial; he outlined his intent, introduced that a few new witnesses would take the stand, and asserted that the red bandana found wedged in Addie Roper's throat would play a larger role. Noethe passed on opening remarks, choosing to wait until later in the trial. The first day brought testimony from the same witnesses of Dell's trial with very similar answers. Nothing new was offered, but the crowded courtroom hung on every word.

A caricature of Watts in an apple orchard, as depicted by the Seattle Times', "Mystery of the Spinster."
Seattle Times, March 28, 1948.

John R. Roper, brother of Addie Roper, along with his wife, child and two sisters sat in the courtroom. Watts had the support of his mother and sister, who sat close by.

Noethe knew he was up against overwhelming odds. He gave a brief opening statement to a court he considered ready to convict. He pointed out that the state's evidence was purely circumstantial, riddled with unreliable eyewitnesses who saw nothing more than shadows moving in the night. He declared there was an open conspiracy aiming to railroad his client, as no credible evidence was ever presented against Watts. Directly after his opening, Noethe proceeded to call witnesses to the stand, many of who refuted previous eyewitness testimonies. Throughout, Noethe did not entertain in courtroom dramatics.

It wasn't until December 10th that testimony became interesting and most incriminating for Watts; that was the day testimony focused on the handkerchief. Salvation Army officer Stewart M. Wile, a 42 year-old widower formally of Canada was called to the stand. Wile claimed to have visited the county jail in April where Watts had confessed to him. He was accustomed to visiting the jail on Sundays, holding religious services for the prisoners. Wile said that one Sunday in April he was urging Watts to lead a better life. Watts commented that if he had lived in a Christian environment, he wouldn't have found himself in such a situation, to which Wile responded, "It's never too late." Watts hung his head before looking back into Wile's eyes. "That handkerchief found in Miss Addie Roper's mouth is mine, and it's a giveaway," reported Wile.

Under cross-examination by Noethe, addressing this particular conversation, Wile said that those were not the exact words he had heard, but that they were very close from what he could remember. Noethe continued his questioning, becoming aggressive toward Wile. Peringer protested the line of questioning and demanded the court stop Noethe from "bulldozing the witness." Noethe denied the use of any such tactics. A verbal argument ensued and intensified between the attorneys until Judge Neterer ceased the bickering. Noethe was able to string out that although Wile said that he had received the "alleged" confession in April, he did not tell Sheriff Williams or anyone about it until Dell's trial, at which point he forwarded the information to Dell's attorney. But, in the case of Dell, Abrams never called Wile as a witness. Noethe asked Wile if he knew there was a reward for the conviction of the murderer, to which Wile said that he neither knew, nor wanted any such reward.

Noethe tried discrediting Wile by having him relay to the jury how he had to resign from the Salvation Army because of his actions at the jail, neglecting services to others in order to spend more of his time talking with Dell and Watts. He was asked whether he had attempted to get Watts to write a confession, to which he denied.

Bessie Stuart of Mount Vernon and Rae Brown's laundress took the stand, offering that she had occasionally found items in the laundry belonging to Harry Watts when he stayed with Brown. She stated with certainty that the handkerchief found in Addie's throat belonged to Watts, of which she could be sure for its uniqueness – a red apple blossom design along the edge, and because her laundry mark was on it. She had washed it many times, and had last washed it just a week or two prior to the crime.

Sixty-two witnesses were brought before the jury in efforts to convict or free Watts. Whenever the jury seemed to waiver their attention, Peringer would bring up William Dell to tie the relationship to Watts. Noethe, in a bitter fight to save Watts, recognized the importance of disproving any ties between his client and the red handkerchief. Noethe called several witness to the stand who declared never to have seen the handkerchief before. Though they may have lacked credibility, the Blaine sporting house Mistress Mildred Neilson and inmate Rita Calvert took the stand, swearing that they had never seen the red handkerchief, and furthermore, that the defendant had been with them playing cards at the time of the murder.

At noon the prosecution was put to rest.

On the morning of Friday, December 13th, Harry Watts took the stand to defend himself. He denied all allegations made against him by the state's witnesses. He claimed to not know anything about the death of Addie Roper or the fire, and that he never owned a red handkerchief, let alone one with blossoms on it. He declared the witnesses as liars, and denied confessing anything to Stewart Wile while in the county jail.

On the stand he relayed his background, which gradually led up to his association with Rae Brown and Raymond Lange, and that his only ambition had been to open a restaurant in the back of the saloon. In the first hour, Watts' defense attorney, Noethe maintained a rather mundane line of questioning until Watts relayed his activities the night of the murder, upon which testimony picked up pace. Noethe said, "Now you may tell the jury what you did…on the night of the fire, until train time."

"I think it was about 5 o'clock when I went down to the mill at the foot of the wharf and stayed for a while. It must have been about 6 o'clock when I went to the electric company to get some light globes for Mrs. Neilson…I went to the house to fix the lights and ate lunch. I went to the parlor and sat down near Rita Calvert…but she wasn't interested in talking so I went upstairs to my room and lay for a while. It must have been about 8:30 or 9 when I got up and went down stairs. I was talking to one of the girls, and then we proposed to play cards. She suggested the game of 'coon can.'[17] Mrs. Neilson coached me. About an hour later the 'Jap' cook came in and hollered fire. We rushed to the

17   "Coon can" or "Conquian" is a card game of either Mexican or Spanish origins, thought mistakenly to have racial condemnations. Played with a 40-card deck, the object is to be the first to meld eleven cards, including the last card drawn.

door and could see flames. Later Lange came in and we arranged to go to Mount Vernon on the Owl train. I was to meet Rae Brown and get some money with which to start a restaurant."

Noethe interrupted Watts and asked if it were possible for anyone to have exited the building from anywhere other than the front door. Watts said it wasn't possible; there wasn't a viable walkway around the building as it was erected on pilings and projected out over the tide flats, which could be surrounded by water at high tide.

"It was about midnight when I left the place to meet Lange at the Reception Saloon, as planned. When I asked for him I found he was gone. I stayed in the saloon for a time fixing some electric lights. From either Manning or Snavely...I borrowed $1.50 in order to go to Mount Vernon. I remember someone told me I would have to hurry if I wanted to make the train. I started down to the depot, and when I was halfway there, overtook Dick Dorr, who is a cripple and uses crutches...it was raining, and tried to hold my umbrella over him, but he objected saying it was in his way...Upon reaching the depot I stood outside, Dorr saying it was too hot inside. Through a window I could see William Tierney, Doan Dell, George Shaw and William Walton inside the waiting room talking together. My coat was wet and I took it off and hung it over the back of a chair to dry. I then went in and got a drink. I did not have anything with me in the nature of a sack, except my tobacco sack. I never carried tobacco in my vest pocket. I then stood around talking and cutting my fingernails with a small manicuring knife. When the train came in I got aboard and met Lange. Dell came up to him and said he would have to detain him. I said to Lange, 'If you are not going to use your ticket, give it to me,' and he handed it over."

"I got to Mount Vernon about 5 o'clock and met Ray Allen[18] and Rae Brown. We had several drinks with a traveling man and then Ray Allen wanted to know why Lange was detained. I replied that that is what he got for being first at the fire and giving the alarm, and that when they held an inquest he would be wanted as a witness. I guessed he would be down Sunday."

"I stayed in Mount Vernon all day Sunday. Ray Allen apparently was drunk, as she staggered about. Sunday night I got a telephone call from Blaine asking me if I was coming back. They said they wanted me, but I didn't know what for."

"I went up to Blaine on the Owl train Sunday morning. Two policemen arrested me as I got off.[19] They took me to the city jail. There, Tierney told me that I was wanted for the murder of Miss Roper. He said Lange had confessed. I replied that Lange was either drunk or crazy."

"They then took me to Bellingham where I was held in the city jail for five days and then placed in the county jail. I remained there until the preliminary hearing in Blaine, about

18   Allen, an African-American, born in Winnipeg in 1887, continuously crossed from Vancouver, B.C. into Blaine working the waterfront and at houses from Skagit County to Seattle.

19   A different story compared to Deputy Sheriff Thomas DeHaven's going to Mount Vernon to retrieve Harry Watts.

May 1, when I was discharged. I was arrested on September 5 at Anacortes, and have been held ever since."

Noethe asked Watts if he knew Stewart Wile, to which he replied, "He came to me as a total stranger. I think I met him three times." He told the jury he never told Wile that the handkerchief used to gag Roper was his, nor that it was a "dead give-away." Noethe then asked, "Did you murder Miss Roper?" "No, sir" came the unflinching answer.

After seven days of testimony, the prosecution and defense gave counter-statements and closing arguments on the evening of the 13th and the 14th. Newspapers reported the largest crowd since the trial had opened. So great was "the jam" in the courtroom that women were forced to stand. Many were afraid of losing their seats and brought baskets of food so that they wouldn't have to leave.

Deputy Prosecutor Livesey dragged the jury and spectators through the entire proceedings again, dwelling heavily upon Dell, who in his trusted capacity of night watchman for Blaine, had permitted Watts to leave the city, indicating that there had been an association.

Livesey went on the attack against the credibility of the defense's witnesses. Raising his finger to the air, the deputy prosecutor hollered, "They attack the reputation of Mrs. Mollie Allen in regard to her truth and veracity. And who do they bring to say that it is bad?…The class of people for whom you care little what they think of you."

Noethe did all he could to refute the state's case. In his closing remarks he told the jury that the state showed no motive for murder, or his client's involvement. He stated Watts could not be attributed the motive alleged against Dell, namely, criminal assault, or rape. Noethe declared that robbery had been hinted, but the state failed to prove that Addie Roper had any money, nor that his client prospered from the crime.

On Sunday, December 15th at 10 o'clock in the morning, the verdict was read to the courtroom - guilty of murder in the second degree. There was an ominous silence as the verdict was read. The judgment came as a surprise, as the case against Watts was far weaker than that against William Dell. It took the jury only four and a half hours to make their decision, while the jury of Dell's had taken more than forty-two hours.

Watts took the decision stoically, but his father, standing close by, looked at his son with tears running down his cheeks. He seemed dazed, and nearly collapsed. The following day Noethe filed a motion for a new trial, claiming jury prejudice and judicial error, which was denied on January 4, 1908.

Watts sat in the courtroom throughout the trial. He appeared confident while Noethe was arguing his case, but when the court overruled the motion he showed signs of nervousness and heavy strain. He appeared ill at ease and when taken from the courtroom he lost his air of jaunty indifference and wore a troubled expression.

On Saturday, January 11th, Judge Neterer asked Watts if he had anything to say before passing judgment. Watts said, "I don't think anything I can say will have any effect on this case!" With that, Neterer sentenced Watts to life imprisonment at hard labor in the state penitentiary.

Watts did his best to appear nonchalant, but was deeply affected in his preparation to be transferred on April 14th. He shaved off his trademark mustache. His hands had a noticeable tremor as his escort Aaron B. Estabrook adjusted the "steel darbies" to his wrists. Although he appeared shattered, Watts remained composed as he bid goodbye to his fellow cellmates. He shook the hands of the sheriff and deputies alike. Officer Trimble made the last remarks beside Watts' name in the jailers' ledger, stating "Disposition made, turned over to guard from state penitentiary to serve out a life sentence."

Epilogue - William Allen "Doan" Dell

William Allen "Doan" Dell, Washington State Penitentiary at Walla Walla.
Washington State Archives.

William Dell was received at the Washington State Penitentiary in
Walla Walla on December 18, 1907; his paperwork was filed on the 28th, and
he became prisoner No. 4741. Dell's medical examination form describes
him as having gonorrhea.

Dell's prison file produces one bit of interest - a letter from Virgil
Peringer dated December 1908, who on the behalf of the state, was sending former Salvation Army officer Steward Wile on a mission to speak with
Dell. This meeting came about as a result of letters Dell had been writing
to Peringer. What was Peringer hoping to gain from Dell, the man he had
already put away for life? Was he looking for a confession? Did he hope that
Dell would offer him his accomplices?

Peringer asked Warden Reed to give Wile alone time with Dell so
that they could talk confidentially, promising that if Wile produced positive

results or obtained statements of value, Reed would send for a stenographer and a notary public. Peringer made it clear to Reed that, "This effort is not at this time subject to publicity of any character, and hence favor us if you prevent this becoming generally known at this time."

All expenses were forwarded to the Whatcom County prosecutor's office. This is all the information secured from Wile's mission, the results of which have never been known.

It has been speculated that the correspondence, between Dell and Peringer marked the beginning of Dell's mental deterioration. Dell also maintained correspondence with a Jessie Boyd of Kirkland. In 1924 she wrote Warden Clarence Long for answers regarding Dell.

"He somehow got my name, having heard I was interested in prison work, and wrote to me asking me to help him, as he had not a friend in the world. He told me he was in for murder, but had been there for 16 years. Well, I have a queer feeling naturally, when it comes to men who have committed such a crime, yet my sympathy, was somehow aroused, because he had appealed directly to me. He writes very illiterate letters, and in his last addressed me by my first name. What I am debating is - am I really doing this man any good, writing him every month a friendly letter…and since you have spoken of his bad record in prison (indicating prior communication), it has given me pause. But I do not want to give him up if I can do him any good. Has his record improved lately? Does he write his own letters? Does he really work in a greenhouse? Did he have a trip outside prison walls to dig 'spuds?'"

Clarence Long, in response,

"…We should have mentioned that, while he has not been charged with many infractions of our institutional rules, he has not established a record of diligence in labor, etc. He is not well-balanced mentally, and the statements he has made to you relative to his work here, are erroneous. He has not worked outside the prison walls since he was admitted here. We have had him under observation for sometime past, and if his aberrations become more pronounced than they are at the present time, he will undoubtedly be transferred to the Eastern State Hospital for treatment. We are always glad to have the inmates of this institution receive helpful letters, and encourage the correspondents of the men here to write as often as is possible. However, in the case of Dell, we believe he would not be susceptible to such refining influences and you would not be compensated for your efforts…"

As predicted by Long in his letter, Dell's mental state deteriorated. He was transferred to the Eastern State Hospital, Medical Lake on Thursday, January 7, 1932. The prison physician claimed Dell demonstrated "senile dementia with marked delusions. He is boisterous, yells and sings continuously night and day and is totally unmanageable. He, in all probability, will not survive for many days." Dell was transferred, but died on Monday, January 11th, and was buried on the prison grounds.

In February 1949, Dell's daughter, Sophie Dell Peabody wrote the warden asking for any personal information regarding her father. She received a curt answer that he was dead. She wrote again in 1957 as Sophie Bennett, inquiring about her father once more, but received little more.

Harry Watts

Harry Watts, Washington State Penitentiary at Walla Walla. Watts was so traumatized by the verdict that he shaved off his trademark mustache. Washington State Archives.

Harry Watts was received April 15, 1908 as prisoner No. 4897. His medical examination revealed gonorrhea, soft chancres and venereal warts, no doubt the result of his experiences in the restricted district. When asked what contributed to his present troubles, Watts answered that he "married too young."

Watts lived behind bars for less than a year and a half, all the while severely depressed. On Saturday, August 14, 1909, after weeks of illness revolving around a throat infection, Watts died a painful death of phlegmonous tonsillitis.

In the last paragraph of his article in, "True Detective Mysteries," regarding the Roper case, William DeHaven wrote, "As one dreary day after another passed, his calm gave way to apathy. Watts had thrived in an atmosphere of gayety - bright lights, music, drinking and dancing [sic]...His life in prison was a steady routine of hard labor with a barren cell awaiting him at dark... Watts turned his face to the wall and died."

On April 19, 1913, Watts' ex-wife Mamie (Olmsted), who at the time resided in Bellevue, wrote Harry Drum, who was the warden at the penitentiary. She had heard conflicting reports of her former husband's death and wanted to confirm the rumors. Although he wasn't a good husband, she never believed he was guilty of the crime. Mamie pleaded that she "would like to know, as he was the father of my children." The answer she received was brief. She was given a date of death, and that his father, John Watts, had claimed the body in Everett.

Through 1964 and 1965, Harry Watts' eldest daughter, Greta Evans who was living in Bellevue, and was 63 years old made a concerted effort to learn more about her father. The family had separated for what reason is unknown, and Greta's mother had regained contact in 1914. After years of searching, Greta miraculously found her sister in 1962, living in California. She discovered her father's grave in 1964 with no name or marker.

John Watts claimed the body of his son, who was interned in Everett, Washington, but had no means to purchase a headstone. findagrave.com

Greta told the governor that since the age of 16, she had read the court records over and over. As a child, and now as a woman, she found the trial a "mockery" convicting her father on circumstantial evidence. Though many of the family had died since her father's incarceration, including her mother, she wanted his name cleared. She had heard a family rumor that 24-hours after his death, a pardon, long in progress, had come through. If this weren't the case, Greta was prepared to fight for it before she died, which was imminent, she revealed, having been ill for quite some time.

On Tuesday, February 23, 1965, Greta learned for the first time that her father, on August 15, 1909, was indeed granted a pardon by Governor Marion E. Hay. Who it was that initiated the process is unknown. Sadly, the information, which would have put the family at ease over so many years, was never divulged to them in all their correspondence.

Chapter 2
Death on the Border

Sumas, Washington. Circa: 1900s. Courtesy of Jim Doidge

In 1908, a truly atrocious murder occurred at the U.S. Immigration detention facility in Sumas, Washington. At the time, as it was culturally, Asian populations were met with general disdain; media reporting was often racist and degrading[1], and incidents regarding Chinese immigrants rarely made headlines. Such was the murder in 1908; it made few headlines in local papers before interest was eventually lost. Even the trial received little attention.

The story of Lee (Li) Wing Wah and Young Shee takes place shortly after the turn of the twentieth century, when rigid immigration laws unfairly persecuted Chinese immigrants who sought to enter the United States. In no place was this mistreatment more evident than on the west coast from California to Washington State, where Asian populations were greatest. By 1903, entry points at the US/Canadian border, such as Sumas in Whatcom

1   The racially charged writing style of that era has been retained, to read as reported.

87

County, had detention centers that housed immigrant "undesirables" until a determination was made for entry or deportation.

The Chinese Exclusion Act passed in 1882, barring the majority of Chinese immigrants, primarily laborers, from entering the United States. In addition, the law prohibited Chinese people, no matter how long they had legally resided in the U.S., from becoming naturalized citizens. This Act followed the earlier Page Act of 1875, which prohibited the immigration of forced laborers and prostitutes. Chinese who traveled outside the United States were required to obtain reentry certifications. The Scott Act of 1888 reinforced the prohibition of reentry. The next significant exclusionary legislation prohibiting Chinese from reentering the United States, the Geary Act, was passed in 1892. It required Chinese to register and secure a certificate as proof of their right to be in the United States. Imprisonment or deportation was the penalty for those failing to have the required documents in their possession.

And Now a Chinaman in California Has Invented a Practical Airship

A caricature of a "Chinaman Airship" crossing the border is an example of the national mood to keep Chinese nationals from immigrating into the United States. Bellingham Herald, September 25, 1909.

"CHINK" SEASON WILL OPEN TOMORROW

Enthusiastic Hunters Prepare to Get Away Early In the Morning Before the Young Birds are All Dead or Educated In the Methods of Men With Guns.

Derogatory announcement regarding the opening of pheasant hunting season gives an indication of accepted racism during the early 1900s. The last sentence ends the article: "A large quota of hunters will invade Skagit county for quail, but the main body of the army will hunt in the northern part of the county for 'Chinks.'" These remarks were not uncommon in newspapers at the time. Bellingham Herald, September 29, 1909.

Such exclusionary legislation led to a thriving underground railroad, which was created to smuggle Chinese nationals from the British Crown Colony of Hong Kong, where they would suffer depravity and dismal conditions while sailing aboard steamers bound for Vancouver, British Columbia. From Canada, many were illegally smuggled across the U.S. border in small boats or over land through the region's densely forested interior. Unscrupulous smugglers demanded outrageous amounts of money to move their human cargo, with little concern or regard for the safety of their clientele.

One notorious Chinese-trafficking corridor extended from the U.S. border town of Sumas and ran 35 miles south into Sedro-Woolley in Skagit County. This route was a highway for nighttime smuggling activities abetting the entrance of Chinese nationals. Undoubtedly, many Chinese were left to their own demise once they made it across the border. During one infamous smuggling run just outside of Sedro-Woolley, tipped-off authorities lying in wait engaged in a fierce gun battle with the smugglers, as forty Chinese nationals scrambled to escape the line of fire and their subsequent capture.

If a Chinese national was entering the U.S. legally, through a border port of entry, the experience was a harsh reality of injustice. The length of time immigrants were detained varied depending on how long officials could extend their interrogation process. If an immigrant were fortunate, the delay would only last a few days. For others it could last months. If detainees were under suspicion of lying or were discovered to hold false paperwork, interrogations would grow lengthy and brutal. The entry process was purposely designed to be very difficult and grueling in order to weed out fraudulent individuals, and likely, to wield power over a nationality in particular need.

The interrogation procedure involved calling the applicant before a Board of Special Inquiry, composed of immigration inspectors; a stenographer and translator were also called upon it necessary. Over the course of several hours, days, or months, the individual would be subjected to specific questions regarding their family history, location of their village and homes and so on. The process was long and tedious, and made more so if the inspectors had cause for concern. However, there was a way to expedite the questioning – the applicant could prepare with their sponsor in advance by memorizing potential answers to questions. If under suspicion of falsifying their identity the process became longer, witnesses from the United States, or settled family members were called in to corroborate the applicant's story. Verifying the testimony of family members who lived great distances across the country extended the process even more. If further suspected of falsification and deceit, the applicant and the resident family faced potential deportation.

Wah and Shee

On Wednesday, March 3, 1908, two Chinese nationals, 43 year-old Lee Wing Wah, and his 21 year-old wife, Young Shee, attempted to cross the border at Sumas. The two were without proper identification or certificates of residency. Wah, speaking through a U.S. interpreter by the name of Quan Foy, nervously explained to the lead inspector in charge, Harry Edsell, that Young Shee was his wife and that they lived in San Francisco, California where he was a wealthy merchant.[2] Edsell sensed a ruse, and held the couple for further questioning. They were offered quarters on the detention center's second floor, which was reserved for family. Local newspapers did not mention any other couples or families occupying the second floor, thus, it is assumed the Wahs were alone.

The detention center at the Sumas port of entry into the United States. Circa: 1900s. Whatcom Museum

Lee Wing Wah and Young Shee underwent fifty-five days of detention and interrogation, during which time the couple increasingly argued and fought with one another. The discord continued until the night of April 26th when Young Shee was murdered.

---

2   Wah claimed that he was a merchant for the Hipp On Company, at 216 Second Street, Oakland, California.

Lee Wing Wah admitted to killing his wife, Young Shee, but for what reason, and under what circumstance, remains in question. Wah maintained that he only fulfilled his wife's "fervent wish to die," claiming she tried to cut her own throat, and that he was only helping her complete the gruesome task. However, under questioning it became apparent that Lee Wing Wah was psychotic. Amidst incoherent gibberish, his story would change continuously.

Harry Edsell had several theories as to why Young Shee would seek to commit suicide, theories developed from his experience working the border. The first, he suspected, was that Shee didn't want to be deported back to China, which could mean losing the respect of her family. The second was that Wah was attempting to bring Shee into the country as a concubine or to be sold into a brothel.[3] Third, he supposed, was that she was married against her will, and was severely depressed, preferring death to Wah.

The Deed

Lee Wing Wah admitted to quarreling with his wife, and that she repeatedly expressed a wish to die. He said she nagged at him about wanting to die so often that he decided to help her.

It was after midnight on Saturday, he claimed, that he heard a noise, which woke him from his slumber. Looking over toward his wife, he saw her lying on her cot gripping his straightedge razor and attempting to cut her own throat. She was having a difficult time of it, he would later claim. Wah watched her for a few moments, noting the feeble mess she was making of it. Her hand trembled, making only a shallow three-inch jagged gash along her small throat. A moment later she dropped the razor to the floor next to her cot. He heard gurgling sounds.

Wah knew she had the will, but not the courage to take her own life. They were married in China barely a year before, and Wah would claim

3   This may have been the price of her ship passage and U.S. entry, paid into Wah's pocket, with future earnings from prostitution sent to her family as income or for her passage to Canada.

that it was because of his love for her that he could not deny her desire to end her life. Observing her difficulties, Wah lifted himself from his cot and walked over to Young Shee. Looking at his beautiful young wife, he reached down, gently taking her hand into his own, while reaching to the floor for the bloodied razor with the other. In Wah's mind it was simple – he was fulfilling his wife's wishes. He believed that she had closed her eyes and tilted her head back for him.

Looking down at her for one last moment, Wah gripped the razor tightly and drew a deep slash across Shee's throat, so deeply that he could feel the resistance of her cervical vertebrae against the blade, and he nearly decapitated his wife. Severing the jugular vein, Shee's blood sprayed all over the canvas cot and onto the wooden fir floorboards with each pulsation of her heart.

It is possible that Lee Wing Wah murdered his wife to dispose of her, for in his madness, perhaps, he felt like it would relieve the burden of their detention. It is also possible that she may have threatened to expose him for whatever secret they shared.

Wah carried her corpse out of the room, through a long hallway, and down a set of stairs to the main floor landing. The door at the bottom of the stairs was locked and Wah was unable to force it open. He left Shee's body in the stairwell and went back to the second floor room to clean up the blood. When he was finished he climbed onto his canvas cot and slept until Sunday morning.

A detention officer discovered Young Shee the next morning, fully clothed, minus her shoes and stockings. Whatcom County Coroner Henry Thompson, who was in Everson at the time, was notified at once of the potential murder. He left for Sumas immediately. Whatcom County Sheriff Andrew Williams boarded the train from Bellingham to Sumas a short time thereafter.

CHINAMAN MURDERS WIFE

Crazed Oriental Who Is Held at the Government Detention House in Sumas, Pending Deportation Proceedings, Cuts the Throat of Woman Who Occupied Room iWth Him.

PRISONER PARTIALLY ADMITS HIS GUILT

Says Woman Tried to Cut Her Own Threat, and That He Helped to Complete Gruesome Work.

Bellingham Herald, April 27, 1908.

At first Wah denied killing Young Shee, but later confessed to Sheriff Williams that when she had started to cut her own throat with his straight-edge razor, and as she was making poor work of it, he decided to help her out. Williams found the murder weapon in the room, hidden inside one of the many foldaway cots stacked against a wall.

With Wah's confession and the weapon retrieved, Coroner Thompson decided that no inquest would be required. Instead, he assembled an examination of Wah that day, with Harry Edsell, Chinese Inspector in Charge at the Port of Sumas, along with Quan Foy as official interpreter and John Wetering, stenographer.

In trying to establish his background, Thompson put forth a list of questions for Wah. He asked about his first wife, whom Wah said had passed away in China while he was in America, four years prior. He said that they had been married for over 20 years and had two daughters and a son, who had all died young. After mentioning the death of his first wife and his children, Wah exclaimed, "…but I heard her[4] voice last night, asking me to come back to China." Thompson asked if he had heard other voices besides his daughter's. Wah said, "She has been talking a great deal, but last night she told me to come back to China."

Following Thompson, Inspector Edsell asked a series of questions. "Do you remember talking to me yesterday afternoon?" Wah said yes, but admitted that he couldn't remember their conversation. Edsell reminded Wah that he had sent him back to his room after that day's interrogation had ended, and had told him to tell Young Shee to come to the office. Wah agreed to Edsell's description of events. Edsell asked what happened after Young Shee had returned to the room, upon which Wah replied,

> "Nothing happened, she just went to her room and scolded me, and also in early times I heard that she would like to die. She started talking a little too loud and I stopped her. I just talked to her asking her to stop talking so loud. After dark we sat in the room, and then went to bed till after midnight and she cut herself to death – Several days ago she intended to die when she dressed up and combed her hair."

---

4   His daughter's voice.

95

Edsell interjected bluntly, "Where was she when you cut her to death?"

Wah calmly answered through the interpreter, "In bed, in the room. Her own bed."

Henry Thompson cut in, asking what Wah had done between the time he took her body downstairs until the next morning. Wah admitted to wiping up the blood and falling asleep before getting up to wash himself. A towel and two cloths covered with blood were found on a bench, still wet; another was draped against the faucet of the sink. "Why did you not call for help?" asked Thompson.

Wah's eyes darted about. He looked confused. He told the men that his brother-in-law was a prisoner in the basement, and offered, "I heard the voice of a pistol shot outside and also my wife's brother and mother are here. They began to have a shooting again this morning." Edsell paused, looking at Wah, unsure of the man's lucidity.

Edsell asked Wah to remove his outer clothes; Wah complied. There were no bloodstains on his underclothes, but the bottoms of his socks were caked in blood. Edsell asked if Wah had noticed what Young Shee had used to cut herself with. Wah looked at him, and speaking through Foy said, "She cut herself first, and after that I found the razor and I cut the rest of it...I wanted to separate it entirely."[5] Wah was asked once more why he didn't try to get help; he repeated that she wanted to die. Edsell produced the razor, asking where it was from and Wah admitted to having purchased it in Hong Kong.

Then Lee Wing Wah made the following statement,

"Many days ago she was talking to me and said, we cannot be admitted into the United States, and we cannot go back to China right away now...I am willing to die. We have a law

---

5   Grabbing the razor from the floor, he sought to sever her neck completely.

suit of the same case in China too, and we have a law suit in this case here, but the woman is dead now and the officers can give me a pass, and I wish you would tell George that I want to go back to China with my mother."

Thompson asked who George was. "All of these men," replied Wah.

A confused Thompson then asked, "Are your mother, your son and daughter here?"

Wah said, "They must be here this morning, because I heard the voice of my mother, brother and daughter."

After the examination, Coroner Thompson told Sheriff Williams, "that to his mind there is no doubt that the Chinaman is crazy and that he committed the deed, for he admitted it."

Williams' official statement to the local newspapers read:

"The tragedy was enacted in the sleeping room, while the woman was lying on a cot. After the cutting had been done Wah picked up the corpse and dragged it out of the room downstairs. At the end of the stairway Wah was stopped by a locked door. He evidently tried to force the door, as the panels looked as if he tried to break through. He was brought to a halt here. He then dropped the body on the steps where it was found and went back and started to clean up the room. He offered no explanation as to why he dragged the body down the hallway, but did say he was too tired and sleepy to give the alarm after he had assisted the woman to slay herself. He wiped the blood off the floor with some cloths, and these he washed in the sink. He also used some newspapers to remove evidence of the crime, but could not make away with these. They were found hidden in the corner."

"Yellow Slayer Tells Wild Tales"

Wah was placed under arrest and transported to the Whatcom County Jail in Bellingham. He did not like having the handcuffs placed on him and protested, offering to give the sheriff $1,000 dollars, which the sheriff considered intended to be a bribe. "When he saw that the officer meant business he came along without further trouble."

Wah was incarcerated with a fellow national, Mah Ah John, who was serving a year sentence for assaulting a cannery foreman with a fillet knife. Wah told his fellow cellmate a strange tale about how Quan Foy, the Sumas interpreter, intended to deport him back to China, and that he had sought to take Shee as his own. Ma Ah John was bewildered, noticing Wah's long fingernails as he spoke, his hands waving about in great excitement. Before Sheriff Williams left the cell, Ma Ah John called him over and handed him a small pair of scissors and a tack hammer that he had found in the room, and said, "Wah heap [sic] bad."

On Tuesday April 28, 1908, the *Bellingham Herald* headlined a column, "Yellow Slayer Tells Wild Tales: Chinese Who Murdered Wife At Sumas Talks Like Insane Man." The article stated that whenever anyone attempted to talk with "Lee Wing Wah, the Chink…the Oriental flies into violent fits of passion." Cellmate Mah Ah John told a reporter that his violent fits were so fierce that he feared on several occasions that Wah would suffer a stroke. He admitted that he was afraid of Wah, claiming he was a "crazy man, rambling along on many subjects, but never telling anything about himself or the wife he killed."

YELLOW SLAYER TELLS WILD TALES

Chinese Who Murdered Wife At Sumas Talks Like Insane Man— Refuses to Tell Anything About Himself Or Woman He Killed— Murder Is the Charge.

6 Bellingham Herald, April 28, 1908.

A reporter who sat down with Wah profited from a series of wild tales. One such story was that he had lived for twenty years as a merchant in California, though he could not speak a word of English. He also intimated that he had a lot of money, but that it couldn't be located, and that Shee had rich parents in China. Lee Wing Wah did have some connections in both business and family within the San Francisco Bay area, but to what extent was unclear. It was perhaps such business or family who contacted the Chinese Embassy or Consulate on Wah's behalf.

When asked what arrangements he wanted made of his wife's body, which at the time still lay in the undertaking parlors at Sumas, Wah said to "fix it up so that it would keep three or four days" so that he could take it back to China. At the same time, a telegram was forwarded through official channels asking that Young Shee's body be preserved and prepared for shipment to San Francisco, where it would be forwarded on to China for proper internment. Expenses were to be covered by an envoy coming to Bellingham.

99

Soon after the telegram was received, Sun Chong, a San Francisco agent claiming to represent the relatives of Lee Wing Wah, arrived in the city for the purpose of inquiring into the murder case. Newspapers claimed Chong was acquainted with neither Wah nor his wife, but was supported by a business of interest in the Bay Area's Chinese community, and would present $10,000 for Wah's defense. Chong may have been sent as a representative through the Hipp On Company of Oakland. The firm was prepared to fight Wah's legal battle in the court system. The *Herald* declared, "…the Chink will have plenty of financial backing and some of the best legal talent in this part of the state will be engaged to defend him."

It was briefly contemplated as to whether Wah's case fell under state or federal jurisdiction, but Whatcom County Prosecuting Attorney Virgil Peringer concluded that there was no difficulty under the law. "The Chink was in this county at the time he committed the crime, so he is amenable to the laws of the state." On May 2nd, Peringer and Deputy Prosecuting Attorney George Livesey filed Information against Wah for murder in the first degree in Superior Court. Wah was arraigned three days later, entering a plea of not guilty before Superior Court Judge Jeremiah Neterer. The trial was set to start on June 1, 1908. Neterer appointed Bellingham attorneys Hans Bugge and Charles Swartz of Bugge & Swartz Law Partners to represent Wah's defense. 40 year-old Bugge had established a practice out of the Pike Building in Bellingham. Though his name was Harris, he went by the name of Hans, so many mistook him as German. It was when he spoke that it was obvious he was from Norway. His partner, Swartz was 46 years old at the time, a proud Ohioan and well versed in the law.

As the trial was set to begin, an interpreter had yet to be found who could translate Wah's commentary into English, as each invariably ended up with the same assertion that the prisoner was unbalanced and that they couldn't make sense of what he was saying. Neterer requested that Low Sam, a local merchant, act as court interpreter on the case. Sam, who really didn't want to be associated with Wah, reluctantly gave in to the court's needs and agreed to translate. After the plea had been entered, Low Sam declared that the prisoner had "wheels in his head" and that Wah talked "crazy."

Amidst the plea, Wah maintained that Shee had cut her own throat. He was said to be as erratic as ever while being hauled back to his cell, making wild and unintelligible statements. Low Sam said that he spoke relentlessly of his wealth while in the detention house, and how he wanted to give it away. Even Bugge and Swartz couldn't make sense of Wah, and as was the same for all others involved in the case, had to depend upon an interpreter to compile a tangible defense.

Sun Chong held a meeting with Bugge and Swartz, regarding defense strategy and expenses. The attorneys later assisted Chong in securing details regarding the location of the crime in Sumas, and inquiring on the status of Shee's body, which had been embalmed in preparation for shipment back to China.

After a thorough investigation, Chong called upon Lee Wing Wah at the county jail for an interview. Until then neither had met before, although Chong knew of Wah and his family, as they had lived in adjoining provinces in China. Chong was expecting to facilitate Wah's attorneys with translation and to take down in writing Wah's version of events. Chong might have sympathized with Wah, acknowledging that frustration or feeling stir-crazy from two months of detention could be viable reasons for his acts of insanity and wanted to make sure the documentation on his character wasn't misleading and mistaken as malcontent. By now it was said that Wah had grown somewhat calmer, but had developed a "non-talkative mood." He had shut down and refused to communicate with Chong, who was doing his best to help him. Wah had no interest in assistance from the Chinese community of San Francisco, the firm, or the money offered for his defense.

Low Sam arrived on the scene with a letter from Wah's brother, Lee Wing Sam, who lived in San Francisco. Wah was not interested in its contents, or his brother. Breaking his silence, he became violent and verbally assaulted Low Sam, threatening to blow off his head. He complained of fraud and growing even more furious, stomped around his cell. After witnessing the episode, Chong had to conclude that Wah was truly insane. Along with Bugge and Swartz, all agreed that the man was not well in the head. Low Sam, being highly respected by Bellingham's Chinese community, stated that Wah was mentally unsound, and declared that no one of his ethnicity would think that he was being persecuted for being Chinese; that this was a case of insanity as opposed to race. It was suggested by Low Sam that Chong could do no more for Wah, and that spending the Chinese community' money would be a waste on his defense. Sun Chong agreed and departed for San Francisco.

Bugge and Swartz made further attempts to communicate with Wah, but he sat in the cell and rebuffed their efforts. In a last endeavor, Wah's council asked the court that a psychiatrist examine him. It's questionable as to whether the defense was laying the groundwork for an insanity plea, or to discover the depth of Wah's mental illness. On Friday, May 29th, Judge Neterer appointed Bellingham physicians Homer J. Birney and John Reed Morrison to examine Wah's mental state. After conducting the examination, the two stated that they had no definitive report for the court. They claimed they could not gather from the examination whether the man was sane or insane, as Wah refused to talk.

A Short Trial

Judge Jeremiah Neterer called Superior Court into session on Monday morning, June 1, 1908. The fate of Lee Wing Wah would be at the mercy of a 12-man jury.

The state rested its case in the early morning and by 11 o'clock, the defense had only put three witnesses on the stand, all of which were previously called by the state. In his opening argument, Prosecuting Attorney

Peringer stated that he would show that the defendant slit the throat of Young Shee, killing her at the detention center at Sumas. Peringer would call eight witnesses for the state. Attorney Hans Bugge, with little to work with, kept his opening argument simple, confirming that Lee Wing Wah did in fact kill Shee, but that he was clearly insane, and because of his mental instability, he should not be held responsible.

LEE WING WAH'S DEFENSE IS WEAKENED

Chinaman Declines to Talk and Expert Alienists Refuse to Say Whether His Acts Indicate Insanity Or Not—He Has But Three Witnesses.

Bellingham Herald, June 2, 1908.

Harry Edsell, the lead immigration inspector at Sumas, was the principal witness in the trial for both sides. While his testimony illustrated mental irregularities on the part of the prisoner, he himself was no professional regarding mental illness and could not determine whether Wah was sane or insane. He testified that on the night of the murder he had called the woman who was killed into his office and asked if she was afraid of Wah, who was said to have been acting strangely. She said that she was not afraid to stay with him, so Edsell dropped the matter. But, before going home for the evening, he decided to call a Dr. Clark and another physician to request an examination of Wah as to his sanity on Sunday, just to be sure. It was Sunday morning that Shee's body was found.

Edsell testified that Wah had insisted that he heard voices and had demanded to be taken to his brother-in-law, whom Wah believed was being held prisoner in the basement of the detention center. Edsell also recalled that Wah had accused authorities of holding up letters that came for him, which was untrue.

Edsell read extracts from the official examination of Wah's request to enter the United States, and in such documentation was proof that he had lied to immigration officials. It was learned that Wah was not a rich merchant, but a fisherman and a diver for seaweed at Cayucas and Cambria, California, and had done so for 14 years. As such, he had no right to enter the United States with his wife, as only merchants were allowed that privilege. Furthermore and for reasons unknown, he had overstayed his time in China, as laborers were only permitted to stay away from the United States for one year. Wah had been away eighteen months.

When Wah and his wife were rejected at the border and refused re-entry to the United States, he grew "perturbed and anxious." Wah and Shee argued continuously, and it was their arguing that the prosecuting attorney highlighted. Peringer pointed out to the jury that Wah, in an interview after he had killed his wife, said "She talked too much," and intimated that it was only natural for Wah to hold a grudge against the one woman to whom he could trace all his troubles. He urged that Wah was not insane and that it was only "the cunning Oriental mind at work when voices were heard and he burst into fits of violet passion."

The defense called on Edsell, Sheriff Andrew Williams and Quan Foy, official interpreter at Sumas, as witnesses. They offered testimony regarding Wah's alleged wealth, even though he only had two Chinese $5 bills, a silver dollar and a dime to his name. They also relayed to the jury Wah's imaginary stories that his brother-in-law was detained in the basement, the fact that he heard voices, and his frantic demands for alleged letters that had never come, all to show that the prisoner was unbalanced.

Wah, refusing the stand, sat silent throughout the trial.

> "One of the features of the trial," said the *Herald*, "is the speed with which it is being completed…The examination of jurors started yesterday morning and was completed by 3 o'clock. Before noon today the state had finished its opening arguments and before night the twelve good and true men will be considering the law and the evidence. The trial has attracted but little attention, only a few spectators being present during the day."

Closing arguments were equally short, Peringer declaring in short order that the murder of Young Shee was premeditated and demanded the jury come back to the court with a verdict of murder in the first degree. Bugge and Swartz, well aware of their eventual defeat, reiterated that their client was mad; they seemed on the verge of asking for mercy.

After final remarks, Judge Neterer instructed the jury before retiring to consider the evidence. Deliberation took little time. A mere one hour and five minutes later, the jurors returned. The verdict was a surprise; it truly demonstrated the equality and fairness of Bellingham's justice system during a time of extreme anti-Asian sentiment. Lee Wing Wah was found guilty of manslaughter, a reasonable compromise from a society with no qualms in applying the death penalty to a "Chinaman" of that era.

The Road Toward Deportation

Judge Neterer pronounced Wah's sentence on Thursday, August 28th after denying the defense's motion for a new trial. Wah received an indeterminate sentence of one to 20 years and a $250 fine. Before the prisoner was taken away, Neterer spent a moment talking directly to Wah, through interpreter Low Sam. Neterer made it clear to Wah that he had received an honest and fair trial with a verdict uncommonly merciful. In return, Wah offered no emotion and seemed uninterested in what Neterer had to say.

Lee Wing Wah was held in the Whatcom County jail as Bugge and Swartz made a last appeal attempt for a new trial through the Washington State Supreme Court. This was denied on May 27, 1909, upholding the Whatcom County Superior Court's decision. On Wednesday, June 30, 1909, Whatcom County Judge John A. Kellogg signed Wah's commitment papers and a few days later Wah was transported to the Washington State Penitentiary at Walla Walla.

Lee Wing Wah became prisoner No. 5451 on July 13, 1909. His prison admittance record described him as 5-foot 6-inches in height and 180-pounds with black hair and brown eyes. It was claimed that his birthplace was China, his nationality, Mongol and his race, Mongolian. It was documented that the last place he had worked was in San Francisco as a shoemaker. No education was cited. He declared that he used opium and that he had been using tobacco since infancy.

Lee Wing Wah, Washington State Penitentiary at Walla Walla. Washington State Archives.

While in prison, Wah was quickly placed under close observation by the penitentiary physician William M. Van Patten for a month, and was declared to be suffering from dementia. On October 28, 1909, Wah was brought before a hearing of members of the State Board of Control at the Washington State Penitentiary. It was determined necessary that he be removed from the general population and committed. On March 1, 1910, Wah was transferred to Eastern State Hospital for the Insane at Medical Lake, Washington, for treatment and indefinite confinement.

While incarcerated at Walla Walla, the process was in play for Wah's deportation. A letter in his prison file dated Jun 6, 1909,[6] by the Department of Commerce and Labor's Immigration Service, written by the Office of Chinese, Inspector in Charge in Sumas, Washington stated:

Sirs:

I beg to advise you that Chinese LEE WING WAH, whom I understand was recently taken to the Walla Walla prison to begin serving a 1 to 20 year indeterminate sentence for killing his alleged wife while in detention at the station, is under order of deportation from the United States, and when released from your keeping, should be delivered to the United States Immigration officers.

Respectfully,
H. Edsell

An interesting letter arrived on the desk of the warden at Walla Walla, dated October 2, 1913. It was addressed to the "Head Man" from Chinese national. T. S. Mark, of the T. S. Mark Company, 900 Broadway N. Seattle. In longhand, Mark wrote an inquiry in regard to the health and

6   Author's Note: I suspect that the letter's date conflicts with Wah's admittance, as he was held over, awaiting notice of his appeal.

welfare of Lee Wing Wah. He was in communication with the prisoner, he said, and had "received a letter from Wah's home[7] from his old mother, wife and children…" The letter clearly states "wife," putting forth the question – who was Young Shee to Lee Wing Wah? Was Wah smuggling her across the border for a price? Was she part of a sex trade? What would motivate Wah, who was eight months beyond legal entry into the United States, to claim Shee as his wife and attempt the border entry?

On November 19, 1913, Washington State Governor Ernest Lister, upon recommendation of the Assistant Secretary of the Interior, Sanford Beauregard "Bo" Sweeney, granted Wah a pardon, enabling his deportation to China. On November 22nd, Acting State Penitentiary Warden Alfred S. Oliver Jr. forwarded the release to Warden Henry Drum at the Eastern Hospital for the Insane.

The Chinese Exclusion Act was repealed in 1943 with the passage of the Magnuson Act.[8] It was an uncomfortable law to sustain after China and the United States had become allies in fighting the Japanese during World War II. Passage of the Magnuson Act permitted some Chinese nationals already residing in the country to become naturalized citizens, but maintained that they were not allowed ownership of property or businesses. The Magnuson Act opened the doors for immigration, however there was an annual cap – a national quota of 105 Chinese immigrants allowed per year. Additional action to eliminate discrimination against the Chinese would have to wait until the Immigration and Nationality Act of 1965.

---

7   In China.

8   The Magnuson Act was proposed by U.S. Representative (later Senator) Warren G. Magnuson of Washington, and signed into law on December 17, 1943 in the United States.

Chapter 3
The Lynching of Louie Sam

The Lynching of Louie Sam, 1884 by Wayne T. Sorenson, May 3, 2013. Courtesy of Jim Berg.

I'm most grateful to Jim Berg for providing The Lynching of Louie Sam, from his expanded work "Tuxedo." This chapter has been slightly edited and reformatted from its original form for the purposes of this book. Berg's version of the story comes from heavily documented sources, years of meticulous research of The Crossing and of the Nooksack region, and by way of a personal connection – his distant cousin, William Pritts, who was his only relative to admit to being a part of the posse who lynched Louie Sam.

— T.A. Warger

Louie Sam was only 14 years old when the events below occurred one cold February in 1884. Sam was a Stó:lō native, of what is today the Sumas First Nation at Kilgard, British Columbia, near Abbotsford. On March 1, 2006, the Washington state government acknowledged in an official apology, that an "unfortunate injustice" was done to both Louie Sam and the Stó:lō Nation.

Period maps of the Nooksack region provided at the end of this chapter.

Sunday, February 24, 1884 dawned bright and clear with a dusting of new snow, creating a Currier and Ives setting on the New Frontier. The drop in temperature was a sudden change from a rainy warm spell. The cloud cover during the chilly night hours had covered everything so that the outside world seemed serene and peaceful to the early rising pioneers.

Breakfast was a time for quiet reflection of the summer. The Berg's had arrived, adding many new hard working hands to help in the backbreaking work of creating homesteads in the wooded wilderness of the frontier.

Sam Berg had arrived in October 1883, joining sons, Dave and Fred, who had built an addition onto Samuel Pritts' home to hold the Berg family over until they could establish themselves.

Church that morning was one of thankfulness as the two families gathered in the home of Samuel Pritts who led a reading from the Bible, which was followed by short reports of how the families had been blessed during the previous week. The gathering ended with prayers for continued protection in the frontier.

Their reverie was shattered when Peter Gillies Jr. came pounding on the front door. Breathless, he stated that "Mr. James Bell has been murdered and his home set on fire. Dad sent me to warn all the nearby settlers to be on the lookout for anything suspicious."

"Hurry, we must go help put out the fire before it starts a forest fire we will all regret," said Sam Pritts. All the men "quickly took their axes, shovels and buckets and headed up the trail that led to the Whatcom to Fraser Trail where they turned west back toward The Crossing and Jim Bell's home."[1]

Harkness Ferry, formerly Hampton's Ferry at The Crossing. Circa: 1885. Courtesy of Jim Berg.

They could hear the fire crackling before seeing it through the dense underbrush, but many men were already there thanks to the Gillies boys who had discovered the fire and warned the settlers. It had been raining, which filled the nearby Pritts Slough, so there were buckets of water coming from all directions.

---

1   Before roads and rail transportation tamed the interior of Whatcom County, movement was conducted by horse and foot traffic along a series of trails. Jim Berg's previous work, "The Nooksacht's Trail and Crossing" describes the entire transportation and communication corridor of the Interior Indians. The Trail later became known as the Telegraph Trail and actually had several river crossing points, as the Indians took the easiest way across, but they were all at Everson. In some writings it is called "Nooksack Crossing" and was the place where things were ferried across. The Nooksack Indians left canoes on both sides, so that they could get across. The White Men, however, would come to the bank and shout across to the settler on the opposite side to cross and fetch them. That was Hampton's Ferry, later called the Harkness Ferry when Hampton was drowned and his partner took it over. When he died, his widow (former Mrs. Jim Bell) took it over. The Railroad Bridge built in 1890 caused The Crossing to be obsolete. Gold miners in 1858 used this crossing and even built a cable ferry across, similar to the one Harkness built. Only three trails came off The Crossing: the Stickney Island, which went to Lynden, the Barnes Prairie, which went north, and the Telegraph, which went northeast, formerly known as the Whatcom to Fraser Trail.

Peter Gillies Jr. and his brothers George, William and John were on their way home from Sunday school when they first saw the fire and later said:

> "When we got there we looked inside through the open door and saw Mr. Bell lying on the floor in the doorway to his lean-to kitchen. He was stretched out in a pool of blood with his arms extended over his head so we grabbed his feet and pulled him outside. When we saw the large bullet hole clear through his head we knew he had died quickly. The hole was so large we knew it had NOT been made with the newer rifles we all have so we wondered who might have killed him."

Peter Gillies Jr.'s brother John, added:

> "We decided to get Mr. Bell to a safe place and put out the fire before it started a forest fire as it was too late to save his personal property. By that time Fred Hauser and Indian Charlie had seen the fire or heard our shouts and were coming to help us. We then went to warn others about what happened and to be on the lookout for anything suspicious. We needed more help putting out the fire even though the rain last week that had melted the previous snow making things pretty wet and helped keep the brush from catching on fire. After the fire was under control we all started looking around for any clues that might help us find out who killed Mr. Bell and set the fire."

George Gillies said:

"Yes, we found some faint footprints leading northwest toward the swampy area around Pritts Slough. The footprints led to a big log that had fallen into the swamp so we climbed up on the log and went to the end where we could see that someone had taken a big leap out into the swamp and headed westward. Several neighboring settlers were curious and together followed those tracks but had only gone a short way into the swamp before they found a new handkerchief hanging from a tree branch. The Trail let out of the swamp and into the woods where they found a pair of new suspenders hanging where the brush had snatched them from the thief. Then we noticed some things from Jim Bell's store that had been dropped. I thought it was strange to go in that direction, as there is only dense forest with no trails. Nobody has made a clearing within a mile west of Bell's place."

Sam Berg remembered well the story that was often told how Indians in Pennsylvania murdered his mother's family just over 100 years ago. When he was in Whatcom, he heard stories of the uprising just 30 years ago near Olympia that killed many white settlers and another story of the Nooksack's Chief Telliskannem killing Henry Roeder's servant as a "revenge" killing, just because he was a Northern Indian. He wondered out loud, "Do you think this might be the start of another Indian uprising?"

Peter Gillies Sr., responded:

"We had similar thoughts when we saw the size of the bullet hole in Jim's head, as some of the Indians still have Hudson Bay muskets which shoot a ball that would make a hole that size. But the Nooksack Indians have been so friendly and helpful that we could not imagine any of them doing anything like this."

"I saw Louie Sam on The Trail headed toward Jim's place last night and when he went by my place he had his musket on his shoulder," Robert Breckenridge said, and then added, "Did anybody see him down by The Crossing or on The Trail this way?" But nobody had.

"We cannot determine who is guilty now and someone has to notify his widow Annette up in New Westminster as well as Sheriff (Stuart) Leckie," said Peter Gillies Sr. He then asked, "Will someone go over to The Crossing and let Bill Osterman know what has happened so he can send a message to Mrs. Bell and Sheriff Leckie?"

Ever Everson was quick to respond, "I'll go right back to The Crossing and tell Bill to put the wires through as I am headed back home anyhow."

Bill Osterman was very surprised when Ever reached his home. After Ever stated the purpose of his visit Bill said, "I just saw Jim not more than an hour ago when he stopped me on my way back home and asked me to drop this letter at the Post Office in Moultray's store. I thought I heard someone calling rather loudly from the back room when Jim came out to give me the letter. I assumed he was feeding someone at the table in his living quarters, which he often does. I did not see anybody, and Jim did not seemed concerned about anything."

Moultray's Store. Circa: 1880s. Courtesy of Jim Berg.

Annette Bell's Journey

Annette was teaching school in New Westminster to help with expenses as Jim's store made very little money, and he was not much of a farmer. Their son Jim, who had been born in California before they came to The Crossing, was with her. She was surprised to get a "Telegraph Wire" that Sunday afternoon and when she saw that it said, "Jim murdered. Come quickly!" she made immediate plans to return to The Crossing.

She told the school board that she had an emergency and needed to go back home. They understood and bid her God Speed, urging her to return with haste, as the students needed her. She arranged with the local Indians to take her upriver to the south shore of Sumas Lake where she and her son would walk the rest of the way. It was winter and there was little else to do but hunt; the young men who would help transport Annette and her son were eager for adventure and readied a canoe for the trip. Two paddlers, Annette, young Jim and their few belongings were loaded in. Annette wasn't

115

sure if she would be coming back, so she took all her belongings with her even though she knew they would have to carry them down the trail if they could not find an Indian packer at Sumas Lake.

Early Monday morning the paddlers set out northeasterly up the Fraser River; there were a lot of sandbars to steer around. They stopped at Wades Landing (the north end of the Whatcom to Fraser Trail), as it was a good place to camp for the night and fix themselves something to eat. They could intersect The Trail some 11 miles farther south at York's place and avoid the difficult climb over Sumas Mountain. Annette decided to go on by canoe in the morning, rather than start their walk there.

Meanwhile, back at The Crossing, that Monday proved to be a busy day for Coroner Manley, who had been called to conduct a Coroner's inquest into the death of James Bell. Sheriff Stuart Leckie accompanied the doctor, as circumstances were pointing toward robbery as the motive for the murder.

Sheriff Leckie found several agitated men willing to help track down the killer; he took charge of the group and they started searching from where the group had ceased their search the night before. They followed a trail that led near the James Harkness place and they stopped in to see if anyone had seen anything the day before. 17 year old Billy said he had seen Me-sah-chie[2] or Bad Jack (Louie) Sam on The Trail from Lynden. He added, "I met him on the road about half way to Lynden and I was alone. The look on his face as he approached me struck me with terror so I moved to the far side of the road and passed him. Then I hurried home as fast as I could and when I got home my mom told me about Mr. Bell's murder."

Sheriff Leckie and the men continued on toward Lynden and stopped at Tyee Jim's village[3] to inquire about Jack or Louie Sam. Jim was not willing to offer much about Jack even though he had a bad reputation and

---

2   There are multiple spellings from the record that are "white man" interpretations: "Mesahchee," "Mesacee," and "Mesachie." The editor of Jim Berg's story has taken liberty to use "Me-sah-chie." My apologies if I have interpreted the wrong meaning.

3   Tyee Jim's village was on Stickney Island, south of Lynden, across from what is now Kamm's Creek on the Hampton Road.

was causing trouble for the Nooksack Indians with his insidious activities in the area.

Tyee Jim did offer that Louie had come in Sunday afternoon to stay the night. Rumors of the murder and the search for Louie had reached him, and Jim warned Louie that the white men were looking for him. Louie left after dark, and Sheriff Leckie assumed he had fled northward on the Barnes Prairie trail back to Canada. He and the posse returned to The Crossing to see what the coroner had concluded.

While on the hunt for Jack Sam, Coroner Manley had examined Jim Bell's body, searched the damaged cabin, looked at the footprints and found goods in stock from the store. He impaneled a jury of good men who examined witnesses and inquired into the case. The Jury of Peter Gillis Sr., (foreman) Josephus Swinehart, William Van Buren, Samuel Lindsay, William Bishop and Ever Everson returned the following verdict:

Nooksack, W.T. February 26, 1884

We, the jury, impaneled and sworn to true verdict render, in the inquest of James Bell, find that on the evidence introduced, the said deceased came to his death on Sunday, February 24, 1884 and that his death was caused by a bullet passing through his head, supposed to be by the hand of an Indian by the name of Jack Sam.[4]

Tuesday morning dawned on the Fraser at Wades Landing and the young Indian canoe paddlers were anxious to get started, so they could get Annette and her son Jim to their destination and return to their homes before it got dark that night. They went a short distance to Indian Reserve 12 (the Stó:lō Tribal burial grounds) at the mouth of the Sumas River where they turned southerly into the River. The river was 200 feet wide and 20 feet

4   Author's Note: It is sad that the Coroner's Inquest records were not properly safeguarded so we could read them today and see what evidence the witnesses revealed to the jury before they rendered their verdict.

deep where it came out of Sumas Lake. They crossed the lake along the west shore, passing the "old village," also known as Naneets, which was built on stilts to avoid the hordes of hungry mosquitoes. The mosquitoes prevented others from settling near the lake, including the local Stó:lō Indians.

Immediately south of the Naneets, the party turned into the Sumas River where it emptied into the lake. It was much narrower and shallower, so the going was slow all the way to Thomas York's place where The Trail and Sumas River intersect. The Indians were able to beach the canoe so that Annette and 10 year-old Jim could step out on dry land with their belongings. That was as far as the Indians went. They pushed off and headed north, back across the lake and downriver to their homes.

Thomas York was hired by the Hudson Bay Company at the Staffordshire colliery in England as an experienced coal miner, to help open up the new Coal Mines at Naniamo. The trip from England to Naniamo aboard the new ship *Princess Royal* was described as "a gloomy history of death, misery and dissatisfaction." It took over six months, and Thomas' wife Anna Marie with their three year-old daughter Phoebe despaired of ever arriving. They and the other 21 miners arrived in Naniamo on a gray November day in 1854. Their arrival at Pioneer Rock was said to have been highlighted by a sudden gleam of sunlight, which lit up the sky to welcome them.

Thomas had intended to continue as a coal miner the rest of his working life, but in 1858, for the first time, white men had found gold in the Fraser River. He was down in Washington Territory helping to open the Sehome Coal Mines and was able to throw down his tools and walk up The Trail to the gold diggings on the Fraser to "take a look." He was satisfied that the stories were true, so he returned for his wife and daughter. Impatient as he was to get started, he hired the first transportation available and the family made the entire journey in an Indian dugout canoe. The Indian paddlers took two weeks to get from Whatcom to Yale in their dugout cedar canoe, up Puget's Sound and then along the precarious Fraser River. They arrived at Yale in May 1858 where Tom immediately started panning. He soon discovered that the place was teeming with thousands of miners, with no place to stay and that there were business opportunities staring him in the face. Tom and Maria built the first boarding house in Yale, finishing the roof just before the onset of winter. When it was half finished their son, Thomas Fraser York, was born "Under the roof" on October 21, 1858. He became the first white baby born in mainland British Columbia. The entire town of Yale had a big celebration for this event, and decided he should be named to reflect his place in British Columbian history, so the name Fraser became his. Fraser's seven year-old sister, Phoebe also set a record, becoming the first white child in British Columbia when they arrived at Yale.

In 1879, after finishing boarding school, 20 year-old Fraser and a partner ran the Oriental Hotel in Yale. In November 1880, he married an Upper Sumas schoolteacher, Josephine Macdonald, whom he had first met in Yale. On his trips home from school he got to know her as she taught school near his parents' place in Upper Sumas. In an interview on June 10, 1945, Josephine stated that," Louie Sam went over to Nooksack in the United States and shot a man." Some Canadians believed that Louie Sam had killed James Bell.

In 1859, Tom invested money in a boat building business, figuring that they could compete with the monopoly priced steamers. They built the *Hope* and the *Yale*, but in 1860 the *Yale* blew up at Union, killing the captain and five crewmembers. After the boat was destroyed, he operated a cable and scow ferry at Spuzzum where the miners had to cross on their way to Lytton. This venture ended when the new Alexandra Bridge opened in 1863. The Yorks returned to Yale where there was a school that Fraser could attend. Phoebe was at a boarding school in Victoria, as education was very important to Tom, who could neither read nor write.

By 1865, on his way to and from Whatcom for supplies, Tom had noted the rich prairie land around Sumas Lake and decided that a good profit could be made selling cattle raised on the lush prairie grasses. He had no farming experience so it would be a complete change in his lifestyle. His land claim was on the Sumas River, south of the lake, far enough so he wouldn't have to worry about annual flooding and the mosquitoes. It was also along The Trail, which he had traversed many times on his way between Whatcom and Yale. He built a small home and began to gather a herd of cattle, pigs and chickens, all of which were in demand by the miners.

Thomas was successful enough in his farming that by 1871 he and Marie decided to build a 14-room hotel. He floated the lumber from the mills on the Fraser up the Sumas River to his preemption claim. They also started a small store. Four years later the Yale Road was built, just north of their hotel and store, connecting New Westminster with Yale. This new road was barely usable when it was not frozen. The hotel was now located at the intersection of the only east to west road and the only north to south trail. Phoebe or young Tom were assumed to be the bookkeepers.

Having heard of Jim's murder and his family's imminent return, Tom and Marie welcomed Annette Bell and her son Jim and offered them a horse to ride down to The Crossing. Tom had seen Jim on his travels to and from Whatcom and might have eaten with him a time or two; he barely remembered Annette when she was still in town. Annette and Jim put their few belongings on the horse, mounted and headed for The Crossing, passing under a tree that in one day would become famous.

The first home they passed, just a mile below the International Boundary, was that of Joe Steele, who appeared to be absent. Three miles later, they came to the Robert Breckenridge homestead where they stopped to spend the night. Mrs. Breckenridge made her old neighbors comfortable and Robert told them about what had occurred over the past three days.

They made arrangements for a funeral the next day. The Gillies' had already contacted their Presbyterian pastor, Rev. B.K. McElmon, to officiate. He was the only clergy in the area and was willing to help the family with the final arrangements. Robert and various neighbors had already picked out a site on the neighboring Welch homestead at the top of Telegraph Hill.[5] Neighbors had helped dig a grave on the north side of The Trail; everything was set for the funeral to be held the next day, Wednesday, in Fred Hauser's cabin, as he was Bell's closest neighbor.

Louie Sam

After Sheriff Stuart Leckie heard the Coroner's jury verdict he asked Robert Breckenridge if he would ride up with him the next day and swear out a complaint against Louie Sam. Robert agreed and on Wednesday he saddled a horse and rode with the sheriff across the border where they contacted William Campbell, the provincial Justice of the Peace for that area.

At 17 years old, William Campbell emigrated from Ireland to Philadelphia where he worked as a drug clerk, before the lure of the Gold Rush of 1858 brought him to the West Coast. He married[6] Mathilda Allard and had two girls before he went to the Cariboo for a couple of years.[7] When he returned from the Cariboo he settled just east of Tom York's place. He fell in love and married Tom's daughter, Phoebe, in 1869 when she was 17 years old.[8] It is likely that his first wife Mathilda had taken the girls back to live with her Indian family while William was in the Cariboo, and that their "marriage" was never legalized.

---

5   Named years before, when the Telegraph line first ran up The Trail.

6   We can't be sure that he was in fact married to Mathilda Allard.

7   The Campbell story is confusing; he supposedly married the native girl, Allard, and had two girls. Then he left for Cariboo, where he stayed for a few years before coming back and marrying Phoebe York. Allard had returned to her people at Fort Langley and Campbell never saw her again.

8   There was a 15-year difference between them; Campbell was 32 years old at the time.

The Yorks and Campbells owned well over a thousand acres, and had the finest ranches in the Sumas Lake region. Mr. Campbell became a prominent citizen and was appointed Postmaster of Upper Sumas in 1883 and could be counted on to perform at all concerts with his fine singing voice.

Sheriff Leckie and Robert Breckenridge explained their complaint against Louie Sam and Campbell took the two Americans at their word and filed a warrant for Louie's arrest for murder. He then mounted his mule and rode with Sheriff Leckie the short distance to Kilgard where Louie Sam lived. Robert Breckenridge went back to The Crossing to attend the funeral.

Kilgard was also known as Indian Reserve No. 6, but was little more than a collection of squalid shacks on the 600-plus acre reserve where Me-sah-chie ("bad" in Chinook trading jargon) Jim Louie and his two sons lived with maybe another 18 or more Indians. Jim was in jail for murder and would die there the next year. His two sons were home alone. Newspaper accounts of that time indicate that (young) Louie was a known thief and had been suspected of many crimes including murder. The family lived in poverty, but was known in all the nearby communities as thieves. Louie's most valuable possession was his Hudson Bay musket, and he was rarely seen without it. The musket may have been his dad's.

Justice Campbell found Louie in the house and questioned him. He also inspected the house and found a new shirt, new suspenders, socks and a new knife. Justice Campbell arrested Louie, putting handcuffs on him and taking him back to Thomas York's place for safe keeping, as the hotel was the most substantial home in the area. Louie Sam made no protest of innocence that has been noted.

On Wednesday, Justice of the Peace Campbell conducted a hearing and several men from the American side of the boundary line gave evidence which implicated his prisoner was the murderer. Therefore, Sheriff Leckie requested to extradite him to Whatcom and let him be tried in an

American court, seeing as it was where the murder took place. However, Justice Campbell would not hear of it, and replied, "He must have his day in a Canadian court first. You can extradite him from there."

Campbell deputized Thomas York and Joe Steele[9] and posted them as guards for safekeeping until Constable Moresby could take Louie to New Westminster the next morning (Thursday) and turn him over to authorities there for trial.

Sheriff Leckie finally decided he had done all he could and headed back to Whatcom. He knew the funeral was over, but he was surprised when he met a group of horsemen followed by others on foot. He said, "How do you do boys? You'll find him up there, alright." With that, he continued on toward Whatcom knowing that the "boys" might "extradite" Louie and bring him to Whatcom without his help.

Back at The Crossing that afternoon the men transported the coffin, made of recently hand-hewn cedar, up the hill with young Jim Bell on top so "the lid would not fall off."[10]

News had traveled fast and people from as far as Ten Mile and Lynden attended the funeral. James Bell was the first person to have been killed in the area and there was much concern about the event. The gathered men were especially concerned that an Indian uprising might start and they were very frightened for the safety of their families.

"Do you believe the Coroner's jury verdict that the young Indian boy from Canada killed him? What would lead him to kill? Why would he kill such a nice man? What should we do now to protect ourselves in case this is just the beginning?" the community asked.

They discussed the tracks leading away from the cabin toward Pritts Slough, which had been examined so that they could be compared with any

---

9   There is no explanation why Steele was deputized, as he was American, not Canadian.

10   Young Jim "Bert" Bell told the author about this event some 80 years later when he was in a nursing home in California and still very clear of mind. He also wrote of this memory in a letter to P. R. Jeffcott on September 22, 1950.

future suspect. Things found hanging from the brush near the footprints appeared to have come from Bell's store, so it was assumed that the murderer was also a thief.

Several people had reported that Louie Sam was around the area on Saturday, carrying his Hudson Bay musket and that he was drunk. All pointed to him as the culprit in the killing; William Moultray had already had meetings down at The Crossing Store concerning him. All work had stopped, and the settlers were anxious to find why Jim had been murdered. Those at the funeral had already conspired amongst themselves and became more and more concerned that such a murder might be the beginning of another Indian uprising. Fueled by the fear of this, they decided to band together and put a quick end to the threat.

Sam Berg recalled the chilling story about how Indians had killed his wife's great grandfather's family, and how they had refused to defend themselves against the Indian attack. He offered:

> "If we want to live in peace again we will need to stop whoever is responsible. My wife's family was massacred in 1754 because they were religious people who did not believe in killing other people even in self-defense. They outnumbered the attacking Indians and could have easily driven them off, or killed them from the protection of their home before the Indians started the fire that forced them out of the house. Great grandmother and the small children were murdered. The older boys and great grandfather were taken as slaves."

Others remembered the stories out of the Olympia area where just 30 years before, Indians killed many of the settlers. Sam Caldwell reminded the others of this by saying:

"You remember the Indian uprising nearly thirty years ago that killed so many settlers in the Olympia area and resulted in the Indians being sent to reservations in order to protect the settlers. Even the Canadian Indians are supposed to live on reserves set aside for them and the Louie family is living on a reserve known as Kilgard. You also may remember that Jim Sam, Louie's dad, is in the Penitentiary in New Westminster for murder. I just saw in the paper where two Indians killed two men in Victoria just two weeks ago, and there is a story that Louie had killed one of his brothers. We all have heard the story about Chief Telliskannem killing Henry Roeder's servant just because he was from a different tribe, which started the last Indian uprising when the Nooksacks decided to rescue their chief who was arrested for the murder. That time it took the United States military to quell the uprising."

Nearly all those attending the funeral were settlers who were developing their claims; they realized how possible it was to be exterminated by renegade Indians, one by one, who could then slip back into the woods undetected. Descendants would remember hearing how single men, frightened by the threat of a revolution, did not sleep in their cabins for many months, preferring to sleep on stumps or platforms built well up in the trees.

William Moultray took charge of the conversation by saying, "We can't know based on what we now know whether Louie is the killer or not, but we know he is in custody at least until tomorrow morning. Maybe we can go and question him in person to see if he will confess."

Robert Breckenridge had already told the men that William Campbell had arrested Louie and would put him in the custody of Thomas York and Joe Steele in the hotel, where they felt he would be secure. Many of them knew Thomas York and where his hotel was, so it was decided that after dark that night they would disguise themselves, and all who had horses would ride (the rest would follow on foot) up to York's and take Louie from Canadian custody. They would bring him back into Washington Territory and question him before turning him over to Sheriff Leckie.

It was the growing sentiment of many Indians that the white settlers were mounting in number, settling en masse and driving them from their own land, a situation similar to that of the last Gold Rush in 1858. It was during this gold rush that Judge Tawes overheard some Nooksack Indians (because he understood Chinookan) planning on killing him and his partner. They reacted by putting a pistol to the Chief's head and directing him along until they were safely transported back to New Whatcom. Though this story was common knowledge among the settlers; they had grown complacent, as the last 20 years had led to amiable relations with the local Nooksack Indians.

Jake Berg (the author's grandfather) was the same age as Louie Sam at the time of the murder. He listened in horror as they talked about a boy his age killing Mr. Bell, but couldn't fathom much of what the older men said in drawing up plans to take the Indian's fate into their own hands. He saw Will Pritts that evening with his face blackened, and he asked his mother why "Cousin Will had made his face all black and why are they talking in whispers?" Priscilla Berg answered him by saying, "This is a private matter that some of the men are considering and they do not want anybody to know who is involved, so they are disguising themselves. It is not something you should remember." Until his dying day, he wouldn't forget.

It is thought that the men involved came from as far south as Ten Mile and from as far west as Lynden. Some years later, some identified themselves, some even on their deathbeds. It was Will Pritts, Pete Harkness and George Gillies who openly discussed their involvement with reporters, and their stories can be found in print.

Later that afternoon, the men gathered at Breckenridge's (he was nearest to the Canadian Border) near where they had buried Jim Bell's body just hours before. They rode slowly up The Trail, so those without horses could keep up until they got into Canada. From there, the mounted men rode on ahead to York's Hotel.

Pete Harkness, a 17 year-old boy who was following the walking men on his pony, later told a first person report as follows:

"The funeral over, there was much continued discussion of the events of the past few days, with now and then a suggestion that the murderer ought to be hanged. I noticed a group of men off to one side who seemed more engrossed in discussion than the others. It was made up of the more prominent settlers, among whom I saw Bill Moultray, my brother Allen, W.E. Van Buren, Jim Scott, William Gillies and Bert Hopkins. Soon they seemed to come to some understanding for they mounted their horses and, followed by many others on foot, set out to the north over the Telegraph Road, led by Bert Hopkins, who assumed the leadership. Out of boyish curiosity, I followed them on my pony and as they paid no particular attention to my presence, I continued to trail them. About midway between The Crossing and Sumas Prairie, where the district of Gera later developed, the vigilantes, for such they proved to be, met Sheriff Leckie, returning on horseback from his pursuit of Me-sah-chie Jack Sam in British Columbia. Evidently seeing from their appearance the mission of the party, and not caring to assume any responsibility for their actions, the sheriff merely remarked; 'How do you do, boys? You'll find him up there alright,' and rode on south on his way to

Whatcom. Riding on, we reached and crossed the border into British Columbia. After going on a mile or so[11] the vigilantes stopped and instructed me and William Gillies to go no further, as they did not want any boys mixed up in what they proposed to do. We were disappointed but said nothing while the leader; Bert Hopkins gave instructions and told all to disguise themselves by tying handkerchiefs over their faces.[12] So we remained there, built a fire to keep warm, and awaited their return. But to say that we were uneasy at being left alone is putting it very lightly. In fact, we were fearful of what might happen and darkness having come on did not lessen our apprehensions."

The group would later become known as the "Nooksack Vigilance Committee" and some were said to have worn their wives clothes or jackets put on backwards to disguise themselves. It is pretty certain that most had their faces blackened with charcoal or oil and pulled their hats low so that they could not be individually identified in the dark.

Deputy Constables Thomas York and Joe Steele had been charged with the safekeeping of Louie Sam. The York hotel was the only lodging and venue for food for many miles around and it took in travelers on a regular basis.

On Wednesday evening the house was quite full with Mr. and Mrs. York, the prisoner Louie Sam and Constable Steele. The Yorks had two employees, Owen Hughes and Dick Williams who also lived in the home. In addition, there were two other men at the Yorks' that evening. Court records identify one as "traveler" and the other as "stranger." The Traveler "was a big man with black whiskers" who carried with him only a bedroll. The Stranger

---

11   Within a hundred feet of the border.

12   This detail does not mirror the reports made by other witnesses.

had no blankets at all, but did carry a gun as he had shown up that afternoon from Hatch Prairie looking for work; Anna York asked him to stay and look after the place while they went to New Westminster the next day.

The household became quiet after 8 pm, when they all went to bed, except for Constable Steele, who stayed up to guard the prisoner. Louie had taken off his shoes and was probably seated on a sofa in the parlor. Owen Hughes had made sure all the doors and windows were locked before he went to bed.

About an hour later, Anna Marie heard the horses as they crossed the bridge over the small creek near the hotel, and looked out the window to see a group approaching the house. A banging on the front door awakened the rest of the household. Thomas York, from his bedroom upstairs, heard a man yell, "Open the door, or I will break it in!" By the time he got downstairs with his trousers in his hand, the front door was thrown open and the room filled with armed men with blackened faces. They had their guns drawn and ordered York to stay out of the way. Hughes rushed downstairs, where he had a pistol thrust in his face and was pushed behind a door and told to stay put.

Hughes later estimated that there were twenty men in the front room and Anna Marie York believed there were another 15 men in the kitchen. They guessed there might have been 75 men all together.

The intruders took the time to put Louie Sam's shoes back on him and demanded his musket. Steele, who was armed, sat quietly in the corner of the room. This could have been a way to keep from getting hurt, or he may have been part of the plan.

Hughes, who had locked the doors, believed that the Stranger had not gone to bed with the rest of the household, or at least he had not undressed. He claimed that someone had descended the steps about ten minutes before the mob arrived.

Special Constable York, who estimated that the men "did not stay over three minutes," made a strange request to the mob. Although they had taken a rifle and his prisoner with his musket, it was the handcuffs he demanded they leave behind. The men refused, telling York he "could get them tomorrow." Then, the boy, who was already handcuffed, had a rope thrown over his arms, and was led from the hotel. He was thrown onto a horse and taken away into the darkness, surrounded by the mob of angry, disguised men.

Pete Harness, the young man who had followed on his pony, and who was kept back while the men continued on, stated:

> "After a long wait we heard horses approaching in the darkness from the north, and soon the posse appeared in the moonlight, with the Indian mounted on a horse led by one of the vigilantes. Me-sah-chie Jack was remonstrating that one of his shoes was coming off and he wanted the leader to stop so that he could fasten it. The leader of the horse refused and the Indian exclaimed angrily, 'Me get out this, me fix you — you, Moultray,' recognizing the leader of the horse by his voice."

Pete continues:

> "Coming up to where they left us waiting, the men stopped for consultation. Being confused by the darkness, they supposed they were in United States territory and did not discover their mistake until later. Suddenly they were filled with alarm by sounds coming from back up the road, and fearing pursuit by British Columbia Indians, they hastily drew aside into the brush by the road. No one appeared, so one of the

more venturesome of the party, Bert Hopkins, rode back a short distance and soon returned, reporting no danger from that source. Then the vigilantes, somewhat nervous from their scare, discussed the fate of their prisoner. Some favored returning him to The Crossing while others were for disposing of the Indian at once. The arguments of the latter prevailed, and a tree that leaned well over the road at a convenient height offered opportunity for quick action.[13] While a rope was being thrown over the projecting tree, the horse with the luckless rider was led beneath it, and the noose fastened around the murderer's neck. At a word from the leader, Bert Hopkins, the horse was driven out from under, leaving Me-sah-chie Jack Sam suspended in mid-air. During all the preparations, the doomed young man made no protest by either word or action, and went to his death without a struggle. Leaving the body hanging as a warning to other potential criminals the vigilantes rode away, crossed the line and quickly dispersed."

R.L. Reid wrote a piece in the Washington Historical Quarterly in 1927, which adds, "It is said that the only time the Indian spoke was when he was coming near the tree. There was a fire visible some distance down The Trail. It had been made by a number of men[14] who had been left as a guard to keep themselves warm. The Indian was afraid that it had been made to burn him. He asked his captors if they were going to burn him, and they said, 'No.' He said, 'Hyas kloshe' (very good) and nothing more."

---

13   This was evidently a large uprooted cedar tree that had come to rest on an old stump before it came all the way down, and so, in effect, "bridged" the trail.

14   Author's note: The fire was made by two boys.

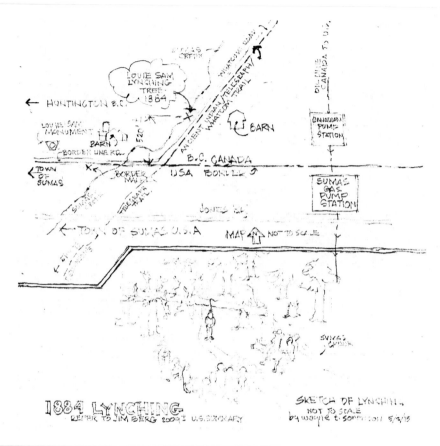

A sketch of the lynching site located along the US-Canadian border. Drawn by Wayne T. Sorenson, May 2, 2013. Courtesy of Jim Berg.

The Investigation

After the disturbance of the mob, the household went back to bed, aware that there wasn't much they could do. On Thursday, the following morning, over breakfast, the Traveler told York that he had known the mob was coming. It has never been discovered how the door was opened to let the intruders in; there was no evidence that it had been broken down. Constable Joe Steele left right after breakfast to see the Justice of the Peace, William Campbell, and told him that a mob had come and taken the prisoner, Jack Louie Sam. Campbell then went to York's place and confirmed the situation.

He took two of Louie Sam's neighbors from Kilgard, Indian Jim (York) and Big Charlie, along with Constable Steele and headed back down the Whatcom Road towards the Nooksack Settlement. He spotted Louie Sam suspended dead and cold, hanging from a tree. "I got the two Indians to hold the body up and cut the rope and took it from around his neck." After removing the noose, on which he detected a "strong smell of musk," he removed the handcuffs, which he kept for the rest of his life; they are now in the Vancouver City Archives. He examined the body and found no signs of violence, except the mark of the rope around his neck. "I told the Indians that they could take the body away but that authorities might call on it in a few days."

A Coroner's Jury was convened on Saturday, March 1, 1884 with Coroner Charles Todd presiding. James Musselwhite acted as Jury Foreman, the rest of which included Antone Roscoe, Neil L. McColl, Cyrus C. Tilton, David Wells, Alfred McDonald, Erastus B. Ackerman and Alonzo Boley. The coroner interviewed the York household, with the exception of the Stranger and the Traveler, who had mysteriously disappeared. Constable Steele had returned to his home just south of the border after he had notified Justice of the Peace Campbell. "The boy was tied with his feet together and handcuffs on his hands," recalled Big Charley. "Campbell came and said, 'I wonder what they took him away for?'"

As part of the coroner's investigation, William Moresby, a Peace Officer in the Province of British Columbia, was sent to measure the distance from the tree to the Boundary Line and found "that said tree to be five hundred and twenty-feet north of the iron post on the Boundary Line. We measured the road with a common tape line, however, the road does not run due north from the Boundary Line, but more in a north easterly direction."

Bad news traveled fast. After the Inquest, that same afternoon, the B.C. Attorney General sent a telegram to the governor of Washington Territory, requesting that his police be prepared to arrest the members of the lynch party, "pending our application for extradition."

The Indians from Sumas and Chilliwack were fuming; they met in ever-larger numbers, until there were over 200 Stó:lō tribesmen from 20 villages between Fort Langley and Yale, conducting a weeklong meeting in Chilliwack to "consider the best means of obtaining justice." Some of the tribe had "summoned" Canadian Indian Agent, Patrick McTiernan, who agreed to attend the meeting.

During the meeting they decided that despite Louie Sam's poor reputation, he had nothing to do with Jim Bell's murder. They conferred that the American telegraph operator, William Osterman, had invited Louie Sam to travel with him along the Whatcom Trail toward Bell's home on the pretext of employing him to repair the telegraph line. Then, as the two men approached the shopkeeper's establishment, the telegraph operator pretended to change his mind and told Louie to "go away." To the Stó:lō tribesmen, it was Osterman who apparently murdered Bell and quickly rode away from the scene of the crime, correctly assuming that others would see Louie near Bell's store both before and after the incident and draw the obvious conclusion.[15]

The Stó:lō version similarly alleges that the murderer headed south, doubling back through the forest to rejoin the Whatcom Trail. The written reports indicate that the owner of the footprints around Bell's house had gone north and then west through the forest, eventually joining the Lynden Trail where Louie Sam had hidden in Tyee Jim's village until he was told that the white men were on the hunt for him. From here he went north to Canada, likely via the Barnes Prairie Trail. He and his brother were reportedly seen late Saturday at Barnes Prairie, a sighting and location which conflicts with the Stó:lō version of the story.

---

15   Author's note: Louie was seen walking alone on The Trail a mile before and headed in the direction of Bell's cabin, sometime before the murder. He was not seen again until late that afternoon some seven miles to the west on The Trail to Lynden. There were footprints leading away from the cabin and store goods dropped going west away from The Trail. The Stó:lō believed there was evidence of a small hole bored in Bell's head and shod hoof prints all around the cabin, which is confusing seeing that none of them ever observed such details. Bell was buried before any of them could have seen the hole in his head. The only tribal person that could have confirmed such details was Louie himself and there is no indication that any of his tribal members ever talked to him before he died. The American Coroner's Jury had seen all the evidence and heard witnesses before they determined that Louie Sam was the probable murderer.

At the meeting with the Stó:lō tribesmen, McTiernan was told, "Some of those present objected to letting you know anything about our intentions until it was all over, but the majority have decided to tell you everything and to take your advice." He was also told that "some of the most determined men" believed the Stó:lō community had "a perfect right to... hang and kill sixty-five Americans" in order to avenge the outrage committed against one of its members.[16]

On his second day at the meeting, McTiernan recorded that those gathered were "unanimous" in feeling "fully justified in going immediately in very large numbers across the boundary line and tak(ing) the first white man (they met) and bring(ing) him to the spot where they hung the Indian and treat(ing him) in the same manner."

The Stó:lō leaders told McTiernan, "Let the Government know how sick our hearts are...and we all promise you that we will go back to our homes and leave the matter at present in the hands of the Dominion Government. We hope you will meet us again about the 1st of May."

The Detectives Go Undercover

On March 11th, Detectives Charles Russell and Clark set out from Victoria to walk through The Crossing area to ask questions of the surrounding communities to determine if any additional information could be obtained. By the 14th they had reached Langley Prairie, where they split up. Detective Clark went south to Lynden and Russell continued on to Upper Sumas. On the 15th, Russell stopped at York's place and found it had changed hands and was now the Ackerman Ranch. It was said that the Yorks had leased the farm to the Ackermans because they were afraid of Indian reprisals, and that they had left for Canada. Mr. Ackerman returned from the Nooksack Crossing at about 8 pm and told Russell that the settlers were

---

16   Author's note: By this reasoning, the Americans were following Stó:lō tradition in killing the suspected murderer of one of their members.

talking about the Indian trouble and were saying that if they were to start something, people from as far away as Seattle would come and "kill every Indian they got their hands on."

On the 16th Russell stopped at the Tallhamers', but they were away "on a visit" and the children were being taken care of by a neighbor. He pushed on to James "Old Man" Harkness' place, who was the administrator of James Bell's estate; Russell arrived at about 4 pm and stayed the night. While the two were talking, Russell remarked on a place he had passed on The Trail where meals were advertised, and how it appeared that the area had recently been burned. James Harkness replied, "That was Mr. Bell's place, an Indian had killed him and set fire to the place."

Russell replied, "I had heard about it and seen the tree they hung the Indian from."

"My boy (Pete) said that over 100 neighbors turned out and hung the murderer," responded Harkness.

From there on out in the area, Russell could not get anybody else to talk even though he "led with the subject at every opportunity. They appear reticent and suspicious."

The morning of the 17th, Russell met Detective Clark on the road from Lynden as Clark was headed for The Crossing. Russell continued on to Lynden, and found the old-time settler and storekeeper, Holden Judson, who was quite willing to talk. Judson asked, "What are they saying about the Indian trouble on the British side?"

Russell replied, "I told him Mrs. Ackerman had said that York was afraid that the Indians were going to kill him."

Holden confirmed that he knew that York was frightened "for the Indians had threatened him the very same afternoon we went across to hang the Indian." He went on to say, "he knew the Indian well" because "on one occasion Louie had robbed or tried to rob" him.

Clark returned from the Nooksack Crossing that evening and Russell noticed that people regarded him with great suspicion and would not talk when he was present. He kept overhearing the word "spy." At the dinner table that evening, rumors or threats were thrown about that people who came to spy out the land were "sometimes troubled with a throat disease from which they never recover."

The following day, on the 18th, Russell sent Clark to Whatcom "as he was useless to him" in a town where people were so suspicious of him. Upon returning, Clark met Bonty Judson, Holden and Phoebe's son, who asked, "Did you come from the British side?" To which Russell confirmed, "Yes."

Bonty then asked, "Are they kicking up much of a stink there about that Indian we hung?"

Russell said, "No, but Mrs. Ackerman said the Yorks had left because they were afraid the Indians were going to kill them."

"He be damned," exclaimed Bonty, "It was him, York, that sent for us to hang the Indian. He was afraid the British Government would find it out and that is why he skinned out to Whatcom."

Russell then said, "The Indians have threatened to kill Justice of the Peace Campbell also."

"The Indians know they had a hand in it." said Bonty and added, "The American boys never would have gone over if old York and the settlers around there had not sent for them."

The morning of the 19th, Russell went on to Ferndale and determined that the settlers in the Ferndale area had not been involved.

Word had gotten to Russell that the Yorks were headed for Seattle on a boat that left the next day, the 20th, so he went to Whatcom and boarded alongside them without their knowing. He "shadowed" them to the New England Hotel with the hope that he would have an opportunity to "work him," and to get to the bottom of York's involvement. He "kept the run on them" for four days but never got the opportunity, as York stuck like glue to his wife's side.

While Russell was in Seattle he wrote all the above information to the Victoria Chief of Police, Roycroft, and added that if the Inspector were disposed to send another man, he would give him some information to start interviewing other settlers. Russell concluded that the vigilantes were settlers from Hogg's (Barnes) Prairie, Lynden and the Nooksack Crossing.

He returned to Whatcom from Seattle on the 26th and met Clark's replacement, a man named Quincy. Quincy was sent on to Lynden on the first riverboat, but Holden Judson "bluffed him straight out," so he returned to Whatcom and Russell sent him back to Victoria.

Russell then went to Mars (Lynden), which was where the boat for Lynden docked, but hurried on to Mrs. Sarah Eddy's, who was widowed, on The Trail on the south side of the Nooksack Ferry landing. Mrs. Eddy was "easily worked" and gave him considerable information. She felt "sorry for Mr. Breckenridge as he is such a nice man. I am sure he would not sell his farm and leave here if it were not for this Indian trouble."

Russell played dumb and asked her, "What trouble?"

Mrs. Sarah Eddy then described the entire incident, which was hear-say, and went on to say, "They don't talk about it on this side as they have been warned not to, but they do on the other side. They have sent to Washington (D.C.) about it and they have detectives now in the country so the people are very frightened." Apparently, she was unaware that she was talking to one of the detectives.

Asked how she knew all this, she said, "The settlers at The Crossing have many friends in Seattle and they got the news."

Russell went on, "I made friends with a man named Sefton, whose holding adjoins Breckenridge's. I promised to work for him and told him to meet me at Breckenridge's at 10 am the following morning."

Tallhamer was contacted on the way to Breckenridge's but, "was too scared to commit himself." He did say, "No, the Indians are not bad on this side. One came over from British Columbia and murdered Mr. Bell. The people from here went over and hung the Indian and it has caused a bit of a mess."

Russell was at Breckenridge's the next morning and told Robert he was going to meet Sefton there. Mr. Breckenridge was in the woodshed and two men, who were looking for work on the Canadian Pacific Railroad, came out of the house. Russell turned the conversation to the murder and asked, "Did the Indian confess?"

"No," said Breckenridge and added, "I had an opportunity to see him (the Indian) some time after Bell's murder and we could get nothing out of him. He was as dumb as a brute." Later that night Robert stated, "I would kill a Chinaman as quick as I would kill an Indian, and I would kill an Indian as quick as I would kill a dog."

That afternoon during a two-hour conversation with Mrs. Breckenridge, Detective Russell heard a few more stories[17] regarding the troubles Mr. Bell had been having with his wife, Annette, and with the Harknesses, and how it was said that Osterman had been seen coming from Bell's place in "less than three minutes after the fire was discovered and the murder committed."

Russell asked her, "Don't the settlers suspect Osterman?"

"Some do, some don't," was Mrs. Breckenridge's reply, "but I feel sure it was the Indian killed him." She went on to give a full account of the funeral and how some of the men had gathered at their place afterwards to blacken their faces and tie sacks over their heads before going over to hang the Indian. Some of the men she identified at having seen at the funeral were Breckenridge, Osterman, Tallhamer, Reinhart, Swinehart, and the Harkness boys, Woorell and Wuscher.

---

17   The following are direct "spy" notes, as incoherent as they might be.

It was said that Mr. Breckenridge had intended to leave the Nooksack district after he sold his homestead, and that he would have it "proved up" on the 15th and could sell anytime after that.[18]

Detective Clark returned to The Crossing on March 28th and interviewed David Harkness, who confirmed that he had been one of the vigilantes. He claimed, "The Indian would not tell them anything, only curse and swear." His dad, James Harkness, repeated what Davis had told Russell, but added, "William Osterman passed Bell's place 15 or 20 minutes before the murder of Bell."

The next day Clark contacted Mr. Tallhamer, who confirmed that he was with the group, and that Mr. Eden, who was a settler in the White River Settlement, had heard the group but had not gone with them.

On March 30th, Clark was back at the White River Settlement and met Mr. Perry. He said to Perry, "I see you have a scaffold on the road."

Perry responded, "Yes, there was a man found hanging there. He came over across the line and shot an old man named Bell. I saw the Indian pass my place the day Bell was shot, and he tried to hide his face. I was one of the constables that arrested him.[19] He has a brother; if he ever comes across he will not go back alive. He will be shot first."

Detective Clark contacted Mrs. Sarah Eddy at some point and reported the following: "An old lady, Mrs. Eddy, a Presbyterian preacher's wife, said that she did not believe the Indian killed Bell at all.[20] Sarah Eddy also said that Osterman passed and afterward said that he could hear the Indian talking in Bell's house. (She did not think he could hear so far). Osterman said that Bell came out with a letter or parcel to the road and gave it to him."

Clark then quoted Mrs. Eddy as saying, "I heard that there was four hundred dollars in Bell's house and the Indian had no money." She also said,

18   Breckenridge "proved up" on May 13, 1884, got his patent on December 4, 1884 and sold on January 19, 1892. He then went on to develop the town of Everson and never left the Nooksack district.

19   Which means Perry was actually Joe Steele.

20   There were no Presbyterian preachers in Whatcom County prior to 1882. Mrs. Eddy was there as early as 1870 and no Presbyterian minister in Whatcom County was ever named "Eddy."

" I heard that Bell was going to (the) law with Harkness for taking his wife. Mrs. Osterman and Harkness (David) are brother and sister. The families are not on good terms with each other. The settlers all through here are a hard crowd."[21]

On April 19th, Clark went back to The Crossing to gather more information and to talk with Whittier, a settler in the Nooksack Settlement near the 10 mile crossing on the Whatcom Road.[22] Whittier said, "Old York and his son-in-law, Campbell sent for the American boys or they would never have gone across to hang the Indian. That was the reason York has left his place. He was afraid of the British Government."

Clark again visited Mrs. Harkness, who told Clark that she knew that he "was one of the detectives," and that he "had come in by (way of) Seattle from Victoria" and that he had "been traced all around." She warned him that he "had better look out or (he) would get hung up like the Indian."

Epilogue

On April 5, 1884, the British Columbia Attorney General's report stated that:

"It is unlikely that anyone would come forward to give evidence when the result would be the inculpating of some 70 to 100 white men, his own neighbors. More motives than one – and many of the obvious ones readily suggest themselves as deterring people from giving any information. Even our own people, who engaged on the coroner's jury,

---

21   Mrs. Eddy is the first and only known American to implicate Osterman as the murderer. However, her information is primarily apocryphal ("I heard") rather than from first hand observations. She freely implicates others and states that they were a "hard crowd" even though she claims to be the Presbyterian preacher's wife.

22   He was actually in 10 mile, some seven miles from The Crossing.

would seem to have been primarily animated by a desire to preserve the good will of their American neighbors."

Papers were forwarded from Lord Lansdowne, Governor General, for British Columbia to His Majesty's Minister, L.S. Sackville West, in Washington (D.C.) on April 25, 1884. West placed the case before the Secretary of State who was already aware of the incident.

The federal authorities of the United States appeared anxious to co-operate and willing to turn over those responsible for the lynching, if the men could be identified. All efforts to trace them failed, for as General Newell, Governor of the Washington Territory, reported to the Secretary of the Interior, the community was surrounded by forest and all members were interested in preserving secrecy.

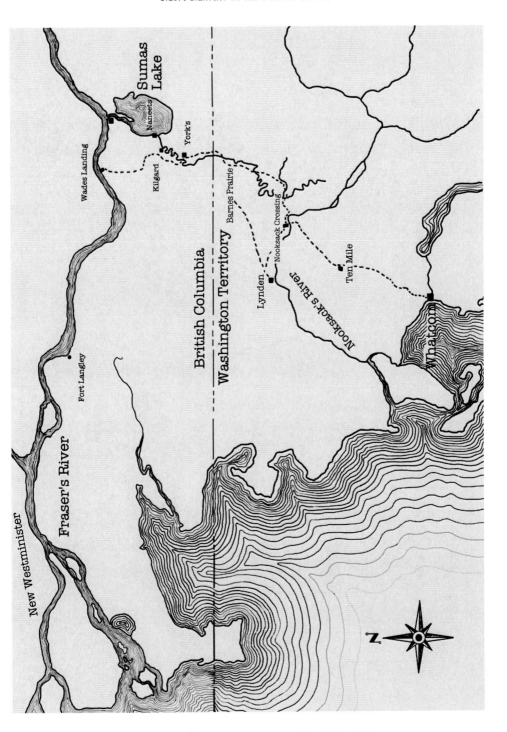

Maps drawn by Jim Berg and enhanced for the author by Sierra Ellingson.

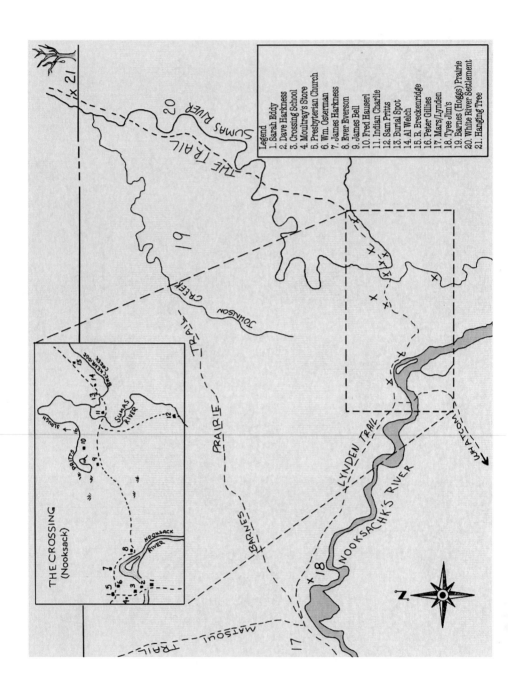

Maps drawn by Jim Berg and enhanced for the author by Sierra Ellingson.

Chapter 4
Bulldog

On January 9, 1917 Charles Wilson, a "transfer" employee of the Bloedel Donovan Lumber Mill, drove his beat-up truck home for lunch. A "transfer" was what they called a contract worker who went from mill to mill picking up whatever work was available for short periods. When the job was finished, they hoped to grab another few weeks at one of the other local mills.

It was the morning of January 9th that fellow transfer workers were excited to hear about news coming from Europe; it was reported that the Kaiser's generals were trying to persuade the German monarch to declare unrestricted submarine warfare against Britain. The Great War had been raging for over two years at this point, and it was believed that cutting off England's shipping would break the stalemate. The transfer employees were excited because it was this policy that nearly brought America into the war in May 1915, when a German torpedo sank the Cunard ocean liner, RMS *Lusitania*. The incident caused a national outcry as 128 U.S. citizens were killed in the tragedy. The contract workers believed that if America entered the war, there would be full-time employment for all of them.[1]

World events mattered little to Charles L. Wilson. The mill foreman declared him giftedly lazy, and fellow coworkers knew him as "not a steady worker" and as someone who "often quit after working a few days." They claimed that he had a violent temper, and that he seemed unbalanced

---

1   They would get their wish. By February 1, 1917 German U-Boats commenced unrestricted submarine warfare, and America entered the Great War on April 6, 1917.

at times, unbalanced. He was short-fused and would fly off the handle with little provocation. Many had heard of his domestic quarrels at home with his new wife. In spite all of this, Wilson was more or less tolerated by the foreman and his coworkers, and he continued to be hired on by area mills.

Wilson pulled into the driveway at 3841 Idaho Street, and sat in his cab listening to his new wife Ada's yellow bulldog barking at him through the kitchen window. He hated that dog; all it did was bark and growl at him. Wilson was determined to get rid of it one way or another.

QUARREL OVER PET BULLDOG BELIEVED TO HAVE LED LAKE WHATCOM LABORER TO KILL WIFE AND HIMSELF

Bellingham Herald, January 9, 1917.

Uncle and Nephew

Howard S. LeBarron, 24 years old, married his wife Ada Borssee, 18 years old, in Dayton, Cattaraugus County, New York, in 1887. Through the following eighteen years the couple would have six children, three boys by the names of Erwin, Clifford and Vern, and three girls, Pearl, Fern and Gladys. In 1907 the family packed their bags and moved out west to Bellingham, where Howard would secure a position at the Silver Beach Shingle Company on Lake Whatcom. The family moved into a mill company town at Larson Station, until they rented a home of their own on Silver Beach. By 1911, Howard, an exceptional carpenter by trade, gained a position as a cooper, or a barrel maker and wagon-builder for Curtin Brothers. Eventually, LeBarron moved his family into a new house at 3841 Idaho Street, after earning financial success as a blacksmith. By that time Erwin, Pearl and Fern were married and on their own.

It was just before 1908 when Charles Wilson moved to Bellingham, living in an Elk Street hotel. Wilson was born in Wisconsin in 1882, the son of LeBarron's kid sister, Della. He worked as a laborer, picking up any odd job he could find. Wilson had moved out from Wisconsin in hopes that his Uncle Howard would help him out, which he did, helping him to secure a job at the Larson Mill. Unfortunately, Wilson proved to be lazy and uninterested in working. He wanted to move in with the family, but LeBarron wouldn't allow it. As it was, the home was overcrowded, and at that time LeBarron was barely making ends meet.

The Past Catches Up

The LeBarron household had a torrid history of infidelity and jealousy that stemmed from their lives in New York. By May 17, 1916 Ada had enough of her husband and hired attorneys Bixby & Nightingale to sue for divorce. Although she claimed to have conducted herself as a faithful, dutiful and chaste wife, such may not have been the case. Ada insisted that her husband had disregarded his marital duties for the past nine years and was guilty of cruel treatment towards her "that rendered life burdensome." She also claimed that during their time in New York, he would go into jealous rages, accusing her unfoundedly of immoral and improper conduct.

Howard believed that during the years 1906 and 1907 she committed adultery with one Bert Hollenbeck. Furthermore, in Bellingham from 1911 through 1915, he accused her of associating with his nephew. On various occasions, Howard would point out his wife's infidelity to fellow neighbors and at family gatherings.

In August of 1911, Howard seized her, threw her down, and started choking her. It's possible that this was the first occasion her husband caught her and Wilson alone, and whether or not it was the first of physical abuse between them, it was when Ada declared their domestic troubles began. She

147

went on to claim that in July 1912 Howard struck her in the face and mouth, bruising her face and cutting her lips. Ada stated, "At the time…I was pushed about with great violence, and held against the wall, and (Howard) roughly seized my hands and arms in his attempts to inflict severe bruises on my limbs and body."

LeBarron recounted his own version of the fight he had with his wife in 1912, but in his, it was she who struck him in the face, and that when she was about to strike again, he grabbed her hands. Somewhat legitimizing his story of mutual abuse, LeBarron's arm had scars, visible even four years later, from when Ada had bitten him.

In August 1915, Ada was confined to her bed for some time with a severe illness, while Howard made cruel insinuations that "she was suffering from a disease to the nature of her exploits."

Howard LeBarron refuted the allegations placed upon him by his wife, claiming her "unmindful of her marriage vows" and that she had "treated him in a cruel and inhuman manner…" Regarding Bert Hollenbeck, LeBarron claimed that "Yes indeed he had a problem, and his wife, who kept having Hollenbeck come over to their home when he wasn't home caused it." LeBarron forbade Hollenbeck from coming to his home, because of the special attention he paid her. One time, when Ada and Hollenbeck thought that LeBarron was away, he caught them in bed "hugging and kissing." LeBarron said this went on for some time, until one day, Ada disappeared for several days. He said that she returned, begging for forgiveness.

It's possible that Hollenbeck was the cause for the family's move to Washington State in 1907. One year after their move, trouble found the family once more. LeBarron's nephew, Charlie Wilson, was aggressively making the moves on his eldest daughter. Although court documents do not mention her by name, the girl was believed to have been Pearl, age 14. Ada threatened to go to the probation officer and have her daughter sent to the house of correction. LeBarron, objecting to this course of action, said they needed to take care of her, and instead ordered Wilson to refrain from coming by the home.

Ada was averse to this decision. It was likely she was jealous of the relationship between Wilson and her daughter. Court records show that she did not agree to keeping Wilson away and "preferred that the said Wilson should continue to come to the house where she could keep watch over them" and "this continued for some time...in 1912 the daughter married and moved away."

After Pearl moved, Wilson continued to come to the house, partaking in meals without contributing to the family's finances. LeBarron told Wilson to go elsewhere as he didn't have the money to take care of him. After much confrontation, Wilson grudgingly left.

Soon thereafter, LeBarron went to work at a camp in Alger in Skagit County for two weeks. When he returned home Wilson was back in the house. Once again he kicked him out and told Ada that he was not allowed to return. She would continue to let Wilson in whenever LeBarron was away, all the way up to divorce proceedings.

Ada LeBarron countered that during the past few years her husband "was with improper conduct with other women," and that it had been since August that he "refused to have (sexual) relations" with her.

In the end, Ada LeBarron got her divorce, custody of the youngest daughter, Gladys, $20.00 a month in alimony and the property in the Whatcom Falls addition on 3841 Idaho Street.

Charles Wilson, twelve years Ada's junior, enjoyed the thrill of the four-year chase of his aunt; perhaps he fed off the suffering he caused the family. It was likely that Ada, at 46 years old and after having bared six children, enjoyed the flirtation and eventual sexual attention of a younger man. Wilson moved into her home on Idaho St. and married Ada on November 18, 1916. Her son, Vern LeBarron, then 18 years old and working at the

Larson mill, along with 13 year-old Gladys and the big yellow bulldog, moved in with them.

With the excitement of the chase now past, Wilson quickly tired of his new life and proved to possess a foul disposition. He now had to work to support a house, wife and family, and working, which he had never enjoyed, made him all the more irritable. Almost immediately, the couple quarreled about anything and everything. He hated Ada's dog, which would defend her when they fought, by growling, barking or biting at him; he threatened countless times to kill her bulldog. Neighbors complained of late night arguments and threats directed at Ada and the dog.

Doggie Defender

On January 9, 1917 Charles Wilson headed home for lunch. Although the sky was clearing, the temperature had dropped and a wild wind was picking up. The dirt drive leading to their home had collected deep puddles of rain. Wilson sat in the cab of his truck, dreading entering his home, where Ada was waiting for him. What happened over their lunch has been developed from the Bellingham police investigation reports and from remarks made by neighbors and family members.

Charles Wilson had come home for lunch; Ada had prepared a meal for two, which was laid out on the table upon his arrival. There was a pot of potato dumplings on the stove. Charles sat at the kitchen table as Ada poured two cups of coffee and turned to the stove to retrieve a dumpling for her husband. He started drinking his hot brew. For whatever reason, a quarrel broke out; it could have been the continuation of a previous argument that morning. Charles became aggressive, possibly violent, and the bulldog intervened, defending Ada. His barking and nipping fueled the fire. Charles leapt to his feet, yelling that he had had enough, and went for his loaded Winchester .32-caliber special carbine. It was likely that Ada attempted to stop him. Charles ran into the bedroom, just off from the kitchen, with the barking dog following him. Before the bulldog entered the bedroom, Wilson was ready, drawing a bead on the animal, and then he fired. The canine yelped and collapsed in a heap from the lead bullet.

Ada screamed and fled into the dining room. In running away from her wounded bulldog instead of trying to save the animal, it was assumed that Wilson uttered references indicating that she was next. She wasn't fast enough to reach the door that led outside and hid between a wall and a cot-bed, lying on the floor. Wilson followed her into the room and fired two bullets into her left side from underneath the cot. These penetrated her chest and emerged from her shoulder. Ada didn't move. She died on the spot ,between the cot and the dining room wall.

It was theorized that Wilson might have sat down in the kitchen for a time to calm down; he may have even finished his coffee as he considered how he had home-wrecked his uncle's family, caused a wider family scandal, and was stuck with a life he didn't want. He walked into his bedroom and placing the butt of his gun against the floor and the muzzle over his heart, he stooped over and pulled the trigger.

American Reveille, January 9, 1917.

Epilogue

It was Ada's 13 year-old daughter Gladys, who discovered the bloody bodies. When she came home from school she found the doors to her home locked. She borrowed a key from the neighbor, entering through the kitchen where she first spotted the bulldog lying dead on the floor. In the dining room to the right, her mother lay dead near the window and behind the cot. The police were not notified until after 6 o'clock that evening. After an investigation, they found Wilson in the bedroom, dead, with the gun beside him. A rather large wound was located in his back where the bullet had exited.

The police would later claim that Wilson might have been mentally unbalanced. They told the *Bellingham Herald* that:

> "There was no sign of struggle in any of the rooms. Evidently the quarrel began at the dinner table in the kitchen. Two places were set at the table and the meal was in place. Mrs. Wilson had not eaten anything. Her coffee was undisturbed in the cup and no food had been placed on her plate. Wilson had eaten a potato dumpling and had drank his coffee."

An investigation launched by Whatcom County Coroner Dr. N. Whitney Wear, Bellingham Police Chief James Dorr and Whatcom County Sheriff William D. Wallace failed to show just what happened before the fatal shots were fired. It was by no means certain that the quarrel was caused by differences over the dog; many confirmed that it was common for the animal to defend Ada. Ada's children, Gladys and Vern corroborated that Wilson and their mother had quarreled frequently and that the bulldog always attempted to protect her from their stepfather's violence. They and the neighbors often overheard Wilson threaten to kill Ada and then himself.

When interviewed by reporters, Howard LeBarron thought the bull-dog played a critical roll in the tragedy. He believed that while the couple was quarreling at the table, the dog had growled at Wilson and that he became angry and shot him. He proposed that Ada would have defended her pet, which would have then escalated the quarrel until Wilson killed her and then committed suicide.

What kind of impact the murder might have had on Howard LeBarron, if any, is unknown. He relocated after the divorce, first to 2413 F Street in the Lettered Streets neighborhood, and by 1919 he moved again to 2514 Ellis Street. Never to remarry, Howard died in a Seattle nursing home on January 6, 1945, at the age of 81.

Chapter 5
Murder at the Turf Saloon

The Turf Saloon, 1905.

A "Wet" Season

Long before the Volstead Act[1] cast the dark shadow of Prohibition across the United States in 1920, Bellingham went dry on January 1, 1911. Before that, the city was wetter than wet. In 1909, forty-nine known saloons, taverns and bars, along with one substantial brewery, were flourishing in

---

1   The National Prohibition Act, known informally as the Volstead Act, was created as a means of implementing the Eighteenth Amendment in the United States.

Bellingham. This does not include the restaurants, hotels, elitist social clubs or illegal sales through the seedy Restricted District, where sex and spirits flowed nightly.

The twenty-eight saloons lining Holly Street were considered the more socialite establishments of the city. Patrons of good character could be found with a foot on the rail of "The Club" or "Dock & Dicks." Sport fans could cozy up to a pint of suds at Bellingham's first sports bar, "The Senate," which was located next to the telegraph office. A runner would come through and post baseball scores, boxing bout rounds and anything else of sporting interest on the bar's chalkboard.

The bars along Elk Street[2] closest to Holly were suitable establishments, but the further away from Holly towards Forest, State and the Boulevard, the clientele descended from working class and blue-collar to waterfront dock laborers, merchant crewmen, sailors, coal miners and lumbermen. The "watering-holes" they occupied would have been such dives as "The Coin," "Diamond Bar" and the "Sehome Bar." There were card houses like "The Turf," "Starvold & Anderson's," and "A. O. Ottestad's." Drinks were also poured at the Byron or Washington Hotels nearby.

Behind the doors of any such establishment at any given moment, a drunken brawl could break out, usually revolving around a card game, a dispute over a woman, or perhaps just good-ole-boys having a raucous time.

Late on the night of Tuesday, September 7, 1909 in the Turf Saloon at 1217 Dock Street, an innocent card game in the backroom would escalate into a brutal stabbing. One old logger would stab another, half his age, with a rusty-bladed pocketknife, as the two were standing in the middle of Dock Street, between the Byron Hotel and the Turf Saloon. At 12:30 am the victim walked into the saloon; he died fifteen minutes later. The rusty blade had severed the left auricle of his heart.

---

2   Now, State St.

The fracas had originated in connection with a game of Solo,[3] which was being played in the cigar smoke filled rear of the Turf Saloon. Around a felt green card table were four players, Hugh Finnan, George Ralph Shoemaker, Charles Reynolds and Theodore Zingg, all of whom were lumbermen. The men had been playing since 9:30 pm; rounds of beer and whiskey shots circled the table.

You Can't Play Solo!

Hugh Finnan joined the game at 9:45 pm. Finnan was born of Irish parents in Caledonia, Racine County, Wisconsin in 1853, and was one of seven siblings. At eighteen, he worked in a sawmill in Manistee, Michigan, before moving to Washington State. Since 1898, he had been working the woods and mills of Whatcom County, stomping through the forests year 'round. By September 7, 1909, at age 56, the logger felt the weariness of old age; he was weather beaten and tired from a lifetime of logging. He was tall, lean, gray and very strong, although he weighed only 130-pounds.[4] The *Morning Reveille* would later describe him thus:

"His head being rather narrow in front and swelling at the back, and long, is covered with a mass of semi-curly, coarse gray hair. The little red lines under the skin, and swollen veins of the face, in which beats visibly his pulse, bare witness of much drinking intoxicants. Above the mouth, and hiding it so that only occasionally can its absence of curve be noted, is a mustache corresponding in color to the hair. The nose is semi-aquiline, his eyes are set well apart and

3   The genesis of Solo Whist is obscure, but the game has German origins. Commonly abbreviated to "Solo," the objective is to gain points (chips) by declaring an intention, sometimes in partnership with another player, to win a specified number of "tricks" and to achieve this against the combined opposition. Solo is basically a gambling game.

4   The Bellingham Police Records claim that (at the time) Finnan was 56 years old, 5'7" in height, with gray hair and eyes, medium complexion, and was born in Wisconsin.

over these are thick eyelashes, dark brown, long and droop-
ing, half-hiding the steely blue of the optic. The eyebrows
are dark brown."

George Ralph Shoemaker, 33 years old, was also at the table that
night, playing several hands. Shoemaker was born in May 1876 in Pleasanton,
Linn County, Kansas, just a month before General Custer's last stand at the
Little Bighorn, and was one of five siblings. By 1900, Shoemaker was working as a shingle weaver in Lyman, Skagit County before moving north to
Bellingham, where he lived at 1417 Central Avenue for several years. Until a
few days before, he was a sawyer in the Whatcom Falls Mill Company, before
transitioning to acting foreman. It's possible he was celebrating his rise in status. Shoemaker had a wife and child living in Castle Rock, Washington. There
she had family, and Shoemaker thought it best for her to remain, as she was
soon due to give birth.

The "Dutchman" Charles Reynolds, 37 years old, had emigrated
from Holland in 1880. Considered the quiet one at the table, Reynolds was
a shingle mill packer at the Whatcom Falls Mill. His English was proficient
with only a slight accent of his former country of origin. He was married
with two children and lived in Bellingham.

Next to the "Dutchman" sat 40 year old Swiss-born Theodore
Zingg, who had arrived in the United States in 1894. Zingg had a good head
for numbers, and quickly secured a position as a tallyman in the mill town,
and was proprietor of the Whatcom Dairy.

Five or six hands of Solo were played when an inebriated Lynden
County Commissioner, A. H. Fraiser, crossed through the card room to relieve himself in the back. On his return, Fraiser stood awkwardly against
the doorframe watching the men play cards. Moments later, Finnan, leaning
back against his chair, looking at his hand, declared he had a Solo. Shoemaker

looked toward Finnan and told him that he could not possibly have a "Solo hand." "You don't have the points," he said.

A drunken Fraiser scoffed, "You don't know how to play Solo, do you?" Finnan took offense, stating he did indeed know how the game was played. Fraiser said, "Cut me in and I'll show you how it's played," to which Finnan remarked, if Fraiser knew how to play the game, then he would know that only four players could play at a time. Turning to Shoemaker, Finnan again claimed he had a Solo.

"I'll bet you $4 you can't show me the points," replied Shoemaker. Finnan grunted, ignoring the bet and continued to play.

"You can't ____ play Solo," replied Fraiser loudly.

"I can play Solo," Finnan remarked with increasing irritation toward the county commissioner.

Frustrated with Fraiser breathing down his neck, Finnan's tone became hostile with the other players. He told Fraiser to get the hell out of the card room. The game soon ended and the men all stepped up to the bar. Finnan had to pay for the drinks as a result of losing the round. Commissioner Fraiser walked over and stood alongside Finnan with his foot on the brass rail. Here again, he insisted that Finnan did not know how to play, continuing to egg him on. "I don't think you had a ____ Solo," he said to Finnan.

Finnan, tired of Fraiser's remarks, struck out at him with his fist. The Commissioner warded off the blow and Shoemaker stepped in shoving Finnan away from Fraiser. Finnan broke loose, and came back toward Fraiser, attempting to strike him a second time. Again, Shoemaker interfered with the attack and pushed the irate Finnan away, grabbing his wrist and wrenching it around. Finnan screamed in pain, his head flat against the bar. He yelled for Shoemaker to let go and leave him alone. The bartender, Otto Kienast, told the men that there was to be no yelling in the saloon and that they would have to go out on the street to settle their troubles.

Reynolds decided it was high time to take his leave. He drank up quickly, and then hustled home to his wife, Nell, and his sons, Paul and Harry. The "Dutchman" didn't want any trouble.

The Stabbing

Having been asked to leave the bar, Finnan and Shoemaker walked outside. Witnesses would say everything happened so fast; at first Finnan turned and struck Shoemaker in the chest, then taking a knife as he would a dirk, he struck Shoemaker with a downward plunge. The powerful thrust ripped a jagged hole through Shoemaker's vest, two shirts, and passed between his third and fourth ribs. The knife was described to have had a black handle with an old rusty blade, about three-and-one-half inches in length, and appeared well used. After he was stabbed, Shoemaker walked back into the saloon without assistance and told bystanders what had happened and to fetch him a doctor.

Shoemaker was lifted onto a table, his upper clothing pulled open and a bar towel stuffed over his wound. The police were telephoned from the Turf Saloon. Patrolman McDonald was taking the "dogwatch," having temporarily relieved Jailer Charles Schysler for his dinner. McDonald took the call, locked the station door and raced toward Dock Street.

Upon arrival, he found Hugh Finnan waiting, with no means to run. He gave McDonald the knife, claiming he was forced to use it on Shoemaker. McDonald placed the man under arrest. Whatcom County Coroner Dr. N. Whitney Wear happened to be across the street at the Byron Hotel at the time, and was also summoned immediately. Sadly, Shoemaker was dead before his arrival. Patrolman Patrick Jessup was close by and appeared shortly after Wear; he took Finnan into custody.

Whatcom County Coroner Dr. N. Whitney Wear was just across the street at the Byron Hotel nursing a drink when he heard word of the stabbing. He was too late to offer any assistance in the tragedy. Laura Jacoby's Galen Biery Collection.

All witnesses surrounding the incident were questioned. Theodore Zingg had watched the fight from the saloon entrance. J. W. Rose, an attorney from Lynden, who was standing on the sidewalk in front of the Byron Hotel, also saw Finnan swing his fist into Shoemaker, but he did not know at the time that the man had a weapon; he thought that Finnan had simply punched Shoemaker.

Bellingham awakens to another slaying. Morning Reveille, September 8, 1909.

Morning

In the city jail that following morning, September 8th, Finnan readily admitted that he had stabbed Shoemaker, acknowledging that although he had been drinking, he was not intoxicated when the fight took place. He stated that it was done in self-defense, and if he had not done so, he could have been injured. When asked if he would make this plea when charges were filed against him, he consented yes.

FINAN WILL SET UP SELF DEFENSE PLEA

Ralph G. Shoemaker Receives a Mortal Thrust From Rusty Knife In Hands of Hugh Finan —Killing Occurs on Dock Street as Result of Quarrel Over Game of Cards In Turf Saloon.

KNIFE BLADE IS DRIVEN THROUGH HEART

Bellingham Herald, September 8, 1909.

Finnan was said to have come to the city four days earlier from Emil Track's Lumber Camp, and had then driven back, taking a room at the Washington Hotel.

A reporter for the *Bellingham Herald* claimed that Finnan appeared to be a quiet, harmless man who answered all questions put to him. He came away thinking that Finnan "did not appear to realize the enormity of the charge that will be lodged against him, or was confident that he was in the right." This followed observations that Finnan seemed somewhat worried.

A reporter from the *Morning Reveille* was able to flush out more from Finnan, as he revealed:

"I had just been in a fight in the Turf Saloon with another fellow and Shoemaker jumped in and twisted my wrist so it hurt awful. I went out of the saloon and he followed. I told him, 'I'm an old man and you can't twist my wrist that way without suffering for it. Leave me alone!' Then he came after me again."

According to a number of shingle weavers who were questioned by police, George Shoemaker was not belligerent and had never been in trouble before. They were utterly shocked that he was dead. Furthermore, they were equally surprised with Hugh Finnan, saying the same of him. He had never been arrested.

Shortly after 12 pm, County Coroner Dr. Wear held an autopsy. It was found that the knife blade had entered the skin between the third and fourth ribs, severing the third rib. It had passed into the upper left chamber of the heart and was driven entirely through it. None of the other chambers were touched. Shoemaker had walked unassisted, according to one witness, into the saloon, a distance of thirty to forty feet. Wear indicated that the blow must have been tremendous as the blade of the knife was barely three-and-one-half inches long. He indicated that it was very rusty, nicked and that the blade was blunt. Wear announced that there would be no inquest, as Finnan had admitted to the stabbing. Shoemaker's personal effects included $10.05, a watch chain, and a pocketknife. Wear notified Shoemaker's wife of her husband's death, upon which she returned to Bellingham immediately. Shoemaker's corpse was taken to the undertaking parlors of W. H. Mock & Sons.

GEORGE R. SHOEMAKER.

George Ralph Shoemaker, killed on Dock Street. Morning Reveille.

The Trial Begins – State v. Finnan

With Information filed, Finnan was charged with murder in the first degree. On Thursday, November 4, 1909, Whatcom County Prosecuting Attorney George Livesay asserted that the state's side of the case would be short and that he expected to have it go to jury the following afternoon. The court engaged Attorney James B. Abrams as counsel for the defense. Judge John Alonzo Kellogg would oversee the trial, which would take place at the Whatcom County Superior Court.

The examination and selection of potential jurors took place that same day; the final twelve men selected were considered to be fair-minded and impartial by both sides. On Friday morning, November 5th, the first evidence in the State v. Finnan murder trial was introduced by the state. When Superior Court opened, both prosecutor Livesay and Abrams, counsel for the defense, outlined their cases for the jurors.

Livesay revealed the story to the jury, beginning with how Shoemaker, Finnan, Zingg and Reynolds had been playing Solo in the back room of the Turf Saloon on the night of September 7th, and that four or five hands had been played when A. H. Fraiser, county commissioner from the Lynden district, entered the room. While discussing the game, Fraiser told Finnan that he did not have a "Solo hand," as Finnan had claimed. The state would further develop upon the game's end, how Finnan had paid for the drinks as a result of his losing, and the taunting that he received from Fraiser regarding his lack of knowledge of Solo.

Addressing the jury, the prosecutor claimed that Finnan had taken offense to the remark and struck Fraiser. Shoemaker stepped in to dissuade Finnan from further violence, but Finnan was relentless. It was then that the bartender told the men that they would have to go out on the street to settle their squabble.

It was a little past midnight when Shoemaker, Finnan and Zingg left the saloon and went out onto the sidewalk. Fraiser remained inside. When the three men reached the sidewalk, Finnan started down Dock Street toward the Washington Hotel. After a few feet he turned, circling back towards the saloon, passing the front entrance and on up toward Holly Street to where Shoemaker was standing. Livesay stated that it was at this point that Shoemaker extended his hand toward Finnan, and amidst doing so, Finnan struck Shoemaker with the knife, inflicting the injury, which resulted in the man's death in the Turf Saloon. Livesay affirmed that Shoemaker did not strike a single blow, either in the saloon or on the street. With this, Livesay concluded his presentation to the jury.

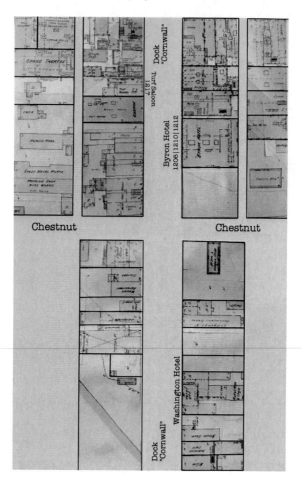

Map of Dock Street (Cornwall) between the Washington Hotel and the Turf Saloon.
Map drawn by Sierra Ellingson.

Abrams took the floor, outlining the evidence on which he hoped to prove that Finnan struck the fatal blow in self-defense. His account of the conversations and actions in the saloon differed little from that of prosecuting attorney Livesay. Instead, he built upon what had happened outside of the bar, offering that after the three men had reached the street, Finnan started down Dock Street toward the Washington Hotel, where he was staying the night. After he had gone a short distance he decided to go back to Holly Street, catch the Eldridge streetcar, and go back to the logging camp. Abrams declared that when Shoemaker and Finnan met a short distance north of the saloon, Shoemaker attacked Finnan, striking several blows, one in the mouth, loosening one of Finnan's teeth, and another to the jaw. Finnan remonstrated, declared Abrams, telling Shoemaker to go away and leave him alone. It was after Shoemaker had struck the alleged blows that Finnan used the knife.

Lynden attorney J. W. Rose was the first witness on the stand. Rose's testimony was as follows:

"I heard and saw the whole affair after the men came out of the saloon. The man they call Zingg was urging Shoemaker to fight with Finnan and I called to them, saying, 'Don't bother him. He's drunk.' But they continued to follow him as he backed off across the street...I heard their voices indistinctly. I had just stepped out of the Byron Hotel. I first saw Finnan leave the Turf Saloon and start toward the docks and then retraced his steps to the saloon where I heard voices engaged in a heated conversation and ugly names, but I could not tell who was speaking. Finnan walked toward Holly, and Shoemaker followed him. Finnan appeared to be drunk. Finnan told Shoemaker to 'cease following me.' About that time somebody in the group in front of the saloon called to Shoemaker or Finnan, to 'Give him a black eye; he's no good anyway.' Shoemaker turned around and shook his head to the advice."

Then, claimed Rose, Shoemaker reached out with his right hand as though to catch Finnan by the left wrist, and the next moment he heard the blow struck by Finnan. Rose saw Shoemaker walk back into the Turf Saloon, where he heard about his death about fifteen minutes later. He went into the Turf, saw the wound in Shoemaker's chest and heard that he had received it from Finnan.

Theodore Zingg was the next witness placed on the stand. He confirmed playing the card game in the back of the saloon, but became badly muddled when cross-examined by the counsel for the defense. He insisted that Rose's story was false, in that he had never urged the two men to fight, and that from what he could remember, Shoemaker had only acted as a peacemaker.

Otto Kienast, bartender at the Turf Saloon, who claimed to have seen the beginning of the fight, disclaimed any knowledge of the brawl. "The men were talking loudly," he said. "I told them to cut out the loud talking or leave the place. They went out. I did not see any fighting in the saloon. If Finnan struck at Fraiser I did not see it."

Lynden County Commissioner, A. H. Fraiser followed on the witness stand. He explained that he had gone to the lavatory at the rear of the saloon and later stopped at the card table, where the game was in progress. "I knew Shoemaker, a friend of mine, and spoke to him. I also knew Finnan by sight and spoke to him and apparently the best of feelings prevailed. I stood there watching them a few minutes." Fraiser admitted to taunting Finnan about his "hand," both in the card room and in the barroom. He confirmed that Shoemaker had offered a bet of $4 to prove his win, and how Finnan had lost.

"Then they all got up and we stepped up to the bar to have a drink, apparently all friendly. There was some good-natured joking and I remarked to Finnan, 'You didn't have a Solo.' Without a word, Finnan struck at me. I dodged and the blow glanced along the side of my face. My first impulse was to strike back, but Shoemaker interfererred [sic] and quieted Finnan down. He went on talking a little while longer and suddenly Finnan hit me again without provocation." Fraiser previously declared that there was no blow struck in the barroom, and that Shoemaker merely shoved Finnan away when he became aggressive.

> "Then I said, 'If you want to fight, I'll fight you,' but Shoemaker interfered again and said, 'Don't have any trouble.' I was a little angry and remarked to Finnan that if he wanted to fight we could go out on the sidewalk. We all started out of the door, but when I got out the door, Finnan ran off up the street, and I just laughed and remarked, 'He doesn't want to fight at all.' Then Shoemaker and two other men went out the door and that was the last I knew that any trouble had occurred until Shoemaker staggered into the saloon and gasped, 'I've been stabbed, send for a doctor.'"

Charles Reynolds, the "Dutchman" who had hurried home, not wanting to participate in the quarrel, believed that Shoemaker was killed because he tried to be the peacemaker. He insisted that Shoemaker's intentions were only to stop the fight in the barroom.

Hugh Finnan, dressed in a light colored, checked suit, a blue woolen shirt, a black and white four-in-hand scarf, and "large room" shoes "fancied by all men employed in the woods," was next on the witness stand, where he told his version of events. His testimony was practically the same as that given by preceding witnesses. He confirmed that he made no effort to escape from the scene and that he had given himself up to patrolman McDonald when the officer appeared. He revealed his story thus:

"I reached the Turf Saloon about 9:30 o'clock, and found the proprietor (Charles Passerini) playing Solo with three men I didn't know. I took the proprietor's place in the game and lost five or six games before the trouble started. I had been beaten. I started to make a heart Solo and the man I learned was Shoemaker said I couldn't make it and offered to bet. I wouldn't bet, but offered to bet the drinks that he couldn't show Solo. Well, he showed me. Fraiser didn't play, but kept saying 'You ___ old fool, you don't know how to play Solo,' and I hit him. The old man that I mentioned, who was not playing at the time, guyed me. He said I couldn't play Solo. I told him Solo was a four-hand game and that five couldn't play. He kept on telling me I couldn't play, and I hit him. That caused the trouble between me and Shoemaker. Shoemaker grabbed my left wrist in both hands and twisted it so, pushing me down beside the bar. I said, 'You just stay away from me.' I told him to stop two or three times. When he let me up Fraiser had his coat off. Then I walked out on the street alone. He followed me. I walked toward the Washington Hotel, intending to go to sleep. I went as far as the livery stable, then concluded to take a streetcar out to camp where I was working and started back up Dock Street to Holly."

"As I passed the saloon Theodore Zingg cursed me, and I called him names and cursed him. Then Shoemaker came running up behind and hit me with his fist behind the ear. I started backing across the street watching him. I told him several times to go away and leave me alone, that I was an old man and didn't want to fight him. He wouldn't leave me alone and I told him if he didn't go off and keep away from me I would stick him with the knife. He said, 'I'll knock the ___ life out of you.' Then he struck me again. He kept after me and caught hold of my wrist once or twice and twisted it until it hurt. I didn't hear anybody there say anything. Shoemaker kept hitting me and one of his blows loosened some of my front teeth. I kept backing away so I could open my knife. Then he rushed at me again and I struck him with the knife. He turned around and walked back into the Turf Saloon, and I went up Dock Street, to the Beck Saloon and heard someone there telephone for the police. When the officer got me I was standing in the middle of Dock Street."

"I don't know whether he saw it (the knife) or not, but I didn't hide it any. I struck him in self-defense. That's all there is to it. I had to do it to get rid of him. I was going to leave the saloon and the crowd I got mixed up with."

With a night off from the logging camp, Hugh Finnan was spending it in town staying at the Washington Hotel. He planned a night of card play and drinks at the Turf saloon.
Laura Jacoby's Galen Biery Collection.

When asked if Finnan felt sorry for what he had done, he said, "I got nothing to say. I did it and that is all there is to it. If they want to hang me they can go ahead. I won't be run over by any young man. I'm old and they wanted to pitch onto me on that account."

Attorney Abrams asked the defendant if he intended to kill Shoemaker when he struck him with the knife. Prosecuting Attorney Livesay called for objection to this question and the objection was sustained. Then, interestingly, Judge Kellogg reversed his decision and encouraged Finnan to answer. Finnan reiterated to the jury that he was defending himself from possible harm when he struck the fatal blow.

Finnan's testimony was said to have been delivered unhurriedly; he seemed to weigh every word. A *Morning Reveille* reporter sitting in on the trial noted Finnan's "strange nervousness, of which he seemed unconscious," and how such nervousness "caused him to move his feet about, tapping the heel of one shoe against the toe of the other, or the heels against the stand." It was described that he was constantly stroking his gray mustache, and would sometimes rest his chin between his finger and thumb, or dig a toothpick under the "long fingernails of a rather bony hand – a hand that is as small as a woman's, but strong as steel." Though the reporter picked up on nerves, others saw him as a man unconcerned with his fate and assured of his innocence.

Towards the end of the trial, Abrams put his most damaging witnesses on the stand against the state. Strong corroborative evidence was introduced during the afternoon to flush out the theory of self-defense. Mrs. Mary Debney, wife of the manager of the Byron Hotel, on the witness stand stated that she heard the quarrel on Dock Street the night of September 7th. The window of her room was open and she could hear Shoemaker and Finnan yelling foul language. Debney went to the window and observed the events below. She described hearing someone, presumably Theodore Zingg, yell out, "Give him a black eye. It will do him good." Other witnesses had testified that Zingg made this remark to Shoemaker, while standing in the entrance to the Turf, as well. Debney also recalled hearing someone crying, "Go away and leave me alone," which was discovered to be Finnan, who uttered this cry as he was backing away from Shoemaker. Mrs. Ida Avery corroborated with Debney; she had also heard the cries on the street and testified to seeing the men from her window.

The defense's character witnesses took up the larger part of the afternoon. Among the witnesses who testified to the good character of Finnan were J. C. McCracken, William McCush, J. E. Rice and J. H. Ball.

At the conclusion of the defense's case that evening, Attorney Abrams presented a motion, based on a new state criminal code, asking that the court instruct the jury to return a verdict of not guilty of the charge of murder in the first degree. At the same time Abrams presented a second petition that the court instruct the jury to bring in a verdict of not guilty of the charge of murder in the second degree, providing the first motion was sustained. Abrams then asked the court to instruct the jury to bring in a verdict of not guilty on the charge of manslaughter, providing the previous motions were sustained. Abrams presented all of the motions without intermission. Judge Kellogg affirmed that he would take the motions under advisement.

The Verdict

At 11 am on the morning of Saturday November 6th, after a two-day trial, evidence in the case was submitted; instructions of the court to the jurors followed thereafter. Kellogg announced that four verdicts were possible under new state laws, as Abrams pointed out the previous day. The state offered murder in the first degree, but Kellogg instructed the jurors that they could also find the defendant guilty of murder in the second degree, of manslaughter, or they could return a verdict of not guilty, in the case that they found the evidence insufficient to warrant a verdict on the more serious charge of murder in the first degree.

FINNAN'S CASE IS IN HANDS OF THE JURY

Twelve Men Now Consider Fate of Man Who Is Charged With Slaying R. G. Shoemaker On Dock Street September 7—Four Verdicts Are Possible Under the Law, According to the Court's Instructions.

Bellingham Herald, November 6, 1909.

After deliberating for twenty-four hours, during which time several ballots were taken, the jury brought in a verdict of not guilty. Finnan was released from custody.

Just what occurred behind closed doors during the twenty-four hours of deliberation will never be known. Jurors who sat on the case were approached by reporters asking for information on what happened during the deliberations, but all refused to talk. "We agreed in the jury room not to say a word outside as to what was said and done. You can ask me as many questions as you please, but I will not answer them," declared one juror the morning of the verdict.

FINNAN JURY FINDS HIM NOT GUILTY

Verdict of Acquittal Is Rendered
After Deliberation of Twenty-
Four Hours—Man Who Was
Charged With Murder of R. G.
Shoemaker Is Released From
Custody.

Bellingham Herald, November 8, 1909.

Epilogue

Around 3 pm on Monday, June 29, 1914, Charles Christie and Andy Hanson were picking berries on the crest of a big hill just south of Bay View cemetery. They had been working their way up the hill for about an hour filling their baskets with fruit. They came upon a large tree and were startled to find a body suspended from its limb.

Christie and Hanson notified acting Bellingham Police Chief, Alexander Callahan. Unable to locate Coroner Wear, Callahan took Deputy Coroner R. B. Stewart and Undertaker A. G. Wickman with him to assess the body. After their examination, the men were certain that the corpse belonged to Hugh Finnan. From all appearances and regarding the decay, Stewart believed Finnan had taken his life nearly two months before; back in April he had disappeared from the Laurel House apartments, leaving no word and all

175

his belongings behind. The working theory was that Finnan had walked up on a log that lay against the tree, and tying one end of the rope around his neck, hung himself by jumping from the log. His feet were just barely touching the ground when the body was found, the tree limb giving way slowly. He had stuffed a handkerchief into his mouth, so as to choke himself in case the hanging was not successful. He wore a suit of new brown cloth, new shoes, a new slouch hat, and had used a piece of new rope to hang himself. On one of his fingers was a gold ring with the initials, "H. F." inscribed within.

The Modern Woodmen of America, a fraternal benefit society founded to support families following the death of a breadwinner, erected a monument to Shoemaker in Bellingham's Bay View Cemetery. Photo taken by the author.

Long since gone now, the Turf Saloon would have stood right of the India Grill. The Leopold (Byron) Hotel is directly across the street. Shoemaker would have been fatally stabbed in the street in front of the bike rack on the far right. Photo taken by the author.

Chapter 6
Terrible Tragedy in Blaine

Author's note: In some murder cases, especially those where the perpetrator doesn't go to trial because they've since died or have never been caught, court room documents, trial transcriptions, arrest records and prisoner files are nonexistent. In this particular story, the McGuire case, the bulk of information available comes directly from newspaper articles, background checks and a few family interviews. In this case, I did my best with available materials to reconstruct the plausible series of events. There is little information regarding any inter-family strife, domestic issues or community knowledge of family life for the McGuire's during the time these events took place.

The weather the week of Monday, November 24, 1919 was not only foul, but it also broke all previous records for the past 25 years in Blaine, for a cold spell to happen as early in the season as it was. Following a week of moderately cold conditions, the temperature fell Sunday night and continued to drop all day Monday, from a government thermometer reading of 25 degrees to 15 degrees by Tuesday morning. A stiff gale blowing continuously day and night bore against the buildings, freezing water pipes and causing considerable bodily discomfort.

It was only a few days before Thanksgiving in 1919, a particularly special year to be thankful for, as it was the first national feast of thanks in three years that the boys were back home from the muddy fields of Europe; a time to celebrate those mercifully saved from death in the Great War. A few weeks earlier, on November 5th, President Woodrow Wilson announced his Thanksgiving proclamation, which began:

"The season of the year has again arrived when the people of the United States are accustomed to unite in giving thanks to Almighty God for the blessings, which He has conferred upon our country during the twelve months that have passed. A year ago our people poured out their hearts in praise and thanksgiving that through divine aid the right was victorious and peace had come to the nations, which had so courageously struggled in defense of human liberty and justice. Now that the stern task is ended and the fruits of achievement are ours, we look forward with confidence to the dawn on an era where the sacrifices of the nations will find recompense in a world at peace."

Aiding in the celebration, national newspapers were notifying veterans that "Victory medals" would be forthwith awarded.

The front page of the *Blaine Journal* reported the daily local, state, national and world news. Beyond reports of the cold snap, there was little else to document. The lack of excitement allotted space for other stories, such as Blaine Marshal David Fraiser's public notice on the front page. It looked rather official:

Notice to whom it may concern:

Notice is hereby given that a buckskin-colored pony, with black mane and tail, right eye out, brand on left shoulder has been taken up while unlawfully running at large in the city of Blaine and was impounded by the chief of police, David Fraiser. If not redeemed soon it would be put up for public auction.

A much longer column ran alongside the pony notice, announcing that the official site for the construction of the Peace Arch had been selected.

The *Blaine Journal's* local news section was about to ignite. One of the city's very own community members was about to commit a monstrous offense, an act so vile the tiny harbor community would have a difficult time processing it.

The *Blaine Journal* on Friday, November 28, 1919, headlined the distressing news, "Father Wipes Out Whole Family: Terrible Tragedy in Blaine Throws Entire Populace into Mourning."[1]

Once again Blaine was aghast by the news of such a vile act, which had occurred at the center of a densely settled part of the city. In a small community where atrocities linger longer in memory, Blaine was having more than its fair share. In 1907, Addie Roper was brutally murdered in her home on G Street. In 1915 Samuel Thomson killed his wife and hired hand outside the city limits. Barely a year before, Edward Gaultier took the lives of his wife and her lover. So, it was with a sorrowful heart that the community braced for the news of the latest slaying.

American Reveille, November 25, 1919.

---

1   At the time the Blaine Journal was a weekly Friday paper, the murder took place Monday, November 24, 1919.

Family Gone

On Tuesday, November 25th, E. P. Bartlett,[2] a boarder at the home of Otis and Orpha McGuire, would have boarded the train for Seattle with plans to attend a government auction, having been sent by the McGuires to purchase items for their children. Considerable quantities of government surplus from the World War were being offered for sale by the war department. These goods, consisting of linens and food, were to be sold cheap, and McGuire and Bartlett pooled nearly $100 between them to bid on some of the lots being offered. Bartlett elected to go to Seattle to do the buying, an offer McGuire might have encouraged in order to get rid of his boarder for a few days.

Before the main trip, Bartlett started out for Bellingham in the morning with the expressed intention of returning in the evening before setting out again for Seattle. McGuire bade him an earnest goodbye, shaking hands at the depot for the Bellingham Stage. Bartlett thought this was "queer" and most unusual.

Returning to Blaine with the goods obtained in Bellingham, Bartlett was back at the McGuire home at 6:40 pm. The house was silent and seeing that there were no lights on, he assumed the family was visiting the Wilder's (Orpha's family). Thinking nothing of their absence, he went into his bedroom, where he remained until 8 pm. He walked into the parlor, struck a match and saw a note written by Otis McGuire lying on the table, in which McGuire confessed to having committed murder.

A shaken Bartlett started looking around the house, going from room to room, not knowing what he would uncover in the dark. The McGuire home had six rooms on a single floor, located at 303 East Boblett Street, where they had lived for nearly a year.

---

2   The Blaine Journal also printed that he went by the name "Gus."

Peering through the open door into the master bedroom, off from the parlor, the boarder discovered that a horrible slaughter had occurred. The bedding and white sheets were saturated in blood and strewn about the top of the mattress in disarray. In a heap at the center of the bed laid the bodies of Orpha and her youngest daughter, eight year-old Gertrude.[3] Their eyes were wide open, and their skin was the color of pale ivory. A bloody hatchet lay on the floor. Without stopping to make an examination of the crime scene, Bartlett ran from the house to alert authorities.

Entire Family Wiped Out By Blaine Slayer; Friend Is In Custody

Otis McGuire, In Jealous Rage, Murders Wife With Hatchet and Knife and Stabs Two Daughters, Aged 8 and 12, Years, to Death, Then Goes to Boathouse On Drayton Harbor and Hangs Himself to Rafter—E. P. Bartlett Friend of Slayer, Taken Into Custody By County Officers.

Bellingham Herald, November 25, 1919.

The Search for Otis McGuire

At the time of her death, Orpha Sarah (Wilder) McGuire, was 33 years old, born September 21, 1886 in Stanwood, Michigan. She was the daughter of James Lindsey and Dora Emeline (Bingham) Wilder. Her father was born in Canada in 1858 and immigrated to the United States in 1870, where he became a farmer. The couple raised seven children between Michigan and Blaine, Washington. By 1919, the last of the family still living at home resided on Adelia Street.

3   Gertrude was born June 11, 1911, although her grave marker claims that she was born in 1910.

Otis Irvin McGuire was born in Kansas on July 27, 1883 to John (Jack) McGuire and Margaret Zalina Fletcher. Margaret died on January 1, 1901 in Los Angeles, California.

The McGuires' arrival in Washington is uncertain, however it is documented that the Minister of the Gospel in Blaine married Otis and Orpha on September 22, 1906, the day after her twentieth birthday. Otis was 23 years old at the time and had written that his occupation was "mill worker" on the marriage certificate; Orpha's was "housekeeper." The most we know regarding Otis' appearance comes from his September 12, 1918 draft registration, which minimally describes him as, "tall, medium build, blue eyes and dark hair."

The Wilder family, with little Orpha standing in the center, about 1889.
Courtesy of Rachel Mehl.

Otis was working as a cannery machinist for the Blaine Cannery Company before losing his position in 1919. Looking for employment, he went to Wenatchee where he worked for a time assembling wooden apple crates. It was claimed that he encouraged Orpha and the children to join him there, but she refused because she did not want to take the children out of school. McGuire returned home on Wednesday, November 19th and had been looking for work up until the present day.

After being notified of the murders, Town Marshal David Fraiser and Deputy Sheriff Barney Hansen investigated the scene. Adding to the horrific tragedy, the officers discovered the corpse of eleven year-old Dorothy in her bedroom.[4] Fraiser notified Whatcom County Sheriff William Wallace and Whatcom County Coroner N. Whitney Wear to come at once.

In their investigation, another note left by McGuire was found. It read, "You will find my body beyond the creek or at Drayton." A citizen posse was hastily organized; it consisted of Deputy Sheriff Barney Hansen, Custom's Officer H. J. Merrill, auto mechanic Bob Smiley, and railroad brakemen William Moore and William Runze. Together, the men started out in search of McGuire.

It was believed that after writing the confession, McGuire left the house followed by his dog, a little white spitz. Witnesses would later claim to have seen him cross California Creek, heading in the direction of Drayton Harbor.

The search party stopped at the home of Otis' father, Jack McGuire, who asserted that he had not seen his son. On the basis of the information in the note, the men went in the direction of the home of Captain "Cap" Hansen, with whom it was known that McGuire had a grudge. The two had a running dispute over a bad boat deal and money was owed. It was theorized that perhaps McGuire set out to settle an old score.

4   Dorothy was born April 3, 1908.

Arriving at "Cap" Hansen's they were told that he was away in Seattle. They heard a dog barking and followed the yelps down a trail leading to Hansen's boathouse, just a few yards from the main house. The dog was McGuire's little white spitz.

Suspecting that McGuire was hiding inside the boathouse, whether dead as he professed in his note, or alive and dangerous, the search party decided that instead of breaking in, they would wait for further developments. It was around midnight and though the dark cast a deeper trepidation, they were comforted by the fact that Deputy Sheriff Chatfield and reinforcements were on the way. Shortly thereafter, David Fraiser, Sheriff Wallace and Deputy Chris Patterson arrived. Together they agreed to await daylight before entering the boathouse.

Asking around Hansen's, they were informed that the dog had been howling dolefully on the south side of the harbor since 4 pm that afternoon. It was evident that the spitz was Otis', and that it had to be him holed up within.

Wallace informed the men that during their search of McGuire's home, they had discovered a .32-caliber pistol and cartridges in a box on the floor, belonging to a heavier handgun. Wallace believed that bullets were missing from the box and that McGuire might have intended to use the gun on Hansen. He warned the men to be cautious; if McGuire were alive, he would be armed and dangerous.

At daybreak the officers returned to the boathouse. They called out for whoever was inside to surrender themselves. Receiving no reply, they began battering the door with heavy stones, trying to elicit a response. They would strike the door, then jump aside to avoid any shots that might be fired through the door. But, nothing happened.

"We didn't know that whoever was inside was dead," the sheriff said. "We thought McGuire might be in there, a raving maniac, and we knew that he was armed with a heavy revolver. That someone was within was evident by the dog's actions. So we worked cautiously until the door was broken open. Swinging it back we saw, in the spots of our pocket flashlights, a body hanging from a rope. The body was still warm," the sheriff said, indicating that rigor mortis had yet to set in. Wallace assessed the suicide scene and claimed:

"Indications were that McGuire had climbed a ladder to the rafters of the boathouse, taken a new, strong rope and tied it to the rafter and bout his neck [sic], then let himself down to one side, on a pile of lumber. Standing there evidently, the man stabbed himself in the right breast with the same knife used in killing the little girls, then fell forward off the lumber pile and swayed at the end of the rope. His feet barely touched, with the neck drawn it is probable the man strangled."

At Otis' feet lay a knife with a seven-inch blade that was undoubtedly the one he had used to kill his wife and children. Inserted in his waistband was a .38 caliber pistol. In one pocket was a tin box containing $101, receipts from purchases and a gold watch in a leather pocket case. In another pocket was a new paper tablet. The first page was inscribed with a note in pencil that read, "You will find a note in the bottom of the buffet in a tablet. God forgive me." The *Bellingham Herald* was quick to point out that the writing was "plain...an unpracticed hand," assessing the lack of capitalization and punctuation. "God" was spelled with a small "g" and "buffet" with two "t's." Otis Irvin McGuire was 36 years old when he murdered his family and took his own life.

Bellingham Herald, November 25, 1919.

Back to the Scene of the Crime

Before he killed himself, McGuire left notes addressed to various persons, with introductions the likes of, "to whom it may concern" and "citizens of blaine. [sic]" One such note offered that if the people of Blaine realized the circumstances they wouldn't blame him for the deed. Two other notes offered that it was E. P. Bartlett, his closest friend, who was at fault for the crimes committed. His notes also implied a sort of jealousy, revealing that he was angry with his wife over rumors of infidelity. Such rumors stemmed from unknown origins, and might have been caused by delusions.[5]

Back at the family home, on the corner of Blaine Avenue and Boblett Street, authorities were combing through the bloodiest crime scene on the city's record. The murders far surpassed any violence in memory, partially because of the children involved. Otis had used a hatchet against Orpha's head and a knife to cut her chest. Those investigating the scene were Lawmen Fraiser, Wallace and Coroner Wear.

---

5   Unsubstantiated claims have pointed toward "Cap" Hansen, Rev. J. R. Phillips of the Free Methodist church, who lived next door to the McGuires, and Otis' good friend, E. P. Bartlett as possible persons with whom Orpha was suspected to have had relations. If this were true, one would think McGuire would have killed them as well.

The *Blaine Journal* stated, "It seems that Blaine has had its share of awful affairs of this kind, but this one eclipses all others, not only in the number of lives snuffed out, but in the way it was carried out. The journal reluctantly reports the details but is forced to give as true an account of it as is possible to obtain in the light of the many and wild rumors floating about."

As closely as could be ascertained, the first murder was committed around 10 am, Monday morning. The children were at school; Bartlett had boarded the Bellingham stage thirty minutes before, and Otis McGuire had personally seen him off. After talking to witnesses, it was understood that Orpha hadn't been feeling well and had stayed in bed to rest. Otis, upon returning from the Bellingham stage depot, entered the bedroom where Orpha lay. We will never know if the two spoke, or whether Orpha was asleep when Otis attacked her. It is certain, however, that Orpha was defenseless and that he held a hatchet in one hand and a heavy, long-bladed breadknife in the other. Orpha was not documented as having defensive wounds.

In the one-sided struggle that ensued, Orpha was struck several times to the right side of her head. Otis must have swung with great force, as it was reported that her head was mutilated and crushed. Head wounds are known to bleed profusely; the scene can only be imagined. The hatchet, which was found thick with blood, lay on the floor beside the bed. Otis then delivered the coup de grace; he stabbed his wife in the heart with the knife.

Within the house, officers found a loaded .32-caliber revolver with several misfired cartridges in the cylinder. If an attempt was made to use the gun on Orpha, it will never be known.

It would have been around 11:30 am that the youngest daughter, Gertrude, came home from school for lunch. There's no telling what Otis was doing between the time he killed Orpha and Gertrude's arrival, but it was speculated that he may have been writing the notes he would leave behind. As Gertrude entered her home, her father seized her and plunged the knife into her chest. It was not recorded where in the house this took place, whether as soon as she entered, or beside her mother, but her body was found on the bed, beside her mother.

Around noon, the eldest daughter, Dorothy, 11 years old, came home. Specific details were not reported, but the local papers indicated that, "Those who viewed the scene, say there was evidence that the oldest daughter fought for her life." Dorothy was found in her bedroom, stabbed to death on her bed.

Shortly thereafter, and after slaughtering his family, Otis McGuire left the house on foot, heading towards Drayton and "Cap" Hansen's. Blaine resident "Red" Custer would later claim to have walked with McGuire for a portion, and offered that he had not detected anything unusual about the man.[6]

Sheriff Wallace took the two revolvers, the bloody hatchet and the knife into evidence. He believed the knife found at the scene of McGuire's suicide was the same one that had been used on his wife and two daughters.

More Notes Found

Two more notes were found by the lawmen in McGuire's home; both mentioned Bartlett's name. One of the notes documented that McGuire had given Bartlett $100, which was not paid back. He also made claim that Bartlett had in his trunk some kind of "India love powder," which he stated looked like sawdust, and that he believed this might have been used on his wife. Though baffled, the officers followed the potential lead and searched Bartlett's trunk; they found nothing. When they questioned Bartlett, he responded that he wasn't aware that such a substance existed, and that he was unable to account for McGuire's actions.

Bartlett told Sheriff Wallace that as far as he was concerned, his relationship with McGuire was on the most amicable basis. He explained the

---

6   It should be noted that no one reported seeing McGuire covered in blood as he walked through town. Why this wasn't regarded more critically is not known.

planned trip to Seattle to purchase government supplies for sale by the war department, and how they had talked the matter over, agreed on who should pay for what, and how he took the commission to place the bids. Bartlett claimed that McGuire was even wrong about the amount; that it wasn't $100 he had given him for the purchase, but $150.

There were many unanswered questions, and the person considered closest to a witness was E. P. Bartlett. Marshal Fraiser took him into custody and handed him over to Deputy Sheriffs Al Callahan and Chris Patterson to be taken to Bellingham for further questioning. Bartlett denied having done anything to cause any trouble in the family.

Bartlett, who was 45 years old at the time, was an umbrella mender. He had come to Blaine in 1889, having lived in other cities in the Northwest beforehand. For several years he was a halibut fisherman. He told a *Bellingham Herald* reporter, who was accompanying the deputy sheriffs as they transported Bartlett to Bellingham about his relationship with the McGuires:

> "I can not imagine," said Bartlett, "why McGuire had such charges as he did in those notes. They are false and I wish he were alive so that I could disprove them, but any of the neighbors will tell you that they cannot be true. McGuire and I were always the best of friends. It was he who suggested to me that I live with his family, with whom I got acquainted when he was working at the Blaine cannery, and I had lived with them since last January. He thought so much of me to join the I.O.O.F., [sic] of which he had been a member about two years."[7]

Bartlett said he was stunned by the sight of Mrs. McGuire on her bed, and declared that he had not been able to eat a thing since he had discovered their bodies. "I went into a Blaine restaurant for breakfast this morning,"

---

7   Independent Order of Odd Fellows.

he continued, "and ordered hot cakes, some boiled eggs and coffee, but I could not eat a thing."

When questioned if the couple fought, he answered:

"I never knew Mr. and Mrs. McGuire to quarrel except on the question of religion," he stated. "Once, I remember, they quarreled over the Bible. He did not want to see her reading it and finally forced her to leave the church to keep peace in the home. His attitude on religion was the same toward the children." But Bartlett added, "He was not a good provider...he was unable to keep a job long because of his proneness to agitate. Furthermore, he had a weakness for gambling and drinking."

Bartlett insisted that he had a good relationship with the family, having even purchased shoes for the girls when they were in strained financial circumstances.

According to Bartlett, McGuire had returned from Wenatchee the previous Wednesday, where he had been working for six weeks building wooden boxes for apple packing. He seemed in the best of spirits and grasped Bartlett warmly by the hand when he returned. Bartlett had also been away for several weeks, working for the Apex Fish Company. He returned home from Seattle and adjacent waters just before McGuire's return from Wenatchee. He recalled that it was the Sunday night following Otis' return when he and the family went to the home of Mrs. McGuire's parents, Mr. and Mrs. James Wilder. Bartlett and the family shared a very pleasant evening. From this get-together to his departure for Bellingham, Bartlett wasn't given the slightest indication that McGuire was on the verge of insanity.[8]

---

8 Some descendents claim Otis' relationship with the Wilder's wasn't as friendly as the newspapers portrayed.

Sitting in the car alongside the deputy sheriffs and the reporter, Bartlett offered a few theories. Perhaps Otis had "been turned by predictions of planetary disturbances, published recently in newspapers in the Northwest...McGuire was a strong believer in planetary influences and probably feared that there would be great floods and other dire happenings as prophesied." Bartlett also suggested that someone may have told McGuire that he, as his boarder, had been "taking undue advantage of his absence, and that this seed of suspicion had grown until it had unbalanced his mind."

Bartlett made claim that McGuire was also paranoid of the Chinese, or "vengeance from Chinamen," and for that reason acquired and carried the small pistol. The previous summer Otis was responsible for the arrest of one or more "Chinamen" on the charge of smuggling, and received a $50 reward. He feared that members of the "Tang" might seek revenge for his hand in the arrest.

McGuire's neighbors, the Reverend Ralph J. Phillips, Pastor of the Free Methodist Church and his wife, who lived in close proximity to the McGuire's kitchen, told the officers that they did not hear signs of struggle at the McGuires' that day.

Other neighbors were interviewed; the information gathered from them supported Bartlett's innocence, as no one had anything negative or incriminating to say about him. Bartlett had not been arrested under any charge, but held pending an examination.

E. P. Bartlett was released on Tuesday, November 26th, after Whatcom County Prosecuting Attorney Loomis Baldrey thoroughly examined him. "We could find that no responsibility rested on Bartlett," said Prosecutor Baldrey. "There was nothing to show that he was in any way responsible. Under such circumstances we concluded it would not be necessary to detain him longer."

Services

Coroner Whitney Wear believed that an inquest was unnecessary and left instructions for the bodies to be turned over to the undertaker. They were then carefully transported to the undertaking parlors of H. B. Potter.

On Tuesday, November 25th, the *Bellingham Herald* headlines read, "Blaine Man Hangs Himself After Killing Wife And Two Daughters – Entire Family Wiped Out By Blaine Slayer; Fiend Is In Custody." The sub-heading of the column read, "The triple murder and suicide, by which an entire family of four persons was annihilated, has stirred Blaine…"

The *Blaine Journal* printed that "words could not express the feeling of the people for those who are left to mourn for the loved ones whose lives have gone out so suddenly. The hearts of everybody have been pierced and go out to the bereaved ones."

The Wilder family, taken in Blaine. Orpha is seen standing on the far right. Standing center is Dorothy, with sister Gertrude kneeling in front of her. Circa: Summer of 1918 or 1919. Courtesy of Rachel Mehl.

At two o'clock on Wednesday the 26th, Reverend Phillips officiated the funeral services at the Free Methodist Church for Orpha and her two little daughters, Gertrude and Dorothy. The church was unable to accommodate all of those who turned out. It was one of the largest funerals Blaine had ever seen, and many had to stand outside. The reverend was said to have spoken as a friend of the deceased and her family, and under such trying circumstances, delivered an eloquent and touching sermon. As many wept, a chorus of the slain daughters' schoolmates sang "Shall We Gather at the River." Interment was made in the Haynie cemetery in the family plot.

On the day of the funeral, the *Bellingham Herald* recorded that "... Victims of Crazed Husband, Laid to Rest – Funeral Services Held Within 100 Feet of Where Triple Murder Occurred – Slayer Will Be Buried Tomorrow Afternoon." The funeral of Otis McGuire, organized by the Odd Fellows and less attended, was held at H. B. Potter's undertaking parlors. Otis' internment was made in the Blaine cemetery, away from his family. The following day would be Thanksgiving.

Included is a poem written by Rachel Mehl, the great-great niece of Orpha Wilder-McGuire:

Family History, 1919

For Orpha Wilder McGuire, my great-great aunt

In the family photo the women's black
shoes blend into the dark earth
and make them float like ghosts.
The outlines of their white
dresses fade into the men's
suits. No one smiles. Orpha's eyes
seem to pop from their sockets.
Her two daughters, at eight and twelve,
are thin as blood grass.

I watch the microfilm blur like an ultrasound.

I slow the crank then stop at the headline,

Entire Family Wiped Out By Blaine Slayer.

I print the article. It comes out dark

and hard to read. It was her husband.

He used a bread knife. He is not in the picture.

Headstones of a fallen family. No explanation of McGuire spelling as "McQuire" on the headstones. Courtesy of Rachel Mehl.

Epilogue

What, if anything, caused Otis McGuire to flip a switch, to kill his family and then himself, will never be known. Only crude and unreliable clippings from local newspapers and a few superior court documents offer the little evidence there is. The local police and sheriff's investigation reports and McGuire's handwritten notes have long since disappeared with history. We know from probate records and letters of administration that the McGuire estate settlement did not commence until July 9, 1925, and did not settle until March 8, 1926. Otis' father, John McGuire, listed as sole heir, turned the estate over to a man by the name of John G. Olson. Aside from a mortgaged home, the McGuire's held no assets and no personal effects were listed.

Consider this Friday, January 24, 1908 article in the *Blaine Journal*, which was printed 11 years prior to McGuire's murder spree:

HURT AT THE STEAM SHOVEL

While working on the Great Northern steam shovel at the ball ground Wednesday morning Otis McGUIRE was struck on the head by a flying sledgehammer and rendered unconscious. At first it was feared that the young man was very seriously injured but he is now reported as recovering. The accident occurred about 8 o'clock in the morning. The crew was preparing to move the shovel and one of the workmen was striking a piece of railroad iron in an effort to drive it into place. The sledgehammer slipped away from him and hit young McGUIRE over the left eye. He was taken home and Dr. REEDY was called. It is thought that Mr. McGUIRE will be around again in a few days.

It is clear that Otis McGuire's mental state shifted, but whether he was mentally ill, unbalanced or receiving medication will remain unanswered as well. It makes one wonder – what if McGuire had a form of brain or other neurological damage, or a slow growing brain tumor and suffered from delusional episodes? Could the blow from the steam shovel incident have acted as catalyst to McGuire family's demise? Only Otis McGuire knows.

Chapter 7
For a Man's House is His Castle

Precedent

Versions of the "Castle Law" or "Castle Doctrine"[1] have a long history, reaching as far back as ancient Rome, and undoubtedly prior to that. In 1628, England was the first modern nation to have a written law that allowed a person to defend their home with lethal force if necessary. Though it was considered justifiable homicide without prosecution within the confines of the law, it would continue to be tested in the courts for centuries past. Today, various laws developed upon the Castle Law are dependant upon what state or country in which you reside; lawmaking continues to evolve regarding the old adage, "an Englishman's home is his castle."

The United Sates has state-by-state laws regarding the defense of an individual's home, property or person. The definition of "a person's home" is ultimately tested daily in the American court system. Today, versions of the Castle Law are better known as "Stand Your Ground" law,[2] "Culpability of Intruder" or the "Make My Day" law.[3]

---

1   A "Castle Law" or "Castle Doctrine" is a legal doctrine that designates a person's home or legally occupied space as a place in which that person is capable of certain protection and immunities allowing him or her to use force to defend himself or herself from an intruder without legal responsibility or prosecution.

2   A "Stand Your Ground" law states that a person may use deadly force in self-defense without the duty to retreat when faced with perceivable threat.

3   Back in 1985, Colorado was the first state to pass a "Make My Day" law, which protects homeowners who use deadly force to repel intruders.

As this book was being written, a verdict was pending from a 2014 garage shooting in Missoula, Montana. Markus Kaarma, alerted by his motion detector, found a nighttime intruder on his property. He rushed outside, firing four shotgun blasts into his garage, which ended up killing 17 year-old German exchange student, Diren Dede. What was later found was that Kaarma had left the door to his garage partially open in hopes of enticing a prowler, which brought forth the question – was this a case of protection or entrapment?[4]

Another such case was that of Katko v. Briney (1971). Briney owned an old, unoccupied farmhouse in Iowa; the property was boarded up and had "No Trespass" signs around it. He dealt with constant break-ins and in his distress he mounted a 20-gauge, spring-loaded shotgun to fire if the door to his farmhouse were to open. Katko went into the farmhouse with the intent of stealing. Upon entering the room, the trigger was tripped and the shotgun fired. The court deemed that an intruder in an unoccupied property was not justified as defending oneself, unless the owner or resident had been present at home during the intrusion.

In the case of Bird v. Holbrook (1825 Eng.), Holbrook set a spring-gun trap in his walled-in valuable tulip garden to catch the culprit who had been stealing his bulbs; he did not post a warning to trespassers. The intruder, Mr. Bird, chased a real bird into the garden and set off the trap, suffering a nasty gunshot wound to his knee. Bird then sued Holbrook for damages. The question was – could Holbrook legally set a trap without posting a warning that he would intentionally harm or kill an intruder?

The answer, according to English law was, no. In the case of Bird v. Holbrook, the court stated that setting traps or "man traps" could be valid as a deterrent only if notice was posted. The court held that in such a case, even an intruder could recover personal damages if injured.

---

4   Markus Kaarma has since been found guilty, despite the state's "Castle Doctrine."

The story regarding Newell S. Barr and John Erickson took place in New Whatcom during 1893-96. It's interesting that today we are still dealing with the same issues as those that occurred a hundred years ago. Really, nothing has changed!

Spring-Gun

John Erickson, a 35 year-old Swede, arrived in New Whatcom from Seattle on Friday, December 8, 1893 in the company of Nels Anderson of Everett, Washington. Erickson and Anderson had known one another for only two months when they came into New Whatcom looking for work. The country was ten months into the "Panic of 1893"[5] and the effects rippled throughout the Pacific Northwest. By all accounts it was turning into the worst economic collapse ever faced by Americans. On Bellingham Bay, it was hoped that the timber and lumber industries were still healthy, but due to bank failings and overbuilding, contracts for building materials were canceled and wood products were piling up on the docks and rotting away. With the region's largest economic product standing idle, unemployment soared to new heights.

Erickson and Anderson found cheap accommodations at the Stockholm Hotel on Elk Street, but time and money were running out for them. Then, a terrific break occurred. The two men were told that E. L. Moran, of Moran & Singleton Construction, was hiring good men and accepting contracts to build the new Northwest Diagonal Road. The two men ran to the Pacific House where George A. Singleton was sizing up potential workers. By four o'clock Tuesday afternoon, on a wet December 12th, the two had their first job in months. Excited, they gathered their bedrolls from the hotel and walked out to the site to see what the job would entail.

5   The Panic of 1893 was a serious economic depression in the United States, the worst it had ever seen. Similar to The Panic of 1873, it was marked by the overbuilding and unstable financing of railroads, which led to a series of bank failures.

They were told that they would be slashing a portion of the right-of-way for the road. Moran was present and showed them a few things, but as it was nearing five o'clock, he finished up and returned to the city.

The Pacific House, located today at the corner of F and Holly Streets, where E. L. Moran, of Moran & Singleton Construction, were hiring good men to build the new Northwest Diagonal Road. Circa: 1880s or 90s. Laura Jacoby's Galen Biery Collection.

An early plank road construction crew, like those hired to build the new Northwest Diagonal Road, laying down heavy timbers. Wood was so plentiful in the Pacific Northwest; it was used to build roads. Circa: 1890s. Laura Jacoby's Galen Biery Collection.

Erickson and Anderson didn't have money or a place to return to. They had noticed a boarded up little cabin just north from where the road crossed Squalicum Creek, about a mile from town and close to the job site. They took their bedrolls and headed back to it, arriving around 5:20 pm as it was nearing dark.

A typical cabin seen throughout the Pacific Northwest, the likes of which would have resembled Newell S. Barr's. Laura Jacoby's Galen Biery Collection.

Erickson went to the door, which was boarded up and solidly nailed across the entry, and preceded to pry the boards loose. He managed to remove them and started to open the door. Anderson looked to his new friend as he grabbed the door handle; a sudden explosion erupted, throwing Erickson into the air. He was struck by something and howled with pain, yelling in his native tongue, "I die." The Swede staggered back and fell heavily onto the ground with a gaping wound in his abdomen. The full impact of the charge had entered Erickson's body below his navel. Anderson ran towards Erickson, but realized it was too late. The wound was as big as a small fist, one of his legs appeared shattered and he was bleeding profusely. Anderson decided to "beat it down the road towards town with the accelerated speed of the wildest dread," with hopes of finding help.

Anderson was scared out of his wits when he got to New Whatcom. Knowing no one in town, he ran to the Stockholm Hotel and asked for the authorities to be summoned. Sheriff Charles G. Requa, Constable M. E. White and Charles Boardman arrived at the cabin about an hour after the shot was fired. They found Erickson dead, lying a few feet from the door, flat on his back.

The door to the cabin was open three inches with a hole blasted through the wood. The door itself was left unlocked, and the boarded planks that Erickson had removed were lying on the ground beside it. On a bed to the rear of the cabin was an old muzzle-loaded, army Springfield musket. Attached from the barrel's end and stock-butt was a string. The muzzle was pointing straight at the door from a distance of about eight feet. It was evident to authorities that Erickson had been the victim of a spring-gun; set purposely for burglars. Erickson's body was brought to Coroner Brackett's undertaking rooms.

The cabin was the property of 39 year-old Newell S. Barr[6] and 18 year-old Walter K. Pixley, who claimed it had been robbed several times in the past year. Barr and Pixley had been living at the cabin, cutting wood for several months. On Monday December 11th, the day before Erickson and Anderson had earned a spot on the Moran & Singleton Construction crew, Barr and Pixley boarded the Bellingham Bay & British Columbia train for Nooksack North Fork country to go deer hunting. They also planned to take part in a prospecting trip in the foothills. They were last seen in the company of "old man" Samuel Bateman near Deming on Tuesday morning, December 12th, 20 miles from their hunting grounds.

In New Whatcom, the authorities were rounding up witnesses. Not knowing if he had any part in the slaying, Walter's father and proprietor of the Chicago House, John L. Pixley, was placed under arrest Tuesday night. He was charged with being an accessory to murder before the fact; the warrant

6   1900 census: Barr born in Michigan, April 1854. Divorced. Living in the home of Frank Littlefield.

was sworn out by Coroner Brackett. It was Pixley's own statements, which he made immediately after the news of Erickson's death, that brought about his arrest; he allegedly asserted that he knew about the spring-gun trap.

Coroner Inquest

UNDERTAKING W. H. BRACKETT, Undertaker, Embalmer and Funeral Director, Undertaking Goods, Burial Robes, Cloth, Metalic and Wood Caskets. Preserving bodies for shipment a specialty. C Street New Whatcom. Telephone No. 42.

Bellingham Bay Express, December 13, 1893.

On the afternoon of Wednesday, December 13th, Coroner Brackett impaneled a jury.[7] Deputy Prosecuting Attorney Howard Boardman, (no known relation to Charles Boardman) represented the state. Court Stenographer Porter, took a stenographic report of the evidence. The witnesses examined were Nels Anderson, Sheriff Charles G. Requa, M. E. White, Charles Boardman, C. W. Stone, John L. Pixley, Morgan Wheeler, W. L. Geer, John Deal, Thomas T. Tyler and Louis Pixley, Walter Pixley's 13 year-old boy brother.

Nels Anderson testified as follows:

"Erickson and himself went out to look at work on the Northwest Diagonal road… taking their blankets, which they left behind a log near the cabin, and after making the examination, returned to the city. They made a contract with Moran & Singleton in the Pacific House at 4 pm. A man named Johnson, who was a friend of Erickson, was party to the contract. Anderson and Erickson then returned to the cabin where they expected to remain over night, not

7   The jurors included: C. G. Hopkins, W. J. Simonds, S. E. Fancy, T. T. Tyler, S. E. Harmon and J. P. Lewis.

having money enough to pay for lodging. Erickson went to the door, succeeded in opening it about three inches, when a gun was discharged from the inside, and he stepped back a few feet and fell with his feet toward the cabin, exclaiming in Swedish, 'I die, I, die.' Anderson ran to the Stockholm Hotel on Elk Street, where they had been stopping since last Friday. The witness had known Erickson about two months."

Sheriff Charles G. Requa testified:

"Anderson, Charles Boardman, Constable M. E. White and himself, went out to the cabin at 7 o'clock Tuesday evening. Erickson was found lying near by and examined him, finding no pulse. The door was ajar and the cabin unoccupied. The musket lay on the bed and there was a hole burnt in the mattress. Two pasteboard shells from which the loads were extracted lay on the floor. C. W. Stone, Deputy Prosecuting Attorney Howard Boardman, White and himself went out yesterday morning making a thorough examination of the cabin. Two gun wads were found outside under the hole made by the shot, which was about two inches in diameter, in that casing of the door. They found a twine string of the exact length of the distance from the hole in the mattress to the door, and found the gun had a string around the stock tied to a small stick of a sufficient length to reach the trigger. A stick about eighteen inches long was found on the bed, which had been broken off the smaller piece. A staple was driven into the casing and a nail in the door, from which the string was passed through the staple and stretched to the burnt spot in the mattress, and was of the right length. A string around the barrel had a nail in one end and had evidently been pulled out of the post of the footboard."

The bed, door, door casing, gun, string and a stick were all brought back to the coroner's office and reassembled. With measurements taken from the cabin, it was found that when one end of the string was tied to the door, passed through the staple and extended to the bed, and the other end tied to a stick (mimicking how it attached to the gun), that a perfect spring was made, so that when the door was opened the gun would discharge.

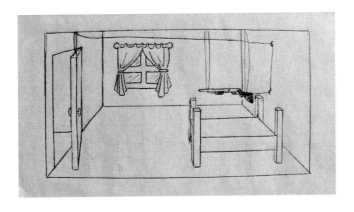

This diagram depicts how Newell S. Barr had his spring-gun rigged to protect his property.
Diagram by Sierra Ellingson

Constable White and Charles Boardman corroborated the sheriff's testimony.

C. W. Stone stated that he saw two footprints beneath one window, as if someone had jumped from it. This further indicated that someone had set the spring-gun aimed at the door, and had left from the window so that it wouldn't set off.

John L. Pixley, who had been locked up until his participation in the investigation was straightened out, testified that he had formally leased the cabin from the BBI Company, had cut wood from the premises and then leased the cabin to Newell S. Barr two months prior. He said his son, Walter, lived with Barr, and that he had told his son to "shift" for himself. He knew nothing of a spring-gun being set, but his youngest son, Louis, told him on Thursday not to go near the cabin as "Barr and Walter were going hunting and were going to play tricks." Other than that, he said, he knew nothing. Mrs. Pixley's knowledge on the matter was no greater than her husbands.

The coroner called Louis Pixley, a bright looking boy, as the next witness. On December 15th, Fairhaven's *Weekly World* reported on his testimony:

"He had all the self-possession of a man matured in years, and answered Prosecuting Attorney Boardman's questions with the promptness of a veteran. The prosecuting attorney evinced a deal of skill in the handling of the young witness, and although the boy at times showed some perturbation he never faltered once during the examination. If he knew that his brother had talked of 'setting a gun to catch burglars' he denied any knowledge of it most emphatically. He said, however, that Barr had told him one day last week that 'he was thinking of setting a gun in the cabin to shoot burglars,' as the cabin had been robbed two or three times, but Walter, the witness' brother, had never mentioned any such thing. The witness had never told his father that Walter had intimated such an intention, although the elder Pixley had testified that Louis had told him of Walter's intention. He also said, that he had never told his mother anything of that nature. Walter, Louis said, had been living in the Squalicum cabin for some three or four months, he and Barr had been cutting wood out there. Louis was firmly of the opinion that if his father or mother had stated that he had told them that Walter had talked of 'setting' a gun in the cabin they were mistaken. He had gone to Sunday school, he said, in California, but never here, and he didn't know what would happen to him if he didn't tell the truth, but he was of the opinion that he might go to jail."

George Pixley, Louis' 11 year-old brother, corroborated his brother's testimony.

Morgan Wheeler, a foreman of BBI Company, testified that on December 5th he settled on a price with Barr for wood he had cut from the land. Barr said, "If you go around the cabin and find a man lying dead, you may know there has been a spring-gun set inside," intimating that he had things fixed for intruders inside the cabin. Wheeler warned Barr that he had better put a sign up outside, warning people of the gun.

W. L. Geer, who had been hauling lumber past the cabin, claimed that a week before Barr had mentioned to him that he and Pixley were going hunting, and that he was going to set a spring-gun pointing toward the door. Barr claimed to have been shown the musket in question. Comparably, John Deal also said that Barr had intimated to him that burglars had better steer clear of his shack.

Thomas Tyler, one of the jurors, testified that the day before the two men had left (Sunday), Pixley had come over to his home and told him that they were going hunting and that Barr was going to set a gun to shoot anybody who attempted to get into the cabin.

Drs. Biggs, Bragg and McPherson held an autopsy on the deceased and testified to the nature of the wound and identified the clothing worn by Erickson. From the abdomen of the deceased, they removed numerous pieces of shot, slugs and most astonishingly of all, a complete .45-90 Sharps loaded brass cartridge. The cartridge was unexploded and had passed through Erickson's thighbone, shattering it. It appeared that whoever had set the spring-gun had loaded the musket with whatever metal they had available.

John Erickson's death certificate. Washington State Digital Archives.

After convening for a short duration, the jury returned a verdict to the effect that John Erickson had met his death by a gunshot wound from a spring-gun.

"Said gun being discharged off and against the body of the said John Erickson, said gun from which the shot was fired being situated in a cabin occupied by one Walter Pixley and

210

Newell S. Barr, said gun being so arranged by a certain device of strings attached to the same in such a manner as to discharge the gun upon the opening of the door of said cabin that the said gun was so arranged by Walter Pixley and Newell S. Barr, and that deceased while endeavoring to enter the cabin door caused the strings attached to the gun to discharge the same, causing the death of said deceased; and that the death of said deceased was occasioned by the act of said Walter Pixley and said Newell S. Barr."

The witnesses were released on their own recognizance. So far as was known, Erickson had no relatives in the United States. Anderson stated that he had only known him for a few months and that he believed Erickson had been in the state for some years, coming directly from Sweden. Erickson's funeral took place at 10 am on December 5th.

Pixley passed the night in jail, but was released the following morning. The inquest would proffer no evidence of his connection in the death of Erickson.

Retrieving Barr and Pixley

As Coroner Brackett convened his coroner's inquest, Deputy Sheriff A. H. Conlin had already departed for the North Fork in pursuit of Barr and Pixley. He rode to within two miles of Hollingsworth and then walked to Kendall, above the North Fork of the Nooksack River and then to Racehorse Creek. At 10 pm that Wednesday evening, he found Barr and Pixley in a cabin belonging to Ed Cleary[8]. At 2 am on Thursday they started on their return trip. Thursday night was spent at Griffin's Hotel, and on Friday morning they

---

8   It appears from testimony during the trial that Samuel Bateman was either at the Cleary cabin when Conlin arrived, or Conlin previously stopped at Bateman's, who followed the deputy to Cleary's. This is never explained during testimony.

walked into Goshen and came in by train. Conlin reported that it was a rough trip, with snow in the North Fork country ten-inches deep.

KILLED BY A SET GUN

RIDDLED WITH BUCKSHOT

John Ericson's Unexpected Death—Shot Through the Door of an Unoccupied Shack—The Inquest.

Bellingham Bay Express, December 13, 1893.

On Friday morning, December 15th, the *Bellingham Bay Express* reported that Conlin had successfully brought in Barr and Pixley from Hollingsworth. The two men, suspected for the homicide of Erickson, were still carrying their rifles when an *Express* reporter saw them walk in off the train. He wrote that they "looked as unconcerned as if they had just returned from an ordinary hunting trip." When asked if they had anything to say for publication, Barr remarked, "Oh, I don't know. I did not think anyone would go into the cabin. I packed what few things I had there and when I left I nailed the door and windows up securely."

"Had your cabin ever been broken into before?" Queried the reporter.

"No, not since I had it. I always left my dog there and he kept good watch. But other cabins in that neighborhood had been robbed."

"And you left the gun there to make sure your stuff was safe?"

"Well, I left the old musket so that if anyone did break in, the neighbors would know who it was. I put in the cartridge and coarse shot because I had no buckshot."

The men walked down to Rhone's livery stable, deposited their rifles and then followed the deputy up to the courthouse. There, they were met by Prosecuting Attorney Thomas Newman, and all proceeded together to Judge Hardin's office. Hardin was out, and while they waited his return, a reporter again called on them, "What will be the charge against the prisoner?" he asked Newman.

"Murder in the first degree" was the prosecutor's answer.

That afternoon, Barr and Pixley appeared before Judge Hardin and had their preliminary hearing fixed for Monday at 10 o'clock in the morning. The complaint was signed by A. H. Conlin and Prosecutor Newman, charging that the prisoners "purposely and of deliberate and premeditated malice shot and mortally wounded John Erickson."

Deputy Sheriff Conlin led the men away to a cell. When a *Weekly World* reporter tried to visit the prisoners that Friday evening, he was told that the prosecutor had given instructions not to allow anyone to converse with the prisoners, even reporters. Nothing of importance was gleaned from Conlin as to any statements that the prisoners may have made. "He was as mum as an oyster," wrote the *World* reporter.

The *Weekly World* described Walter Pixley as "a smooth-faced youth of eighteen years or so, bright looking, and without any trace of viciousness in his countenance. Barr, his companion in the alleged crime, is a stalwart looking man of probably 35 or 40 years of age, also intelligent in appearance, and does not look as though he would, with malice aforethought, seek to encompass the death of anyone."

Conlin stated that when he found Barr and Pixley, they were comfortably "ensconced" in Cleary's cabin, and when he told them that they were wanted for murder, they at once expressed their willingness to accompany him back to Whatcom to clear themselves.

At the preliminary hearing on Monday morning, Prosecuting Attorney Thomas Newman formally presented Information into the Superior Court stating:

> "Then and there, with the motive of mortally wounded and shooting the said John Erickson with a gun loaded with gunpowder, leaden shot and a brass cartridge, which the said Newell S. Barr and Walter K. Pixley, then and there placed and set, which said gun was rigged and equipped with a certain combination and device of nails and springs and a wooden stick whereby said gun was fired and discharged against and upon the person of the said John Erickson, inflicting mortal wounds from which Erickson then and there died."

Prosecutor Newman, who appeared for the state, informed the prisoners that the charge against them was murder in the first degree. On the advice of the prosecutor to the court, the prisoners would be committed to jail without bail.

On Monday, December 18th, the *Bellingham Bay Express* wrote that:

> "N. S. Barr and Walter Pixley…had their preliminary hearing before Judge Hardin this morning. Barr acting under instructions from his attorney, H. A. Fairchild, who was unavoidably absent, waived examination and was committed without bail to await action of a grand jury. Pixley was defended by Kerr & McCord, who introduced evidence to show that the boy…had nothing to do with the running of

the cabin and only inferred that a gun had been set through remarks made by Barr. They had also had plenty of evidence of good character. The judge (Hardin) on the conclusion of the evidence dismissed the charge against him, but put him under $1,000 bond to appear as witness before the grand jury."

Trial

On Monday morning, February 12, 1894, the trial for Newell S. Barr began. A jury had been impaneled and sworn in the day before.[9] Prosecuting Attorney Thomas Newman and his assistant, Deputy Prosecutor Howard Boardman, conducted the case for the state. E. P. Dole of Seattle and C. C. Rogers represented the defense,[10] with Judge John R. Winn presiding. Barr sat quietly, clad in a Prince Albert coat and appeared undaunted.

It was arranged that Deputy Prosecutor Boardman would open for the state, to be followed by Mr. Rogers for the defense. Mr. Dole would continue and Prosecutor Newman would close.

The afternoon was occupied with the examinations of Nels Anderson, who was with Erickson at the time of his death, their brief employer, Moran, as well as Sheriff Requa and Constable White. Their testimonies greatly mirrored that which was introduced at the coroner's inquest.

Attorney Dole did not outline his defense for the court. In his cross-examination of witnesses, it was evident that he did not accept it as "indisputable that Erickson and Anderson were actuated by honest motives" when breaking into the cabin. Dole questioned how it happened that Anderson was not near his companion when the gun was discharged, and

---

9   M. Grant, Charles Stevens, J. H. Harkness, A. M. Smith, A. M. Roby, G. W. Fox, T. C. Monahan, C. W. Owens, J. Hanlon, W. J. Hallock and O. D. McDonald.

10   H. A. Fairchild was no longer representing Barr at this time.

how it was he remained uninjured; this befuddled Anderson, who didn't know how to respond.

Other witnesses for the state included: M. E. White, M. Wheeler, Charles Boardman, C. W. Stone, R. S. Bragg, D. E. Biggs, J. K. Munro, J. P. Smalley and C. M. Logsden.

J. P. Smalley testified on cross that after Pixley and Barr had been arrested, Barr had told him about setting the gun, but that it wasn't his intention to kill anyone; Barr didn't believe the charge would go through the door.

Deputy Sheriff Conlin, one of the key witnesses for the state, was absent serving subpoenas. The attorneys agreed that his testimony should be introduced when he returned. Prosecution was set to rest at 10:30 am.

After a short recess, the defense opened its side of the argument by calling Walter Pixley to the stand. According to Pixley, Barr mentioned that he was going to set a gun several days before the two left for their hunting trip, but that he had not seen him set it. He stated that before he and Barr went to the residence of Samuel Bateman and then on to Ed Cleary's cabin to hunt deer, that Barr had locked the door and nailed boards across it and one window. Pixley said that he told Barr to put a notice on the door with the word "Danger" written on it, and that Barr complied. This sign was introduced as evidence by Attorney Dole and was confirmed by Pixley as corresponding with that which he had written.

On cross examination, Deputy Prosecuting Attorney Boardman asked Pixley whether or not he had testified at the preliminary hearing that he had gathered his blankets and gone away, and upon his return, saw that the back door was closed with Barr nailing it up. Pixley affirmed that this was true. "Did you not testify that you knew nothing about the gun being set?" asked Boardman. Pixley answered yes, that he saw Barr lock the door when he returned with a second load of boards. Boardman asked if, when Deputy Sheriff Conlin came to arrest them, that Barr had said, "It served the man right to get shot if he was trying to break into a fellow's cabin." But Pixley claimed that he did not hear Barr make that statement, rather, that it was Conlin he heard it from.

Concluding his testimony, Pixley said that the cabin had been burglarized three times while he owned it, and that he had let Barr know this.

Judge Harden was called to show that Walter Pixley had testified differently on preliminary examination. The defense objected. Pixley did not have his previous testimony read back to him.

That afternoon Barr's sister, Mrs. Harry Cowden, testified that on January 4th, she and Mrs. Barr found a "Danger" sign tacked to the lower side of a board, lying near the cabin. Mrs. N. S. Barr corroborated this information in her own testimony. The two of them had heard that a notice of the sort was put up, so they went to look for it.

On the stand, Colonel Rawson and W. M. Flanner testified to having seen the danger sign nailed on a board in front of the door, at 4:30 pm on the Saturday before the homicide. Their testimonies do not uphold other testimony, including Pixley's assertion that the signage had been posted on Sunday.

When Benjamin Winkler took the stand, he said that he walked along the road some forty feet from the cabin the day before the killing, and hadn't seen a notice marked "Danger." He figured he should have seen one, had one been posted. F. W. De Lorimier stated that he went by the cabin four times the day before the killing, ranging in proximity of one to ten feet from it. He also claimed that there was no sign on the door, and that he would have seen it.

When George A. Singleton, of Moran & Singleton Construction took the stand, he attested to having signed a contract with Anderson and Erickson in the Pacific House on Monday afternoon, and that he offered for them to stay at his camp until they could build a cabin. Beyond this, all he could submit was that he understood Barr bore a good reputation.

Next on the stand was Samuel Bateman, who said that Barr had stopped at his house on his way up the Nooksack to go hunting, and told him that he had set a gun in his cabin. Bateman denied having heard Barr say, "If the Swedish ____ had kept out of a fellow's cabin he would not have been killed." Instead, Bateman recalled that when the deputy sheriff arrested Barr, Barr had said he was sorry the man was killed and that if he had kept away, he wouldn't have been hurt. Though similar, the vulgarity of the first statement would have painted Barr in malicious light, characterizing him as careless.

The prosecution called Deputy Sheriff A. H. Conlin next, who arrested Barr at Samuel Bateman's. He testified that he heard Barr say that if the "Swede ____ had kept away from the door he would not have been killed." To which Bateman responded with, "Erickson is Norwegian, not Swedish." "Him or any other ____," said Barr.

Conlin reaffirmed that he took Barr to Griffin's Hotel in Deming the night of the arrest, and had charge of him until he was locked up in Whatcom. Barr slept in a different room from him while they were at Deming, and he did not use shackles, as they were unnecessary.

Evening Session

Barr's attorney, Dole, argued a motion to dismiss the case on the ground of inefficiency of indictment. The court released the jury so that he could plead his case.

Dole argued that the indictment alleged that the "killing of John Erickson was deliberate, malicious and premeditated," while the evidence failed to show that the defendant ever knew the deceased. The Information read, and the argument made by the attorney for the defense were that "the case must be proven as alleged in the indictment, and that a man had a right to defend his liberty and property." Dole cited a Kentucky case (pre-Civil War), where a man set a spring-gun in his warehouse to protect his grain from theft. Another man's slave was killed while endeavoring to secure an entrance, and the owner of the slave was unable to recover the value of that slave, much less convict the man criminally for setting the gun.

Attorney Dole also argued that under the indictment, a murder in the first degree or absolute acquittal must follow; he ended up choosing to move for an acquittal. The court overruled all the objections made by the defense and held that such a verdict was not absolutely necessary.

THE BARR MURDER TRIAL

The Testimony all in and the Counsel Before the Jury—The Issue of Fact Remarkably Narrow and Unimportant —Is Every Man's Home His Castle to the Extent Claimed ?

PREVIOUS GOOD RECORD

The Barr murder case was on trial in the superior court all day yesterday.

The Daily Reveille, December 13, 1893.

Is it Manslaughter?

On Tuesday, February 13th, as the second day of court proceedings slugged on into the evening, Deputy Prosecuting Attorney Boardman made his opening argument in the case. Attorney C. C. Rogers followed for the defense, stating that Barr had a right to set the gun to protect his home from intruders.

Attorney Rogers made the principal argument for the defendant. He led with the old adage that every man's house is his castle, which he must protect, and intimated that Erickson and Anderson had intended to burglarize the cabin. Addressing the jury he stated "…that the prosecuting attorney had persecuted witnesses of the defense, and that Mr. Newman had sneeringly asked Mrs. Barr and Mrs. Cowden if they were not relatives of the defendant," bullying them in regards to the potential motivation of their testimonies.

According to Attorney Rogers, Barr did what any other man would have done, in setting the gun to protect his property. He professed finding it very odd that several witnesses testified to having seen the danger sign, while others had passed the cabin several times without observing it. An inordinate amount of time was spent identifying Barr's good character, which was further established by witnesses who had known Barr for years.

Prosecuting Attorney Thomas Newman closed the argument with a two-hour speech, finishing at 5 o'clock that evening. In his speech, he denied persecuting the witnesses and argued that Erickson and Anderson had not presented themselves as likely burglars, but had looked for a place to sleep from out of the cold. He contended:

> "While a man's house was his castle, which he had a perfect right to protect by means of firearms, if necessary…but if that man left his house, he had no right to leave a death trap for anyone who might attempt to enter it…a friend might have endeavored to go in. A law officer might have broken in while in the service to protect the home while the owner was away…the jury must consider the moral effect, for should they return a verdict of acquittal the effect would be

that a man would have the right to set a gun in his office or in his chicken coop. The charge of powder and shot and the .45-90 cartridge placed in the load and the deliberate manner in which the trap was arranged did not look as if the defendant had intended no harm. The case has been tried on the indictment returned by the grand jury of murder in the first degree, but if the jury finds that it was not a case of murder in the first degree they should return a verdict of murder in the second degree, or manslaughter."

Another Evening Session

Judge John Winn began his instructions to the jury by thoroughly defining the various degrees of murder open for them to rule on:

"He told the jury that if they found that the defendant had set the gun maliciously and premeditatedly, with the intent to kill any one who might endeavor to enter for a night's lodging, they must in such case find the defendant guilty of murder in the first degree; that the defendant had the same right to set the gun during his absence as if present at the time; that the attack upon the house must have been sufficient to have justified the defendant in killing had he been present at the time, otherwise the defendant is criminally liable."

Judge Winn defined "burglary" and told the jury to take into consideration the placing of the "Danger" notice on the door, together with the former reputation of the defendant and the credibility of witnesses. He closed his instructions by stating that the question of proof fell upon the state and the charges should be proven beyond a reasonable question of doubt.

The attorneys of the defendant took exception of the courts refusal to instruct on charges as requested:

"And excepted particularly to the ruling of the court that either of the three degrees of murder could be found under the indictment; that malice under the code of this state may be implied; that a man has no more right to set a gun in his house during his absence than when at home; that it was a wise law that gave justice of the peace power to bind over a witness for his appearance."

IS IT MANSLAUGHTER

The Barr Jury Agree on a Verdict After a Deliberation of Two Hours— The Verdict Will Be Rendered This Morning—The Closing Arguments of Counsel—Charge of Court.

JURORS STAY IN COURT ROOM

The Daily Reveille, February 15, 1894.

The Verdict

At 10:30 pm on Tuesday night, after two hours of deliberation, Bailiff T. C. Austin went directly to the residence of Judge Winn with the verdict, but could not arouse him. His bell pull was out of order. From there he went to see Clerk Pierce, who advised him to return to the jury deliberation room, where they should all remain until morning, as the attorneys would need to be present when the verdict was announced. Rumors amassed that the verdict would read "guilty of manslaughter." At 1 am on Wednesday, February 14th, the jurors were lounging around the courtroom; some were asleep on the benches when Bailiff Austin notified them that their verdict would be received.

The courtroom reconvened at 10 am. A sudden silence fell as the verdict was read aloud: guilty of murder in the second degree. Pending Judge Winn's decision, Barr could serve a minimum of ten years in jail. The public considered it a fit ruling for the crime, but the defense, E. P. Dole and C. C. Rogers were displeased; they intended to fight with an appeal.

On March 28th, a motion for a new trial was argued before Judge Winn. Attorney Dole spoke from 10 am until 3:30 pm, stressing that the court refused to admit crucial testimony. An affidavit from J. P. Smalley was introduced that swore that G. W. Fox, one of the jurymen, told them that while arriving at the verdict, the jury took into consideration the idea that Barr set the spring-gun to kill his wife. It was alleged that Barr had papers in the cabin that his wife wanted, documents that would have given her grounds for divorce, and he intended to harm her if she sought them out.

The state introduced affidavits from eleven of the jurymen, Fox among them, denouncing the claim. They did admit to discussing the matter, but swore that it had only been discussed once the verdict was signed and was in the foreman's pocket. They were adamant that, as a jury, they had not committed any form of misconduct.

Newell S. Barr's judgment and sentencing. Washington State Archives.

Judge Winn denied the motion of a new trial and on March 28, 1894 he sentenced Barr to ten years at hard labor. Attorney Dole declared he would appeal to the state Supreme Court. Barr would remain in New Whatcom until further appeals were exhausted.

In May 1895, Newell S. Barr was moved to the Washington State Penitentiary at Walla Walla. The *Daily Reveille* said that it was a "merciful thing to the prisoner (the application of a pardon having been denied), as he has had absolutely nothing to do for nearly a year and one half, and enforced idleness is, in the long run, mental wreck." Dole told Barr that he would keep on fighting, and that "from the tenor of the governor's reply to the prisoner for pardon, it is probable that his sentence will be materially abridged by this executive or his successor."

Newell S. Barr. Washington State Archives.

Barr was received at the penitentiary on May 11, 1895 as prisoner No. 1399.[11] His inmate registration claimed that his parents were from New York, and were deceased at the time he was admitted. His registration also mentioned that he was born in Michigan, was married and had no children. Barr attended grade school long enough to learn to read and write. He was a temperate man who chewed and smoked. Physically, he stood five-foot-nine inches, was heavily set, with a large oval face and sad gray eyes. He was balding, with light hair trimmed short at the sides and a thick heavy handlebar mustache, which framed a set of bad teeth.

11   There are date discrepancies from newspapers, court documents and trial records from this point on. Suffice; I decided to use the dates in Newell Barr's penitentiary records.

Epilogue

Attorney E. P. Dole continued to fight as he had promised. Eventually, he got Newell S. Barr a pardon.

From the House Journal of the Fifth Legislature, Begun and Held at Olympia, The State Capital of the State of Washington, By Washington State Legislature and House of Representatives January 11, 1897. Compiled, Arranged and Indexed by S. P. Carusi, Chief Clerk of the House:

"N. S. Barr, having been found guilty of the crime of murder in the second degree, was on the 28th day of March 1894, sentenced by the superior court of Whatcom County to ten years imprisonment. Pardon granted August 21, 1896, upon the recommendation of several hundred citizens of Whatcom, including the prosecuting attorney and other county officials and nine jurors. Barr's crime consisted in setting a trap gun in a cabin, which he had occupied, just previous to his going into the mountains on a protracted hunting trip. During his absence four [sic] persons affecting an entrance to the house discharged the gun, killing one of them. The prosecuting attorney in recommending pardon said, in part: 'While the conviction in the trial court and its affirmance [sic] in the supreme court in this case is in our opinion fully sustained and warranted by the law and the evidence, however we are free to say that this case for the first time to our knowledge presented for adjudication to an American court of last resort in a criminal case, the question of responsibility for taking human life by setting spring-guns in the habitation. Wide spread erroneous impression undoubtedly existed among the people and no

little misconception on the part of some courts of last resort, as to the right to defend one's property and therefore
one's habitation considered as property by deadly means.'"

Washington State Governor John McGraw signed the pardon on
August 21, 1896. Newell S. Barr was released on August 24th.

Newell S. Barr's pardon and release by the governor, 1894. Washington State Archives.

Chapter 8
Double Murder on Lummi Island

Lummi Island was an ideal location and layover for adventurers heading for the Fraser River. Circa: 1900s.
Courtesy of Jim Doige.

The tiny communities of Sehome and Whatcom had a toehold on the edge of Bellingham Bay in 1858 when the Fraser River gold rush began. In March of that year, the frenzied cry of gold's discovery in the Northwest reached San Francisco, and by June the two hamlets grew from a population of a few hundred to approximately 10,000 inhabitants. The bay communities were the last stop before entering the Dominion of British Columbia. The water's edge quickly turned muddy and the surrounding land was covered in tents. Prospectors searched for transportation to the Fraser, Thompson or Sumas Rivers. Most would travel by boat, while others attempted the very primitive Whatcom Trail to the Chilliwack district. Those adventurers not traveling further north, stayed on the bay selling mining equipment and supplies at inflated prices, and as always, crooks, cheats, gamblers, whores and cheap liquor followed with the influx of people.

Many adventurers didn't waste their time or money in places like Sehome or Whatcom, or on the inflated passenger rates aboard overcrowded steamers. They procured their own waterborne transportation by canoe or skiff and loaded them with supplies from the communities on the lower Sound or at Port Townsend before paddling north. Stopovers along the way may have included any one of the San Juan Islands, or along the shoreline of Lummi Island. The local Indians were fairly courteous on Lummi Island; it was a logical navigational route from either Whatcom or Port Townsend to the mouth of the Fraser, and was thus a popular layover for a night.

It was during the first year of the gold rush, on Wednesday, August 25, 1858 that a mysterious double homicide occurred. Reports of the event were protracted from the sole newspaper in Whatcom at the time, the *Northern Light*,[1] which was just over one month into circulation and founded by editor William Bausman, who had come to Whatcom because of the gold rush. Other reports come from research conducted by the esteemed Percival R. Jeffcott, historian for the Whatcom County Pioneer Association. From these works we garnish the first news of the region.

Sleeping Death

On the morning of Thursday, August 26th, a passerby in a canoe came upon a campsite where he saw a campfire and what appeared to be two campers asleep in bedrolls, presumably around Legoe Bay or Village Point. The passerby, whose name remains undocumented, was either interested in conversation, a hot fire or a cup of coffee and he hailed, but received no response. He decided to beach his craft and say hello in person.

---

1   The Northern Light's first edition was July 3, 1858.

What greeted the caller were the bodies of two men slain in their sleep. It was claimed that their campfire was still burning with hot embers, indicating that whoever fated their death had only just done so. There was no indication of a struggle, or that there were others missing from the party.

The oldest victim of the two took a musket blast to his right breast. A huge portion of his chest cavity was blown out, leaving a gaping hole from which his innards were spilling. The force of the gunshot had left dark clotty blood splatter and meaty tissue scattered about. His younger companion, from what we can assume, jolted awake from the blast, sat upright, and at that instant received a bullet through his back, blowing much of his chest and lungs onto his lap and legs. It was a macabre sight; the man, just sitting there, head bowed and a hole running through his body large enough to see through.

The *Northern Light* submitted that Whatcom Coroner Dr. L. Ridgely "and several persons accompanied him to the island." The "persons," may have been Sheriff William A. Busey and Constables J. E. Jewett and J. G. Chapman, all of whom were elected into their positions on July 17th.

It was suggested that the two men might have been hunters, although nothing but a ramrod of a gun was found to support this. If they had a boat, guns and other necessary appurtenances of a hunter's outfit, such could have been appropriated by the murderers. It was also proposed that they might be prospectors en route to the Fraser.

Ridgely returned to Whatcom by canoe with the bodies wrapped in the same bedrolls they had died in. The verdict of the coroner's jury indicated that the deceased came to their deaths by "shots from a gun, and wounds from a knife, by the hands of persons unknown." Dr. Ridgley held a postmortem examination over their bodies. The elder of the two men was named Joseph Dixon, of Texas, aged 55 years. The name of the other was "unknown; aged 35; bodies first discovered on Thursday; supposed to have been murdered on the previous night…an empty purse found near them."

The Usual Suspects

On Saturday, August 28, 1858 the *Northern Light* printed: "Two White Men Murdered By Indians." They would be the first to propagate possible culprits, though they gave no evidence to the allegations:

> "Soon after these facts – which are chiefly derived from popular rumor – had circulated, a storm of violent indignation was kindled against the Indians. Several were at once arrested and put in the lockup as hostages, till a regular demand could be made upon the chiefs for the delivery of the murderers. A paper was put in circulation for the enrollment of volunteers, quite a number of whom were secured, and six of whom in an hour afterward, departed in a canoe towards the mouth of the Lummi River with two Indian interpreters intending, as we believe, to make further arrests. The arrival of the bodies of the two murdered white men on Friday afternoon, and the consequent excitement in the community, was the signal for a general stampede among the Indian residents along the shore of the bay. Before nightfall most of them had bundled up their efforts and put off in canoes for their fishing grounds near the mouth of the Lummi River.

On Saturday, Indian Agent Colonel M. T. Simmons, C. C. Vail, a Mr. Bailey, and Lieutenant Forsyth, with twenty United States soldiers from Fort Bellingham, "waited on the chief of the Lummi Indians, and made a formal demand for delivering up the Indians who had committed the numerous murders recently perpetrated in the vicinity." Although the demand stated, "the numerous murders," besides the murders on Lummi Island, the only other mysterious death was that of Deputy Surveyor Dominick Hunt, who was claimed to have been murdered on Whidbey Island on July 17th. The *Northern Light* headlined the story regarding Deputy Surveyor Dominick Hunt with "Supposed to be Drowned or Murdered."

A surviving bastion from old Fort Bellingham.
Laura Jacoby's Galen Biery Collection.

Hunt left his camp near Whidbey in a canoe, bound for Whatcom. He was seen passing an Indian camp near the north end of Swinomish Pass, and had not been seen since. His canoe was picked up adrift. Foul play was never proven.

Another article appearing in the *Northern Light* during that summer was the following Coroner's Inquest:

"A coroner's inquest was held Tuesday on the body of a Frenchman, name unknown, found along the shore of the Bay. A post mortem examination by Dr. Ridgley elicited the medical opinion to the following effect: The body displayed three wounds on the back, and one on the point of the shoulder, having the appearance of being inflicted with a hatchet. Neither of the wounds being sufficient to cause death, the supposition is that the man came to his end from drowning, while attempting to escape from further violence. We could not learn the verdict of the inquest."

None of these instances were proven to be "Indian" related, but by the constant reference to the victims as "white men," it would suggest that public opinion had assumed their culpability.

According to the *Northern Light*, on Monday, September 6th, the Lummi Chief, accompanied by Indian Agent Colonel M. T. Simmons' party, and a hundred and twenty "warriors," proceeded to Samish Island and returned with seven captives. It was said that while making the arrest, one Indian resisted, and in an attempt to use his knife, another Indian seized it and inflicted a severe wound in the struggle. "Their canoes drew up in front of Colonel Fitzhugh's residence, and that gentleman was saluted by a general discharge of musketry. The supposed murderers were conducted to Fort Bellingham and placed in close confinement."

The arrest may have been nothing more than a display of force, as the *Northern Light* even admitted, "There is believed to be no evidence to convict the captive Indians of the murder of Dixon and Freeman...but they stand accused of the blood of Deputy Surveyor Hunt and others, by what is said to be incontestable evidence."[2]

No trial or hearing was ever conducted against the captives, but the law and the brigade of men needed to display a show of strength for the settlers, demonstrating that they weren't inept. A closing remark from the *Northern Light* offered, "The sudden exodus of the Indians from Whatcom and vicinity was in obedience to an order from Colonel Simmons to that effect. They have repaired to their several fishing grounds." Jeffcott was quoted to have

2   There is no indication how the Northern Light came by the names of the victims, Dixon and Freeman. During the inquest, Dixon's name was first mentioned, but Freeman was "unknown."

said, "…there was no evidence against the Indians arrested, and in the end they were probably released." It was understood that Simmons made a deal with the local Lummis to quit the area for a time, until things settled down.

Epilogue

In "Nooksack Tales and Trails," Percival Jeffcott wrote that it was unfortunate the story was not further recorded, and that true rest in the matter will never be known. He states that in their reports of 1858-59, Indian Agent, Colonel M. T. Simmons nor Special Agent E. C. Fitzhugh reported the tragedy in its entirety.

In the end, the double-murder on Lummi Island was never solved. The weapons used in 1858 were muzzle-loading guns, which would indicate that two or more men would have had to commit the murders. The inquest mentions the use of a knife in the killings, but not how it was used. It is assumptive but likely that the victims were not men of pioneer stock, as they would have been accustomed to their environment and not so easily approached.

Many questions will remain unanswered. Were Dixon and Freeman hunting? Were they stopping at the island on their way to the Fraser River? Were they returning from the gold rush and had a pursuer shadowing them? Were the killers Indians, murderous thieves, or perhaps men they befriended on their journey who murdered them in the night and took their valuables? It's another local mystery!

Part II
Skagit

Chapter 9
Grimm Murders in Sauk Valley

Concrete Herald November 18, 1937.

On Friday, November 13, 1937, Skagit County Prosecutor Richard Welts disclosed to the local press that an investigation into the theft of a 12-foot Pelton wheel[1] and electric generator from the George Peterson farm at Birdsview had led to the discovery of two murders which took place at the 40-acre farm of Roy Amos Grimm and his wife Ethel, located in the Sauk Valley, approximately eight miles southeast of Concrete. 25 year-old Clifford Hawkins, a farmhand, was being charged with killing Ernest Sylvester Grimm, age 27, and Floyd Hamilton "Sonny" Grimm, age 21, plus the statutory rape of the Grimm's 13 year-old daughter, Edith.

---

1 "Waterwheel."

Investigation of the theft eventually lead Skagit County Sheriff Patrick J. McCarthy and Undersheriff Lester P. Finsen to the Grimm farm, where they found the missing Pelton wheel sitting behind the barn. While pursuing the investigation, however, the officers learned about the mysterious disappearances of the two Grimm boys, Ernest and Floyd, from neighboring farmers. There were also troubling rumors that Hawkins, who was using the assumed name "Toivo Hautaneimi" and known locally as "The Finn," had been having an illicit love affair with the young Edith Grimm.

Clifford Hawkins

Hawkins' background was murky; he had an identity complicated by emigration and an eventual adoption. He claimed to have been born in 1912 in either Finland or Salem, Oregon. At various times he said his name was either "Toivo Hautaneimi" or "Clifford Hawkins." His family supposedly emigrated from Finland to America in 1922, and both parents later died from influenza. He was adopted and given the name "Clifford Hawkins" by his foster father. His adoptive mother was a resident of the Oregon State Mental Hospital in Salem and his father lived in Tacoma, Washington. It was rumored that he had four brothers, but their locations were unknown, and there was no information regarding surviving relatives. The only verifiable information was that Hawkins, while in his middle teens, was arrested in Tacoma for passing forged checks and was sentenced to serve three years at the Washington State Reform School[2] in Chehalis. His name is listed in the 1930 U.S. Census as an inmate at the training school.

The 1930 U.S. Census shows that Roy and Ethel Grimm had nine children living at home, six sons and three daughters, ranging in age from 4 to 21 years old. As time passed, Roy's health deteriorated markedly, and he relied heavily upon his sons to maintain the Sauk Valley farm. Three of the

2   Now the "Green Hill School."

older sons, Ernest, Floyd and Howard, found steady employment at logging camps to earn much needed money for the family. Howard, age 25, remained working full-time at a logging camp near Acme in Whatcom County and only occasionally visited the farm, usually on weekends. The two oldest daughters, Lillian and Eva, married and left the farm, making Jay, the second oldest son, and the three youngest children, Earl, Edith and Roy Jr., responsible for all the routine tasks.

Clifford Hawkins became acquainted with the Grimm family in 1935 while assigned as a medic to the Federal Emergency Relief Administration (FERA) work camp located in the Sauk Valley. He became friendly with Jay Grimm and visited the farm on several occasions. When the FERA program ended in late December 1935, Hawkins was invited to live at the farm to help care for Roy Sr. and with the numerous chores. He received no remuneration other than room and board. Without a job and nowhere else to go, Hawkins stayed on; soon, he had won the family's confidence and virtually ran the farm.

During the investigation into the missing Pelton wheel and generator, Sheriff McCarthy spoke with Hawkins to inquire how the equipment came to be at the farm. During the interview, Hawkins volunteered that Ernest Grimm had suddenly left for California to find work in December of 1936, and that Floyd had followed in March 1937. Neither had told their parents or siblings that they were leaving the state; apparently Hawkins was the only person to have seen them leave. The family was close-knit and self-reliant, and such behavior was uncharacteristic of their sons. The family hadn't heard a word from either Ernest or Floyd since their departure, which was curious since their father was gravely ill.

Roy A. Grimm Sr. died on Wednesday, June 30, 1937, and was buried at the Mount Vernon Cemetery. In September 1937, the Grimm farm was put up for lease or sale. Ethel Grimm and her three youngest children, Earl, age 15, Edith, age 13, and Roy Jr., age 11, moved to Sedro-Woolley, leaving

Jay Grimm, age 22, and Clifford Hawkins at the Sauk Valley farm to maintain the property.

The McCarthy Investigation

Sheriff McCarthy believed Hawkins' alleged affair with Edith was likely criminal and decided to investigate further. In early October of 1937, Sheriff McCarthy, Prosecutor Welts and Reverend Carl A. Lund, Pastor of the Salem Lutheran Church in Mount Vernon, called at the Sedro-Woolley elementary school to question Edith Grimm about her rumored romance with Hawkins. Initially Edith kept mum, but with the encouragement of the school principal, Mary Purcell, she finally relented and told of her ongoing affair with Hawkins. When she was asked about the sudden disappearances of her two older brothers, she fell into silence once more. Following the interview, Hawkins was arrested and taken to the Skagit County Jail. He was charged with statutory rape in a criminal complaint.[3] He made no admissions, but said that he had nothing more than a brotherly interest in Edith's welfare.

Two images are seen here of 13 year-old Edith Grimm, who was taken under the spell of 25 year-old Clifford Hawkins. Taken in 1937. Photo from Holt Photo Service of Mount Vernon.

---

3   A "criminal complaint" is "accusatory instruments" or papers filed in the courts that charge or accuse a person of committing a crime.

Sheriff McCarthy wasn't satisfied; there was a lot of depravity circling the Sauk Valley farm, and something didn't sit well with him regarding Ernest and Floyd Grimm. During questioning, Hawkins claimed that Floyd had brought the Pelton wheel and generator to the farm and denied having been involved in the theft. He also denied knowing the specific whereabouts of the absent Grimm brothers. Unconvinced, Sheriff McCarthy recruited the assistance of 23 year-old Gerald "Jerry" N. Granville, who was serving a sentence for petty offenses, to share a jail cell with Hawkins as a means to gather information from the inside. The two cellmates chatted amiably about various subjects, but nothing was said about the missing Grimm boys. The scheme proved unproductive, until the final day of Granville's sentence, Tuesday, November 9, 1937.

Before Granville was released from custody, Hawkins asked him if he would help "his girlfriend" dispose of a dead body. Hawkins told Granville how Edith had killed a transient who had inadvertently interrupted their secret rendezvous on the farm's back forty. Hawkins, worried that the body might be accidentally discovered, asked Granville to obliterate the grave with dynamite. Then, he surreptitiously passed Granville a handwritten note instructing Edith to show him where the body was buried.

That afternoon, Granville drove to Sedro-Woolley in a borrowed automobile, followed by Sheriff McCarthy, Undersheriff Finsen and Prosecutor Welts in one vehicle and the deputies in another. The convoy arrived at the schoolhouse shortly before the students were dismissed for the afternoon and they waited for Edith to appear. When she exited the building, Granville approached and handed her Hawkins' note. Without hesitation, Edith climbed into the front seat of Granville's automobile and they drove east toward Faber Ferry to cross the Skagit River, trailed loosely by Sheriff McCarthy and his entourage. Granville and Edith crossed on the first available ferry and the Sheriff followed on the next, giving the two of them ample time to reach the Grimm farm.

McCarthy, Finsen and Welts arrived in time to watch Granville and Edith, each with a shovel, walk down a trail that led into a deep ravine, some 300 yards back from the farmhouse. The men followed at a safe distance and quietly crept forward to observe the pair digging. By this time it was approaching dusk and Sheriff McCarthy decided to make his presence known. He stepped out from his place of hiding.

While Finsen and Welts drove Edith back to Sedro-Woolley, Sheriff McCarthy, his deputies and Jerry Granville continued digging; they found nothing but hard-packed dirt and glacial till. Soon, it became dark and the hunt was suspended until the following day.

Discovery

Early Wednesday morning, November 10, 1937, Sheriff McCarthy, accompanied by Undersheriff Finsen, Prosecutor Welts and several deputies, returned to the place where Edith and Granville had been digging. He brought along Jay Grimm and professional photographer John I. Holt to identify and document any evidence they discovered. The search party probed for an hour before they were convinced that the ground hadn't been previously disturbed. Sheriff McCarthy and Jay Grimm meandered up The Trail, looking for other likely places, but found nothing that appeared suspicious. A short distance away, they came across a mound of dirt and rocks by a fallen tree, indicating that something had been buried there, and began to dig. Three-feet down from the surface, they unearthed the lower portion of a human body, still wearing a pair of high-top logging boots which Jay identified as belonging to his brother, Floyd.

Nearby, deputies found another grave containing a badly decomposed human torso. Jay identified a heavy wool Mackinaw found in the hole as Floyd's. After Holt photographed the crime scenes, the body parts were placed in a canvas bag and transported by ambulance to Mount Vernon for a postmortem. At the Dunham Undertaking Parlor, Skagit County Coroner Henry D. Dunham and two physicians, Dr. George E. Boynton and Dr. Walter W. Ebeling, determined that the victim had been shot in the head with a large caliber bullet, which shattered his skull.

From left to right: Prosecutor Richard Welts, Sheriff Pat McCarthy, Jay Grimm and Under-sheriff Les Finsen at the grave of Floyd (Sonny) Grimm. Jay was present to identify his brother's clothing and boots. Photo from Holt Photo Service of Mount Vernon.

Confronted with the evidence, Edith finally broke her silence and confessed that Hawkins had murdered her two brothers and threatened her life if she ever revealed his secret. Hawkins told her that he killed Ernest and then Floyd for attempting to interfere with their courtship. She knew that Ernest's body had been buried in the barnyard, but wasn't sure where exactly it was. Edith claimed to have neither witnessed their deaths, nor helped to conceal their bodies.

Floyd's remains, high-top logging boots and woolen Mackinaw was identified by Jay as belonging to his brother. Photo from Holt Photo Service of Mount Vernon.

On Thursday, November 11, 1937, Sheriff McCarthy and his deputies returned to the Grimm farm to search for Ernest's remains. The group spent the entire day exploring and digging holes in the barnyard and around the farmhouse, but found no trace of his body. Concerned the county might need to excavate the entire 40-acre farm, Sheriff McCarthy decided to coerce Hawkins to confess.

On Friday morning, McCarthy, Finsen and Welts entered Hawkins' cell and asked him again about the sudden departures of Ernest and Floyd Grimm. The suspect stuck to his story that the brothers had left for California at different times to find work. When asked to provide details about Floyd's departure, Hawkins claimed they met on a street corner in Concrete and that Floyd said he was heading south to join Ernest. Sheriff McCarthy asked what

Floyd was wearing and Hawkins gave a description of his clothing, including his Mackinaw coat and high-top logging boots. He was then handed one of Holt's photographs taken at the burial site and asked if he recognized the footwear. "Well, I guess you've got me, boys," Hawkins responded.

Hawkins broke down and confessed that he had killed Ernest and Floyd for trying to interfere in his relationship with Edith, and for having ordered him to leave the farm. He also offered that Howard Grimm, who also expressed concern about the illicit affair, was next on his hit list, but he was logging at Acme and seldom came home to visit. Hawkins then told the officers where he had hidden Ernest's body.

The Crime Unravels

According to Hawkins' lengthy confession, his dalliance with Edith began in September 1936 when she was only 12 years old. Ernest's discovery of Hawkins' sexual advances toward his little sister resulted in violent arguments. Hawkins said he couldn't live without Edith, so he decided to eliminate Ernest from the picture at his earliest opportunity. On Thursday night, December 17, 1936, Hawkins lured Ernest from the house on the pretext that someone was prowling about the barnyard near the chicken coop. When Ernest went outside to investigate, Hawkins followed with a .22 caliber Savage rifle and shot him in the back. He then broke the stock of the rifle over Ernest's skull and hastily buried the body in a large pile of manure. After hiding the broken rifle, he returned to the farmhouse and told family members that Ernest had chased after the intruder, and would be taking the ferry to Concrete after.

The following day, Hawkins told the family that he had seen Ernest on the street in Concrete, who said that he was driving to California to find work. Several weeks later, Hawkins removed the body from the manure pile, wrapped it in canvas and buried it beneath the root house. Later, he burned the root house to the ground to obliterate any evidence of the grave and the body beneath.

Though Ernest was out of the way, Floyd and Howard continued to quarrel with Hawkins over his ongoing relationship with Edith. On Saturday, March 12, 1937, Floyd and Hawkins, carrying a .30-30 Winchester Model-94 carbine, went out to hunt for deer. In a wooded ravine, some 300 yards from the farmhouse, Hawkins shot Floyd in the right temple with a soft-nosed bullet, taking out the left side of his skull.

The Gimm family farm, Sauk, Skagit County. The cross marks where the remains of Ernest Grimm were first buried in a manure pile, before they were removed by Hawkins and placed under the root house to the right of the manure pile. Photo from Holt Photo Service of Mount Vernon.

Hawkins hid Floyd's body in a shallow grave and covered it with underbrush. When he returned to the house, he told the family that Floyd had suddenly decided to leave for California to join Ernest, and they believed him without question. Worried that Floyd's body might be accidentally discovered, Hawkins returned to the site, hacked it in half with the blade of his shovel and buried the pieces separately. In his 37-page confession, he absolved Edith of any complicity in the deaths of her brothers.

On Saturday afternoon, Sheriff McCarthy and a group of deputies returned to the Grimm farm to excavate the site of the root house. There, buried deep beneath the ashes and ruins, they discovered Ernest's decomposing body. Jay was able to identify the remains by virtue of clothing remnants, a house key, a ruler and a distinctive matchbox. The body was transported by ambulance to Mount Vernon where Coroner Dunham and attending physicians determined the victim had died either from a compound fracture of the skull or bullet wounds. Both Ernest and Floyd were buried at the Mount Vernon Cemetery alongside the grave of their father.

The headstones of Floyd and Ernest Grimm.

With both missing Grimm brothers now accounted for, along with a full confession from the killer, the investigation into the murders was closed. On Wednesday, November 24, 1937, Prosecutor Welts filed Information in Skagit County Superior Court before Judge Willard L. Brickey, charging Clifford Hawkins with two counts of first degree murder and one count of statutory rape. Since the defendant was destitute, the court appointed Mount Vernon Attorney Edward E. Knipe to represent him at all court proceedings.

During arraignment, Hawkins surprised his attorney by pleading guilty to the charge of statutory rape, which carried a penalty of life imprisonment. However, he pleaded not guilty to the two charges of first degree murder. Prosecutor Welts asked that sentencing the defendant for the charge of statutory rape be deferred until after the trial; if found guilty of premeditated murder, the mandatory sentence would be either life imprisonment or death. Judge Brickey set the trial during a special session of the court, scheduled for December 1937.

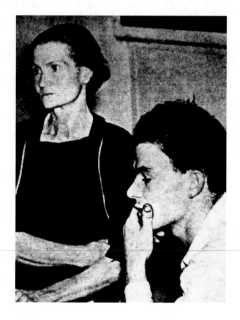

Mother Ethel Grimm and her son Jay shocked by loss. Photo from Holt Photo Service of Mount Vernon.

Edith's Testimony

The trial of Clifford Hawkins commenced in Judge Brickey's courtroom on Tuesday morning, December 15, 1937, with the selection of a death-qualified jury.[4] By noon on Wednesday a jury of 10 men and two women were

4   A "death-qualified jury" is a jury in a criminal law case in the United States in which the death penalty is a prospective sentence. Such a jury will be composed of jurors who 1. Are not categorically opposed to the imposition of capital punishment; 2. Are not of the belief that the death penalty must be imposed in all instances of capital murder – that is, they would consider life imprisonment as a possible penalty.

impaneled to sit in on the case. That afternoon, Prosecutor Welts delivered his opening statement alleging that Hawkins, with malice aforethought, shot and killed the two Grimm brothers because they objected to his continuing intimacies with their underage sister, Edith. Welts revealed that while in custody on the morals charge, Hawkins had willingly revealed the details of his crimes in a lengthy confession. He admonished that Hawkins was guilty of premeditated murder and deserved to be hanged rather than imprisoned for life.

Ethel Grimm, with the last of her sons. Left to Right: Mother Ethel, Jay, Roy Jr., and Earl.
Photo from Holt Photo Service of Mount Vernon.

The state called 24 witnesses to testify, which included the remaining members of the Grimm family that had lived on the farm with Hawkins. Most of the testimony was relatively brief, except for Edith's. As the state's primary witness, she recounted how Hawkins had seduced her, murdered Ernest and Floyd, and then attempted to compel her silence through intimidation. Hawkins informed her that he would have to kill her older brothers for constantly interfering in their love affair. Afterwards, he told Edith about the two slayings and showed her the location in the ravine where he had initially hid Floyd's body. At 2:30 p.m., on Thursday, December 17, 1937, the state rested its case.

On Thursday afternoon, in his opening statement, Attorney Knipe told the jury that Hawkins had admitted to his intimate relationship with Edith and pleaded guilty to a charge of statutory rape, which carried a sentence of life imprisonment. He stated that this was ample punishment for the crime Hawkins had committed, and as for the two deaths – they should be regarded acts of self-defense and considered as justifiable homicide or manslaughter, but certainly not premeditated murder.

Hawkins took the witness stand, and testifying in his own defense, refuted Edith Grimm's graphic testimony. He fabricated a tale about his final confrontations with Ernest and Floyd, and said that both had died as a result of self-defense. He admitted to having buried their bodies on the farm, and in trying to avoid needlessly upsetting the family, how he had made up the story of their travels to California. At the conclusion of his testimony, the defense rested its case.

In rebuttal, Prosecutor Welts introduced into evidence a letter the defendant had written to Edith, which Sheriff McCarthy had intercepted before it left the jail. It read in part:

Edith Darling,

If you want to save yourself and help me a little, please bear in mind what I'm about to tell you. Do you want to be one of the persons to help hang me, and also, dear, if you go against me in court, you will get yourself in the reform school and you know what I told you about that place.

You will have to admit in court that the reason you did not tell on me for killing them was because you loved me and didn't want to lose me, otherwise they will make it look like you helped me.

Then it will force me to tell about something else we did. I will have to tell all that in court if you talk too much. Just imagine what that will do to your reputation.

Read this carefully. Do not say in court that you ever heard me plan to kill Sonny and Ernest.

You must not admit we were intimate more than a couple of times and don't admit that I ever gave you morphine. I still love you with all my heart, but is it true, what I read in the Herald, that you told the attorney you do not love me any more? Do as I say.

Toivo

The introduction of the letter came as a complete surprise to Attorney Knipe, who strongly objected to it being admitted into evidence. Judge Brickey overruled the objection, however, on the grounds that it was rebuttal evidence and therefore not required to be disclosed in advance to the defense counsel. The letter belied Hawkins' sworn testimony he had killed the Grimm brothers in self-defense. Recalled to the stand, the defendant admitted he had written the document.

On Friday morning, December 17, 1937, Judge Brickey delivered his lengthy instructions to the jury, followed by Prosecutor Welts and Attorney Knipe's closing arguments. The case went to the jurors at exactly 2:45 p.m. and after deliberating for only 43 minutes, they returned a verdict of guilty on both counts of first degree murder and recommended the death penalty for each. Hawkins sat unmoved in the courtroom.

Sentenced

Clifford Hawkins' mug shot. Washington State Archives.

On Saturday, December 18, 1937, Attorney Knipe filed a motion in Skagit County Superior Court asking for a new trial on various grounds, including newly discovered exculpatory evidence and the surprise introduction of Hawkins' letter to Edith. However, at his sentencing hearing on Thursday, December 23, 1937, Hawkins withdrew his appeal for a new trial and requested the earliest possible execution date be set. Judge Brickey acquiesced and sentenced the condemned prisoner to be hanged at the Washington State Penitentiary on Wednesday, February 23, 1938. Hawkins was remanded to the custody of the Skagit County sheriff and on Monday, January 3, 1938, he was transferred to the penitentiary at Walla Walla.

While sitting on death row and contemplating his demise, Hawkins had a change of heart. On Tuesday, February 15, 1938, he sent a telegram to Attorney Knipe asking him to file an appeal for a new trial with the Washington State Supreme Court in Olympia. Knipe replied by letter that he had waited too long and that further appeal was impossible. His only recourse, he proposed, was to petition Washington State Governor Clarence D. Martin for executive clemency, but said that in reality there wasn't enough time for that course of action either.

At 5 p.m. on Tuesday, February 22, 1938, Hawkins ate his last meal, consisting of fried chicken, mashed potatoes, pie, ice cream and coffee. Afterward, penitentiary chaplains Rev. Arvid C. Ohrnell and Dr. Eli T. Allen stayed with the condemned prisoner throughout the evening. Just before midnight, Clifford Hawkins was shaved, dressed in a set of new clothes and taken from his cell on death row to the execution chamber. He was accompanied by Warden James M. McCauley, two chaplains and two prison guards.

Hawkins calmly approached the scaffold and climbed the 13 steps to the platform without assistance. After reading aloud the death warrant, Warden McCauley asked the condemned prisoner if he had any last words. "All I have to say is goodbye, Edith," Hawkins murmured. The state executioner stood him on the trap, pulled a cloth hood over his head, and set the hangman's noose. At 12:02 a.m., on Wednesday February 23, the trapdoor dropped beneath Hawkins' feet and at 12:17 a.m., he was pronounced dead by the attending physicians. His body was placed in a cheap pine coffin and taken to the prison morgue.

The execution was attended by a large crowd of 103 people, comprised mostly of law enforcement officers who were in Walla Walla attending the Eastern Washington Sheriffs and Police Chiefs Association conference. After a brief memorial service, his unclaimed body was buried in the penitentiary cemetery with a crude marker identifying the grave only as inmate No. 17265. Hawkins was the 41st prisoner and the first from Skagit County to be executed at the penitentiary since the Washington State Legislature mandated in 1901 that all executions take place there.

What happened to Edith Grimm is unknown. The 1940 U.S. Census shows that her mother, Ethel Grimm, age 55, was living on Warner Street in Sedro-Woolley with sons Jay, Earl and Roy Jr. Edith isn't enumerated in the federal census and her name doesn't reappear in the region's newspapers.

Penalty Is Paid
By Salem Native

Clifford Hawkins, 26, native of Salem, who was hanged at Walla Walla prison early today.

Hawkins Executed As Double Slayer

Walks Quietly to Gallows and Says 'Goodbye' to Cause of Crimes

WALLA WALLA, Feb. 23.— (Wednesday)—(AP)—Clifford Hawkins, 26-year-old farm hand who slew two brothers because they objected to his intimacies with their 13-year-old sister, was hanged on the gallows of the state prison here early today.

Oregon Statesman.

Chapter 10
The Mysterious Hermit Smith

Hermit Who Was
Killed in Woods

T HE above picture was taken of Hermit Smith as he lay in front
of his cabin where he had been shot down from ambush. The
picture was taken by Deputy Sheriff Dunham, of Skagit
County.

Hermit Smith never heard the bullet that hit him. American Reveille, September 10, 1909.

On Friday, September 10, 1909, Swiss born Frank Urfer, accompanied by two women, was working his way back to Wickersham from a fishing
trip. Starting the day before, they had been fishing parts of Skookum Creek

and the South Fork of the Nooksack River under perfect temperatures. They meandered along the Skagit-Whatcom County border, and were about to make the last push over to Whatcom again to head for home.

It was still early in the day; Urfer was probably tired of fishing and wanted to have some fun with the women. He was well acquainted with the terrain, and knew that they were in close vicinity to the infamous Hermit Smith's cabin. A week prior there had been a slight uproar by ranchers that a "Wildman" was purported to be living in the woods. Stories evolved into tall tales of a crazed man carrying cattle from the fields back to his cabin, where he would devour them. Receiving several complaints, the sheriff's office sent a couple of deputies out, and after hours of searching, discovered a harmless hermit living deep in the woods. Proving to be extremely anti-social, they deemed the man no threat and left him in peace. It was Friday that Urfer decided to stop by the hermit's place to take a break.

It took Urfer about an hour to locate the thin path leading to the cabin. The women were nervous, but excited to see the reputed recluse. As the hermit's cabin had been the source of much mystery since he was declared a "Wildman" by the press, they approached the cabin with caution. The small dwelling seemed to be deserted. Urfer called out to the hermit to give him fair warning and so that they wouldn't risk getting shot at. When the trio got closer they found Hermit Smith lying face up near his door, next to a sitting log. He had acquired his own "bouquet" due to a lack of hygiene, but this combined with an influx of insects swarming about, feasting on his corpse signified to the passerby that the hermit was dead. The poor old recluse had a bullet hole through his head. The projectile had entered just below the back of his ear and had exited through the back of his neck, shattering the bones and creating a rather large hole.

Frank Urfer and the two women hiked eight miles to the Ferguson camp of the Bellingham Logging & Timber Co., near Saxon. Urfer left the women there so that he could hurry on to Acme and notify authorities.

Because the cabin most likely lay on the Skagit side of the line, a call went to Skagit Sheriff Charles W. Stevenson.

Stevenson was an unlikely lawman. He was from Illinois, and just how he ended up westward is unknown. At 46 years old, he was still a single man, living alone in a boarding house. Murder or not, Stevenson wasn't about to tromp around the woods for a dead hermit. Instead, he sent an apparently more agile Deputy, Robert K. Dunham, along with Skagit County Coroner Dr. Cassills on the mountainous mission.

A glance through turn-of-the century newspapers reveals an energetic Dunham appearing throughout Skagit County, arresting troublemakers, smugglers and drunks, breaking up brawls and settling domestic troubles. Stevenson was always mentioned, but usually after the fact and seemed quite at ease to work from the office.

On September 10th, Coroner Cassills and Deputy Sheriff Dunham went to Acme in Whatcom County, expecting to find the corpse of the hermit. Before their departure, it had been reported to Dunham that the old man had been found dead by a fisherman and the corpse was carried out to Acme. When they reached Acme, there was no corpse, and no one could be found who knew anything about it. Finally, a man was located who had been notified by Urfer that Smith was dead at his cabin. Cassills and Deputy Sheriff Dunham immediately started into the hills to investigate.

Acme liveryman James C. McCoy offered to guide the men. McCoy knew the area, having traipsed the same hills many times while hunting. The cabin was claimed to be located seven miles into the forest, past the end of the wagon road, which extended a short distance above the mouth of Skookum Creek. On arrival, Dr. Cassills, who would decide if an inquest was in order, would make an examination of the body. If the investigation resulted in no indications of foul play, the corpse would be buried beside the cabin and no inquest would be ordered. Dunham packed a camera to document Smith, the crime scene, and any evidence.

The three men arrived at their destination, and sure enough, Hermit Smith lay dead, just as Urfer had claimed, his eyes glossed over with a white glaze. Cassills determined Smith had been dead four or five days. A grass straw was still sticking between his teeth, which he must have been gnawing on at the time of his death.

Cassills made his observations, hypothesizing based on the bullet's trajectory. He believed that Smith was sitting on the log, perhaps in contemplation or deep meditation, with his head down, sucking on a straw. Smith would have had to be sitting with his head hung low, as the bullet's impact came from an upward angle hitting him high, near the back of the ear and exiting low, out from the neck. Cassills noted no powder burns, so Smith was shot from a distance. He couldn't be sure if it were a hunting accident, a stray bullet, or premeditated murder. Cassills calculated the bullet's direction and ordered Dunham and McCoy to search an area from which he speculated the bullet originated for any clues.

Over a hundred feet away, near a clump of bushes the men found a man-made blind. Limbs were snapped off to create a better line of vision, and the ground was marked up enough to indicate that someone was lying in wait for some time. On the ground an empty rifle cartridge was discovered. Deputy Dunham determined that the cartridge came from a .32 caliber automatic Winchester rifle.

The officers searched for hours in the vicinity of the cabin in hopes of finding other traces of the assassin. Surrounding trails were carefully examined, but nothing out of the ordinary was found. The cabin was searched, but it appeared to have never been entered by the murderer. The interior was sparse with only a bed, minimal furniture, canned food and a crossbow. An examination of Hermit Smith's clothes yielded $20 in gold and silver, which seemed to insinuate that the motive was not theft, but possibly revenge.

With no method of removing the decaying body to Mount Vernon and no witnesses or substantial evidence to present, the coroner decided to forgo an inquest. After photos were taken and statistics about the hermit were noted, McCoy assisted Dunham and Cassills in digging a grave near the cabin, where Hermit Smith was laid to rest. The two Skagit officials were clueless as to where Smith had come from, but believed that he was no true dweller of the woods. He was not living off the land; his cabin was well stocked with canned goods. He kept up a clean appearance, as best as he could under his living conditions. Most notably were Smith's soft hands showing only months of calluses and few blisters; they were not the hands of a hard-working man. After Smith's burial, Coroner Cassills said a few words over his grave. He took Smith's few personal effects back to Mount Vernon, where Deputy Sheriff Dunham would attempt to find some of Smith's relatives.

American Reveille, September 10, 1909.

It was assumed that Smith, whose real name was never discovered, must have been in hiding. The murderer, perhaps an old enemy, might have discovered his hideout and followed hidden trails to Smith's cabin to avoid detection. The murderer would have then found a vantage point and waited for a good mark. A flash, a report, a groan, and the last scene of a mysterious tragedy concluded.

Who Was Hermit Smith?

In the weeks before his death, ranchers who knew nothing of Smith had heard strange reports of a wild man living in the woods. In fear of having livestock and crops stolen they telephoned into the Bellingham and Mount Vernon sheriffs' offices, requesting for them to look into the matter. Deputy Sheriff Wallace Coleman of Whatcom County and a Skagit deputy were sent out to investigate. After a long search, they found Smith's cabin.

Anticipating that they would find a crazed man, they were greatly surprised to find that the recluse was not only sane, but also thoroughly intelligent. He answered their questions politely, but firmly evaded all questions about himself and gave his name only as "Smith".

In appearance, the hermit was of powerful physique, just shy of six-foot, and weighed about 200 pounds. He had medium complexion with blue eyes, light blond hair, a sandy mustache, and a neatly clipped beard. He was neglectful of his clothing; the deputies noted upon their interview that Smith's attire was in filthy condition. Something in the way Smith lived or looked encouraged Coleman to conclude that there was something mentally wrong with him.

Coleman noticed by the narrow trench that had been worn into the ground along the porch, that the man had spent a great deal of time pacing back and forth in front of his cabin. The officers believed Smith was either some fugitive or ex-con in hiding, and though he was living in the woods, it was clearly not due to financial conditions. Regardless of their impression, the man had done nothing illegal and neither deputy saw justification to haul him in.

In Prairie,[1] Saxon, Wickersham and Acme,[2] residents had their own suspicions regarding Hermit Smith. None of them believed that it was a

---

1   Skagit County.

2   Whatcom County.

thief's doing; rather, they speculated that it was a "deadly enemy" who, after years of searching, had found and killed his quarry. Amongst the rumor mill, there was no doubt that it was a revenge slaying. "Smith" villagers said, "had a good reason for concealing himself behind what he thought was an impregnable barrier." When the story of his death was published in newspapers, it was thought "the unknown assassin" seeking the death of Smith learned the whereabouts of his enemy.

HERMIT'S LIFE AND DEATH VEILED IN MYSTERY

Officers Find No Clue That May Serve as Key to Unlock Secret Which Recluse Took With Him to His Grave—Motive for Murder In Hills Baffles Skill of Detectives.

Bellingham Herald.

Those who spoke with Smith before his death said that he had acted strangely and opted out of conversation at every opportunity. Upon reflection, it was opined that he was in constant dread and fear from some unseen fiend. He seemed to be restless and very nervous. Once a week Smith would come into Acme to purchase necessary supplies, and he always paid in cash. People would comment that Smith, seemingly gruff, was in fact approachable, but his attitude was such that curiosity seekers were discouraged from getting any information out of him.

At the time the story was made public, settlers and backwoodsmen believed Smith the Wildman, was either a recluse or an escaped convict seeking concealment from the authorities in the dense forests. Still others believed him to be insane. Now that Smith was murdered, and not by a thief, the story of Hermit Smith's life resembled that of a modern crime novelette. The mystery would play well in local papers as articles soon read like romance crime novels. Part of a *Bellingham Morning Reveille* column read:

> "...all the towns and settlements on the edge of the 'forest primeval' to which the lonely man had fled for refuge in his trouble, are wondering over this new chapter of romance and tragedy of the west. Under the shadowy branches of the lonesome firs, with the whispering wind on tree tops the only requiem...only the firs, spruces and cedars were the silent witnesses of the tragedy. Their wind swept branches struggled uselessly to tell, but their whispers of the secret fell on ears deaf to the languages."

The sheriff's newspaper photographs of Smith were recognized at Big Lake, near Mount Vernon, where the man of mystery was believed to be Frank Tallman, who had been employed at a logging camp in 1905. Beyond discovering the name, authorities attempting to trace the man's history learned little else. While at Big Lake, Tallman was said to be secretive. He was silent about his past and no one knew where he had come from. Tallman was known to never drink or spend money, and just what he did with his wages was never known. He kept to himself, was regarded as miserable and his actions were so eccentric that he was considered slightly demented. He seemed suspicious of all those around him and was always wary of new arrivals. Tallman worked several months steadily, after which he drew his pay and disappeared. The authorities couldn't be sure – was Tallman their Hermit Smith?

The Simpkins Theory

Once the story of a missing Tallman got wind, theories ran rampant as to the hermit's true identity once more. Bellingham Chief of Police, 51 year-old Hiram M. Cade, was sitting behind his desk on Friday, September 17th, when he picked up the sheriff's circular from a few days before. The hermit affair was a case for the sheriff's office, but was more of a Skagit County problem. Still, Cade picked up the circular and looked at some of the photos that Deputy Sheriff Dunham had taken of Smith. Dunham had taken a complete set of photographs of the corpse and the cabin's surroundings. Cade read the description of Smith.

The sheriff's circular set off a buzzing in Cade's head. Why? He couldn't put a finger on it. He stared at the paper for a while, wondering why the photo seemed familiar to him. Then it hit him; the photo was none other than Jack Simpkins, implicated in the brutal Union bombing of ex-Governor Frank J. Steunenberg at Caldwell, Idaho, on the evening of December 30, 1905. At least that was Cade's conclusion. Cade hurried off a message to Seattle for another circular, and for all updates in the search for Simpkins to be forward to him immediately.

The Steunenberg affair[3] was the biggest news in the nation four years prior. It was another episode in a long series of clashes in the war between labor unions and industry. Jack Simpkins, who was an executive committee member of the Western Federation of Miners (WFM), was believed to be an accomplice in the Caldwell bombing. It was alleged he was in Caldwell

---

3   Targeted for his role in quelling a miner's strike in 1899, former Idaho governor Frank Steunenberg was wounded by a powerful bomb that was triggered when he opened the gate to his home in Caldwell, ID. He died shortly afterwards in his own bed. Steunenberg's actions restored order in the Idaho silver mines, but also earned him the lasting enmity of many radical WFM members. Six years later, the radicals took their revenge by sending a professional assassin named Harry Orchard to Caldwell.

to either participate or to keep a watchful eye on Harry Orchard,[4] who was charged with the assassination. This would make sense, as Simpkins was in charge of WFM Idaho operations. Whatever Simpkins' participation was remained a mystery, as he soon disappeared.

Rumors persisted for years that Jack Simpkins was either dead, had committed suicide, or had slipped away and was hiding in a different country.

In the aftermath of the Caldwell bombing, suspects were rounded up and put on trial. Orchard turned state's evidence and accused three WFM union leaders[5] of planning the murder: the President Charles H. Moyer, Secretary-Treasurer "Big Bill" William Haywood[6] and George A. Pettibone. Meanwhile, Pinkerton detective James McParland, noted for his successes against the Molly Maguires,[7] was hot on Simpkins' trail. McParland considered Simpkins the missing link in the affair, as he would have been the man who received the order to kill Steunenberg, and see that it was carried out.

The greatest fear was that Simpkins would turn state's evidence, as Orchard had done. Even the lawyers defending Haywood, Moyer, and Pettibone tried locating Simpkins, but with no success. He simply vanished.

Chief of Police Hiram Cade

Once Chief Cade received updates from Seattle regarding Simpkins, he compared the photos and descriptions, convinced that it was the same man. Simpkins had black hair, but Hermit Smith's hair was a golden blond.

---

4   The professional hitman was responsible for planting the bomb that killed the former governor. Orchard was captured, tried, and sentenced to life in prison, and his guilt has never been seriously disputed.

5   Many were convinced that the plot to kill Steunenberg was supported not just by a radical minority within the WFM, but also by its top leadership."

6   WFM secretary-treasurer William "Big Bill" Haywood was brought up on charges of criminal conspiracy but was found not guilty largely as a result of famous Chicago lawyer Clarence Darrow's brilliant defense.

7   The "Molly Maguires" was an Irish 19th century secret society active in Ireland, Liverpool and United States. They were mostly known for their activism amongst Irish American coal miners in Pennsylvania. After a series of often violent conflicts, twenty suspected members of the Molly Maguires were convicted of murder and other crimes and were executed by hanging in 1877-78.

Otherwise, the two descriptions were identical. Cade suspected that Smith had colored his hair with peroxide and claimed, "If the murdered man was Simpkins, it is more than likely that he had the presence of mind to dye his hair." The face, forehead, nose, prominent upper teeth, thick shoulders, and a peculiar ear were all distinctive marks of identification and were the same in each man's photograph. "If Smith was not the murderer of Steunenberg, then Jack Simpkins had a double in this world, a man who resembled him more closely than a twin could resemble a brother," asserted Cade.

American Reveille, September 19, 1909.

Physical characteristics on the Pinkerton's poster reported Simpkins to have had blue eyes, a medium complexion, with hair that grew high on the forehead. He was 40 years old, 5 feet, 9 or 10 inches in height, thick chested, and had a shifty, peculiar glance. He was described as having a long ear with its inside fold bulging, set well down at the base of the skull and tilted back to the top. These characteristics applied to both Simpkins and Smith alike. The Pinkerton's poster offered a $2,000 reward for his capture and it was declared that it was not safe for him to be alive as the prosecution had evidence in their possession that would convict him of being a part of Steunenberg's assassination.

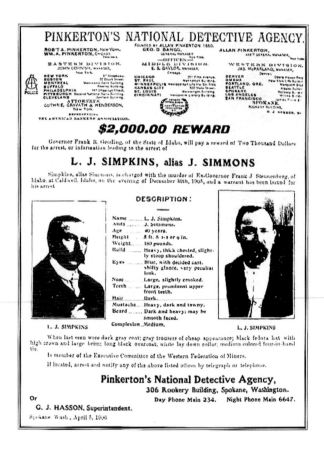

Pinkerton Detective Agency wanted poster for L. J. Simpkins.

Pinkerton Description of Jack Simkins.	Description of "Hermit" Smith Furnished by Deputy Sheriff R. K. Durham, of Skagit County.
Name—L. J. Simpkins. Age—40 years. Height—5 feet 9 or 10 inches. Weight—180 pounds. Build — Heavy, thick chested, slightly stooped. Eyes—Blue, with decided cast, shifty glance, very peculiar look. Nose—Large, hooked. Teeth—Large, prominent upper teeth. Hair—Dark. Mustache—Heavy and dark. Beard—Dark and heavy; may be smooth faced. Complexion—Medium. Ear—Inside coil bulged out, set low on the head, top tilted back.	Name—Unknown. Age—40 years. Height—5 feet 10 inches. Weight 182 pounds. Build—Heavy, broad shouldered, thick chested, stooped. Eyes—Blue, very peculiar look. Nose—Roman, large. Teeth—Big, sound, upper teeth very prominent. Hair—Golden and short. Beard—Blonde, stubble. Complexion—Medium Ear—Inside coil bulged out, set low on the head, top tilted back.

Comparing the information on the Pinkerton wanted poster to the description of Hermit Smith.
American Reveille, September 19, 1909.

Comparing images of L. J. Simpkins and Hermit Smith.
American Reveille, September 19, 1909.

"In vain," said Cade, "did the authorities endeavor to locate and capture Simpkins. Harry Orchard was branded as the most fiendish criminal this country has ever produced and is now a prisoner. Daily it was thought the Pinkerton Agency would nab their man. Unless something comes up to prove the contrary I shall always be convinced that 'Hermit' Smith and Jack Simpkins are one and the same person. If I had been furnished with (Deputy Sheriff Robert) Dunham's description of Smith before the hermit was killed I would have arrested him for Simpkins. But now the hermit's lips are sealed, the descriptions tally perfectly, all but the hair color, and that is often made golden with drugs…besides, why was the hermit shot? What did he fear? What reason can be given for his secluded and unnatural life? Who had a good reason for getting him out of the way? I don't think the Idaho authorities did it. That is entirely beyond the bounds of reason. They would have arrested him. Nothing dealing with man's criminal actions need be a mystery. You read about such mysteries in books and there are some in real life, but I say that when you come to consider what Simpkins had to live down, and the reasons he might have for living just as Smith did, the latter's life and peculiar actions can be accounted for…And now I'm as satisfied of the hermit's identity as any man can be."

Chief Hiram Cade seriously believed he had Jack Simpkins in the ground, and would so for the rest of his life, yet somehow he was unable to convince others. He sent photos and descriptions to the Pinkerton and Idaho authorities, but there is no record of anyone from the Pinkerton Agency ever visiting Bellingham, Mount Vernon or Police Chief Cade. Furthermore, no effort was made by Cade to retrieve Hermit Smith's body from his mountainside grave. Why no action was taken to prove the identity of Smith is not known, which is rather peculiar, as Jack Simpkins was never found, and his fate still remains a mystery. It would be reasonable to assume that Smith's cabin was an ideal place to hide out from the heat of a scandal.

An Alternative Story

If we think about it from all sides, we must ask ourselves – why would anyone assassinate a hermit? While researching what little exists about Smith, I discovered a one-page story from Marie Hamel Royer's, "The Saxon Story," where Chapter 22 reminisces, "The Mystery Man." Although it does not mention Smith by name or any of the participants surrounding his death specifically, I wanted to add it, as it gives another perspective regarding the mysterious hermit:

> "Someone had seen a man with a pack on his back walking up the road along the South Fork of the Nooksack River. Within a few weeks, someone else saw him at a distance headed up the river. Tom Nesset and his family recall seeing the outline of a man in the distance as they were driving along with their horse and buggy. When they reached that place in the road, there was no one there. But they did detect a man behind a small tree. Why was he avoiding detection? It was not long before the sparsely settled area of Saxon became aware of this 'mystery' man who walked with a pack up the river."

> "The owners of the Wickersham store reported that a man paid for groceries with twenty-dollar gold pieces. He

did not communicate other than what few words were required to make his purchases. He did not divulge his name. Sometimes when he got down in the valley, the mystery man changed his route and bought groceries from the store at Acme, which was in the opposite direction. It is also believed that he occasionally went over the Lyman Pass trail into Skagit County to make purchases."

"One evening a local hunter came off the hill from above the Dye area and came upon the old Portrate cabin. He could see by the partly opened door that a stranger occupied it. He knocked but did not get the usual hospitable response. However, he could see the bedroll and food on the table. The hunter went on his way a bit puzzled. Could the man have found gold while prospecting and wanted his identity kept secret? There was no need to report the stranger to the sheriff. He seemed to do no harm and tended only to his affairs."

"One sunny morning as A. O. Nesset approached the front of the cabin, he saw a man lying on the ground beside a chair – dead. An empty cartridge and a man's footprints were found on the ground at a nearby tree. It was surmised that the assailant had taken aim from that tree. Nesset went to Jake Rothenbuhler and another nearby neighbor. They came back, wrapped the corpse in bedding, and buried it by the cabin. The report at the sheriff's office read simply: 'White male about 50, shot with one bullet in the head. Name unknown.'"

There's no definitive answer regarding Hermit Smith or Jack Simpkins. It's wishful thinking that we could combine the two. But imagine, Smith as Simpkins, a wanted fugitive in the backcountry who was behind one of the leading union slayings of the twentieth-century, shot dead, seemingly out of the blue.

Chapter 11
The Marineer's Pageant Murder

The first Marineer Pageant, Anacortes Veneer float, Saturday, August 21, 1937.
Courtesy of the Anacortes Museum, Wally Funk #0349.

Martin Lavine was a black sheep, who grew corrupt with time. Born on November 26, 1900 in Marinette, Wisconsin, Lavine attended school until the 7th grade, where he quit at the age of 14 after several grade level failures, caused no doubt, from a miserable home life. His parents, Edward and Maude, moved to Anacortes, Washington shortly thereafter, leaving him in Wisconsin. At some point they divorced, and Maude would marry two or three times, eventually becoming Maude Spanenberg.[1] Martin's father, Edward, moved to Bothell, where he was a logger until his death in 1932.

Lavine, remaining in Wisconsin, worked at a lumber mill before relocating to South Dakota, where he stayed for two years. Beginning in 1919, he labored as a railroad worker. By the age of 18, he started to get in trouble with the law; most of his offenses were caused by heavy drinking. On October 10, 1920, he was sentenced to three years at the Wisconsin State Reformatory for auto theft. Lavine was granted parole, which was soon revoked, and he was placed back in confinement.

Martin Lavine was again paroled from the reformatory, this time placed in the hands of Sam D. Loper, a farmer in Fond du Lac, Wisconsin. Loper's farm was considered a work release farm, and Lavine fell under Loper's care.

Loper had an attractive 15 year-old daughter named Anna May,[2] who Lavine took a keen liking to. The pair began a sexual relationship and soon enough disappeared with Loper's automobile, so that they could elope in Woodstock, Illinois. Martin Lavine and Anna May Loper married on May 29, 1925.

The newlyweds traveled around the country in Loper's automobile until they reached Skagit County, Washington in October 1925, where Lavine's parents had been living for the previous two years.

On February 12, 1926 Lavine was apprehended for burglary. After the home of Mrs. C. Eddy, in Anacortes was "looted" on February 2nd, a stolen framed photo from the home was sold at a second hand store and traced back to Lavine. In the local newspaper's report of the crime, it was mentioned that Anna May was soon to become a mother.

Mrs. Essie Loper, Anna May's enraged mother, charged Lavine with abduction. Lavine was returned to Fond du Lac to be held by reformatory

---

1   Maude married George Spanenberg; together they lived at 1218 M Avenue.

2   Also known as "Eva."

officers. Nothing more was documented regarding Anna May; a few articles mention that there was an annulment, as she was underage and without parental permission for marriage.

Two years later, in March 1929, 28 year-old Lavine went back to Anacortes, where he immediately met and married 13 year-old Christine Frances Nicholson[3] in Mt. Vernon. At the time, Nicholson's mother, Harriet P. Bridgman, claimed that her daughter was 15 years old. The couple rented a home at 3908 32nd Street. A daughter, Isabella-Fern was born May 12, 1930, followed by Bellade May, Martin Jr., and lastly, Teddy, in 1935.

Lavine worked as a house painter for H. O. Davey of Anacortes in 1930, and did odd jobs in Seattle. He worked briefly for the Works Progress Administration (WPA), but was let go for drunkenness. Squalor, heavy drinking, smoking and fighting were a part of Lavine's daily routine. His children were said to be in deplorable condition, dirty and underfed. In 1934 Lavine received a 20-day sentence from Judge Davis, of King County for drunkenness and reckless driving. Judge Davis expressed the opinion that Lavine was an "immoral degenerate."

There were incessant rumors that Martin and Christine drank excessively. Christine was said to be reluctant to complain about her husband because she was afraid of him. When Lavine was arrested in 1934, Christine was with him, and was intoxicated as well, but she was released to go home to their children, who had been left there alone.

Sometime in 1935, Lavine befriended a man by the name of Frank Rollins, who started hanging out at his home. Rather quickly, it was claimed, Rollins and Christine struck up an affair. Lavine alleged that the two of them would "spike" his drinks to knock him out so that they could go into the bedroom. The situation escalated enough that Lavine moved his family to Kirkland, where he took up work as a logger. Newfound harmony dispelled when Rollins started coming around their new home.

---

3   Born November 26, 1914.

One day Lavine came home to an empty house. Christine and the kids had returned to Anacortes, where they took up at Christine's father, Edgar Nicholson's home. Nicholson was well known in Anacortes as "Dirty Nick," which would indicate that the children were not met with a better environment. The home was located at 1109 3rd Street.[4]

Christine filed divorce proceedings with her attorney, Richard Schacht, and Martin Lavine returned to Anacortes to fight for custody. In her divorce action, Christine claimed that her husband threatened to kill her, that he had brandished a knife in front of the children, and that he had beaten her on various occasions. Lavine, in response to the divorce complaints, denied his wife's charges and asked for custody of the children, alleging his wife was not competent enough to care for them. Through the divorce, Christine would learn for the first time that her husband had served a term in the Wisconsin State prison system.

As the process was in play, the two finally agreed that Martin could see his children and that he would consent to a divorce and pay his wife $25 a month in alimony, pending that she would refrain contact with Rollins. She failed to keep this agreement.

Frank Rollins resumed his visits to the Nicholson home, and then rumors stirred that two other men, Sid Wills and Ted Strawser were paying Christine "extra" attention. Lavine would continually show up at his father-in-law's house drunk and looking to catch his wife in the act with another man. Christine obtained a restraining order to keep Lavine away from the house and children.

On Saturday, August 21, 1937 their quarrels came to a boil. The Anacortes Marineer's Pageant, soon to become an annual three-day event, had begun and Christine took the kids to watch the parade progress down Commercial Avenue. There were events all weekend, which drew thousands of tourists. Martin was not with his family, but attended the festivities with

---

4   Nicholson lived at this address in 1935-40. In 1930 he resided at 1020 17th. Harriet is not mentioned after 1930.

Dick and Mary Tasovac.[5] During the merriment, Martin mentioned that he was angry with his wife and wouldn't mind seeing her dead. Mary responded, "Now Martin, you don't mean that," to which Martin remarked that he didn't give a darn for his wife.

Martin left the Marineer's Pageant and spent the rest of the day hitting bars and drinking beer. In one barroom, Martin saw a snapshot in Ted Strawser's wallet of Strawser with his arm around Christine. Strawser was a 27 year-old Fidalgo laborer, who picked up odd jobs and who was trying to get through the Depression like the rest of society. He had a reputation as being a ladies' man. Seeing the photo was more than Lavine could stand; he grabbed at the billfold, pulled the photo out, tore it up, and stomped out. By evening, all hell broke loose.

The Attack

Martin Lavine arrived at Edgar Nicholson's home with a .32 caliber Colt automatic pistol in his possession at 10 pm that evening. He ran to the rear of the house and rapped on the back kitchen door with the butt of his gun. Edgar and Christine saw Martin, but chose to ignore him when they saw that he had a gun in hand. The children and visiting cousins were upstairs in their beds, sleeping after a long day at the Marineer's Pageant. The door was locked, so Martin ran around to the front. "Go away," yelled Christine.

It was late summer and the sun still hung in the sky. Christine had left the front door open for air. Lavine charged into the house claiming that he wanted to see his kids. It's likely he mentioned finding Strawser's photo of her. He ran toward the kitchen, while Christine demanded that he leave at once. Lavine brought the gun forward and the two struggled; Christine knocked it out of his hand, and it hit the stove before landing on the floor.

5   Some sources mention that it was Richard Tasovac, a Croatian fisherman, and his wife Pauline.

67 year-old Edgar, worried that things would escalate and aware that he wouldn't be able to put up much of fight, ran out the back door for the police station. Lavine reached for the gun. From here on, the story differs throughout the course of the investigation, trial and thereafter. Martin Lavine would later claim that the pistol's safety came ajar when it was dropped, and that it accidentally discharged "several times" when he picked it up. To be exact, five "accidental" shots were fired between the kitchen and the porch.

Edgar's neighbor, 46 year-old Lee Cudmore, heard the shots from his home across the street and ran over to the Nicholson's.[6] By the time he reached the house, Lavine and Christine were struggling in the living room. "Get out of here or he'll drill you," Christine yelled at Cudmore. He raced to a neighbor's to phone the police.

The gun discharged again. Lavine claimed that his wife fainted after one of the shots was fired, and that he didn't think she was hit.[7] A moment later she was up and running out the door. Lavine ran out to the porch, took aim and fired a few more rounds as Christine ran toward the neighbors. Christine didn't make it to the neighbors; she dropped dead on the sidewalk at 22 years old.

Standard Oil Complex, November 1909. To the right of the building marked "Red Crown" is 1108 3rd Street. Behind and to the right is the home of Edgar Nickolson at 1109 3rd Street. You can just make out the roof of the porch from which Lavine shot his estranged wife. Courtesy of the Anacortes Museum Deanna Ammons, #2013.026.002.

---

6   Leo Nicholson, an ALCo. mill worker and his wife, either "Anna" or "Nina."

7   Earlier reports claimed a bullet pierced her heart. It seems unlikely that she would have put up a continued struggle after a bullet had pierced her heart.

The scene of the crime as it is in 2015. Photo taken by the author

Locked Up

Anacortes police department, April 1936. Front row, left to right: Chief Harold Hinshaw, Unknown and Nick Petrish. Back row: Unknown, Lawrence Pollard, J. B. Goff and Marvin Beebe. Courtesy of the Anacortes Museum, Wally Funk #1849.

Shortly after 10 pm three calls came into the police station in rapid succession. Officer Tom, along with State Patrolmen Paul Schmoe and Oscar S. Buehler, who were in Anacortes to assist local police during the Marineer's Pageant responded to the calls. Police Chief Harold H. Hinshaw arrived a few minutes later, having been called from Eagles' Hall, where he was on duty during the festivities. They discovered Christine in front of the Cudmore residence, lying in a pool of blood.

After the shooting, Lavine ran upstairs and aroused two of the five sleeping children. He came out of the house with one child under each arm. One was Martin Jr., the other his little cousin Theodore, who was sleeping over. In the excitement, Lavine may not have noticed that he was carrying the wrong child. Once outside he released the children. A crowd gathered around him and he surrendered without resistance when officers arrived.

Deputy Sheriff Lester P. Finsen quoted Lavine as saying that he was glad that he killed his wife "so no one else could have her." At the police station Lavine asked if his wife was really dead. When it was confirmed, he became hysterical and started to sob.

Anacortes Daily Mercury, August 23, 1937.

Skagit County Prosecutor Richard Welts arrived and questioned Lavine at the police station. Welts held a general law practice for many years in the Skagit Valley. By 1937, he was forty-five years of age, had a small family and was freshly sworn in as the new county prosecutor. With Lavine he would be trying his first murder case. Lavine declared to Welts that he remembered shooting only one bullet at his wife in the parlor of the Nicholson home. He said that he shot her because of the divorce action brought against him by his wife, and because he was afraid that he wouldn't be able to see the children. In his hysteria, Lavine accused Frank Rollins for breaking up his home and pleaded for a "half-hour of liberty so he could get the Anacortes man."

Welts spoke with the county coroner, interviewed witnesses and visited the crime scene. The coroner said that the bullet that killed Mrs. Lavine entered her left side, broke a rib, and went through her heart and out the right side of her body. There were powder burns on her clothing where the bullet had entered, which indicated that the gun had been fired from close range. Lavine had fired several shots in the Nicholson home, three within the house and two from the front porch as Christine ran toward Lee Cudmore's.[8]

In the prosecutor's interview with Edgar Nicholson, Nicholson relayed that Lavine had first come to the backdoor of his home, upon which Christine had screamed. Lavine then ran around to the front door, stormed into the house in a foul mood and confronted Christine. Nicholson said that the two were scuffling in the front room when he heard one shot fired; since he didn't have a phone, he ran to the police station.

Cudmore, Nicholson's neighbor told the prosecutor that he saw Lavine enter the front door and after hearing a gunshot soon thereafter, he went to the Nicholson home. From his vantage point at the Nicholson's, he was able to see Lavine brandishing a gun as Christine struggled with him. He affirmed that Christine had yelled, "Get out of here or he'll drill you," in regards to Lavine, and recalled having heard three shots fired in all. Cudmore said that he raced to phone the police.

Twenty-four year-old Clarence Sherman, who lived across the street, watched the scene from the window of his home, afraid to go outside. He reported hearing two or three shots fired inside the house and three more times as Lavine stood on the front porch.

---

8   The amount of shots fired has differed amidst various accounts. Witnesses, police records, newspapers, court, prison and clemency records all give different numbers for shots fired and where on the property they were fired. The best assessment by the author is that Martin Lavine fired five rounds, three indoors and two from the porch.

On scene, police found four empty casings inside the house – three shell casings on the kitchen floor and one in the front room. One bullet had bounced off the kitchen floor and was lodged in the leg of a table in the dining room. Another was found in a doorsill.

Welts returned to question Lavine further, and found no alterations to his original story. According to Welts, Lavine insisted that what he had done was for his children. He feared that they "wouldn't grow up to be anything if they remained with their mother," claiming that she was not a proper influence on them and that their surroundings at "Dirty Nicks" were not satisfactory. As Lavine sobbed, he asked Welts what would become of his children, to which the prosecutor could not answer.

Prosecutor Welts declared that he would file Information for a first degree murder charge against Lavine within a few days.

Meanwhile, plans for Christine Lavine's funeral were changed three times. Originally she was meant to rest in Anacortes where she had lived until her death, then Mount Vernon, where she was born. At the last minute however, relatives decided to hold the service in Seattle. On the day of Christine's funeral, Lavine turned to Skagit County Jailer Ted Pierson, and said, "I suppose they're burying my old woman today."

Martin Lavine was 36 years old when he shot and killed Christine. He was described as short and stocky, standing at only five feet two and a half inches, and weighing 135 pounds. Ruddy in complexion, with blue eyes and a wreath of brown grey hair crowning the back and sides of his scalp made him look much older than he was. He wore heavy black-rimmed glasses and false upper teeth. There are no descriptions of Christine, but the coroner weighed her body and claimed it to be a pitiable 87 pounds. He reported that her slight weight, lack of nutrition and poor health seemed to be alcohol related.

Trial

On Tuesday, September 14th, Martin Lavine appeared in shirtsleeves and an open collar before Superior Court Judge Willard L. Brickey for arraignment. Brickey told him that his appearance was unacceptable. He asked Lavine if he had an attorney; Lavine said that he didn't and that it would take a day or two to make arrangements. Judge Brickey postponed the arraignment until the following day, Wednesday September 15th at 9:30 am, so that Lavine would have time to procure defense. He had an infected lower lip and complained of having stomach pain, so Welts said that he would see to his request for a doctor in the meantime. Lavine was confident about his case and told reporters that he would "come out all right."

By Wednesday Lavine was still without counsel and acknowledged that he didn't have enough funds to employ an attorney. Judge Brickey appointed former prosecutor, John W. Brisky to defend him. Immediately, Brisky stated that he would base his defense on temporary insanity.

When asked by reporters about the shooting, Lavine contended that it was accidental and that he hadn't intended on killing his wife. A *Mount Vernon Daily Herald* reporter called on Lavine in his cell and was told, "It's wrong to kill anyone, I guess, but what's done can't be helped." Then Lavine declared, "I understand 90 percent of Anacortes is for me." He finished the interview bitterly discussing the Anacortes men responsible for his trouble, reporting, "My little girl told me she saw one of them on the bed with my wife and I certainly objected to such goings on before the children. My wife denied it."

Lavine told the reporter that it was unfair that a restraining order was placed against him, when other men were allowed to go to his wife's home as they pleased. "I didn't think it was right to permit those men to go there and let the children sit on their laps when I wasn't allowed to," he said.

Much to Brisky's displeasure, the *Daily Herald* reporter and city editor Oliver Noce was given an interview with Lavine. The article quoted him thus:

"I ran into the kitchen with the gun in hand, thinking I could scare my wife into letting me see the children. I started to go up the stairs to see the children and we scuffled. My wife knocked the gun out of my hand and it struck the stove before falling to the floor. I think the safety was loose, for when I picked up the gun it fired. There were only two shots. My wife sank to the floor and I thought she had fainted. At the time, a child whose name I don't know came out from under the table, and my little boy came running from downstairs. My wife got up and walked out and as I went to the porch with the two children the cops were there. They told me my wife was dead. Hell, I didn't mean to kill her. I just wanted to scare her."

Lavine told Noce that he had never used a gun before and encouraged him to "give [him] a good write-up so people would know [his] side of the story."

Attorney John Brisky had to work fast in collecting witness names for his defense. He was worried that Lavine would shoot his mouth off to the press beyond that which he had already done. In the end, twenty-three witnesses were subpoenaed, including Pastors Rev. Donald Finlayson of the Presbyterian Church, Rev. R. K. Anderson from Congregational, Lavine's mother Maude Spanenberg, Attorney Richard Schacht,[9] Dick Tasovac, Arnold Walton, Sid Willis, Morgan Twilliger, Frank Rollins, Gab Turner, Harold Hinshaw, Attorney Ben Driftmier, and H. O. Davey, all from Anacortes.

---

9   Attorney Richard Schacht was Christine's attorney during the divorce proceedings.

Skagit County Prosecutor Richard Welts, seen top row far right. He was coach of the 1926 Anacortes High School basketball team. Courtesy of the Anacortes Museum, Wally Funk #1983.

Martin Lavine's defense attorney, John W. Brisky.
Courtesy of the Anacortes Museum, Wally Funk #3572.

On Monday, October 25, 1937, a jury list of 45 names was drawn. There was an original list of thirty-six jurors, but it was increased in an effort to include Skagit residents with "open minds" regarding the death penalty, and to buffer the original list of jurors in the case of exhaustion. Prosecutor Welts revealed for the first time that he would ask them to convict Lavine of first degree murder and send him to the hangman's noose, claiming that Lavine slew his estranged wife during a jealous outburst over her having filed divorce proceedings against him.

At 9:30 am, Judge Willard Brickey opened with the announcement that prospective jurors would be offered rooms on the third floor of the courthouse, as they would be sequestered during the trial. The selection of jurors from the list of forty-five progressed slowly; it was expected to take several days to finalize. In the morning session three were excused, two of which said that they did not believe in capital punishment and the third complained of defective hearing.

On October 28th proceedings were under way. Addressing the finalized jury of ten men and two women,[10] Skagit County Prosecutor Welts charged that Lavine planned to slay his wife Christine several days before she was shot down with a bullet through her heart. The prosecutor gave instructions to the jury as to their roles in the trial, completing shortly after 11 am. Judge Brickey called a recess; Welts was set to deliver his opening address when the court reconvened at 1:30 pm.

Defense Counsel John Brisky made a motion for a directed verdict of "not guilty" in the case against Martin Lavine, to which Judge Brickey denied. Brisky then pled that the charge be reduced from first degree to second degree murder, as the prosecution had not shown that the bullet that killed Mrs. Lavine was from the weapon fired by the accused. The court refused the motion.

---

10   The final jury included: E. A. Sulter, carpenter; M. Engdahl, farmer; A. B. Wilson, farmer; Mrs. Neal McLeod, housewife; I. W. Youngquist, farmer; Mrs. Wallace Sharpe, housewife; Harry E. Mullen, school bus driver; W. Goodwin, Washington Co-op Egg & Poultry plant; Grant Sisson, farmer; F. A. Riebe, farmer; Thomas Ellestade, farmer; and D. M. Munhall, farmer.

Attorney Brisky, in outlining the strategy of the defense, said that his client would maintain that he became temporarily insane because of his separation from his children, and the presence of another suitor at the home of Edgar Nicholson.

Prosecution

The state was well prepared to try its case. Prosecutor Welts spent the first day introducing a long list of witnesses and called Edgar Nicholson to the stand.

"Who pressed the gun?" Welts demanded.

"That man there," Nicholson, remarked, pointing dramatically at Lavine, who was sitting at the counsel's table with his mother.

"Name him!" Welts thundered.

"It was Martin Lavine," Nicholson shouted. Then, in a calmer voice, Nicholson reported how he had fled from the backdoor for the police station to get help, and as he did, he heard two shots fired from inside the house.

Helen McComas, who was the defendant's stepsister and a waitress at the Log Cabin Tavern, told the jury that on the day of the shooting Lavine had come into the tavern and asked for a gun, declaring that he was "going to shoot Christine."

Mr. and Mrs. Tasovac, who had watched the Marineer's Pageant Parade with Lavine on the day of the shooting, also told the jury that the defendant had threatened the life of Christine Lavine. They stated, "He didn't give a darn for his wife."

Deputy Sheriff Lester Finsen quoted Lavine as saying that he was "glad he killed his wife, so no one else could have her."

State Patrolman and Officer Paul Schmoe, who had taken custody of Lavine, said that Lavine reported that he "felt better" after shooting his wife and that "he felt better now that he had killed his wife because he knew she would not now go out with any other man." According to Schmoe, Lavine had asked his wife to come back to him; when she said 'No,' he shot her.

The next witness called by the state was County Clerk Will Ellis, who identified the restraining order issued in the Superior Court in the Lavine divorce case, restraining the defendant from interfering with or molesting his wife.

Former county probation officer Neil Richardson took the stand. He told Welts that Lavine came to him complaining about deplorable conditions at Edgar Nicholson's home. When asked if there was more to the conversation Richardson said, "Yes, I advised Lavine to bring this point out when the divorce action was aired" and that "He left in a high temper, declaring he was going to shoot his wife or the man who was keeping company with her." Richardson said that he visited Lavine in the county jail after the shooting, and offered that Lavine "...did what he said he was going to do."

Former Chief of Police, Alfred Sellenthin, of Anacortes, testified that Lavine had complained to him that other men were going out with his wife, and knew that there was little he could about it. Then both Sellenthin and Attorney Ben Driftmier testified that Lavine seemed nervous just before August 21st.

On cross-examination, defense counsel Brisky asked Richardson to name the "other man" for the record. Richardson replied, "Frank Rollins." Brisky also drew from Richardson an admission that he had investigated the Nicholson home and was convinced that it was indeed "no fit place for children."

William Hopke, an Anacortes apartment manager on 1011 3rd Street told the jury that Lavine had attempted to borrow a gun from him. Hopke said he advised Lavine that he had "better forget it."

John Jacobus, a 68 year-old Anacortes store keeper, told the jury that Lavine had asked to borrow a gun to scare off prowlers who were stealing his mother's geese. He loaned Lavine his Colt automatic. Presented with the gun in the courtroom, Jacobus said it looked like the weapon he loaned Lavine.

Lee Cudmore, Nicholson's neighbor, said that he saw Lavine go toward the Nicholson home on the night in question and that he had previously advised him to "stay away." Cudmore told the jury that when he heard the shots he entered the home and saw Lavine holding Christine by the arm and brandishing the weapon.

Mrs. Anna Cudmore testified that she heard Mrs. Lavine screaming, while Clarence Sherman, who lived directly across the street, told the jury he saw Mrs. Lavine run from the house and fall dead a short distance from the residence. Sherman said that he saw Lavine come out of the house and fire at his wife; he heard five shots and saw three of them.

Oscar Buehler of the state patrol, who took possession of the gun found later in the Nicholson home, identified the weapon and shell casings. He said Lavine was angry and despondent after the shooting.

The last witness called was *Daily Herald* city editor, Oliver Noce, who testified that Lavine contended that the shooting was accidental and did not, at the time, mention mental irresponsibility.

After the prosecution ended its case, Judge Brickey was met once more by the defense's motion for a direct verdict of not guilty, on the decree that prosecution had failed to produce enough evidence to support a guilty verdict. When this was denied, a motion to reduce the charge to second degree murder was brought forth and was further denied by Brickey.

Defense

Counsel John Brisky presented his case for the defense. Neil Richardson was recalled as Brisky's first witness. Brisky asked the former probation officer about prior testimony that Lavine had come to him after the divorce suit had been filed and complained that conditions at the Nicholson home were not fit for the children, as he had stated earlier. Richardson agreed that this was correct. Asked if, in his opinion, Lavine was correct in his statement, Richardson admitted that the Nicholson home was indeed an unfit place for children. Prosecutor Welts strenuously objected to Richardson's testimony, but Judge Brickey ruled it admissible.

Mrs. Maude Spangenberg, Lavine's mother, was the second witness called by defense. She testified that her son was noticeably upset over the separation from his children and the visits other men were paying his wife and could not eat nor sleep because of it.

Two Anacortes Ministers, Rev. R. D. Anderson and Rev. Donald Finlayson, testified that Lavine had complained to them about the Nicholson home's living conditions, claiming that it was not a fit place for his children, and how he had also stressed that his wife was going around with other men, who were interfering in his domestic affairs and making his life miserable.

Other testimony for the defense came from Nellie Hartman, a social worker, who said that she hadn't seen anything to be concerned about over at the Nicholson home, although she hadn't been upstairs.

Hartman's statement was followed by accounts from Attorney Richard Schacht, Christine's attorney in the divorce, who said that there had been an agreement whereby Lavine was granted time with the children.

Morgan Twilliger, a friend of Lavine's, said that he had warned Martin about Rollins and was thrown out of the Lavine home for speaking against Rollins at the time.[11]

The last person on the stand was Martin Lavine himself, speaking in his own defense. Brisky was prepared with his line of questioning. When Brisky brought attention to the shooting of Christine Lavine, he broke down completely and wept. "No man ever thought more of his wife than I did. She's the last person I wanted to see dead," Lavine told the jury with remorse.

---

11   This must have occurred when Lavine and Rollins were still friends, before he suspected Rollins of having relations with his wife, and was brought forth in trial to portray Lavine as sympathetic.

He posited how it could be that he would do such a thing with in-tention, if it meant never seeing his children again. He accused Christine of unfaithfulness, but admonished that it was no fault of hers, as they were happy together up until two years ago when Frank Rollins started coming to their house. Rollins was one of three men he would blame for the estrange-ment between himself and Christine. The other two were Sid Wills and Ted Strawser.

Lavine told the jury that his wife had admitted having intimate rela-tions with Rollins because Lavine had owed him five dollars. He said that he threw Rollins out of the house on several occasions, but that he kept return-ing. He told the jury that Rollins would bring liquor to his house and accused him and Christine of "spiking his drinks so they could go out together."

Lavine relayed the story of how he met Ted Strawser in a beer parlor the day he shot Christine, and how he found a picture of Strawser and his wife in Strawser's billfold, which he proceeded to tear up. Brisky asked the prosecutor to deliver the photo, which was admitted into evidence, taped back together. Welts submitted no objection, declaring that it had been "on the desk here all the time."

Lavine maintained that on the night of the shooting he went to the Nicholson home to see his children. He said that he knocked on the back door with the butt of a .32 Colt automatic pistol; when no one answered, he went around to the front door and walked into the house, casually concealing the weapon in his pocket so he wouldn't frighten the children if they were up.

Lavine said that he asked Christine if he could see the children, to which she refused, so he pushed her aside. At that time, he acknowledged, Nicholson had gone out the back door. He followed his wife into the kitchen, where Christine asked what he did with the gun and accused him of trying to hide it, so he took it out of his pocket.

According to Lavine, Christine knocked the gun from his hand and it struck the stove before falling to the floor, where he picked it up. "I think the safety catch on the weapon was jarred loose, for when I picked up the gun it fired," said Lavine. "I heard a shot and from then on I don't remember anything. She's the last person I wanted to see dead," he repeated, sobbing.

Lavine declared that he didn't know who fired the shot that killed his wife. In response to a question as to whether he had gone to the home with the intent to kill his wife, he answered emphatically, "No." He claimed that he had no recollection of how he got to jail or what he told officers thereafter. Regarding the testimony he had given authorities that he was glad his wife was dead, he denied making such statements.

Continuing to sob, Lavine accused his wife of hard drinking and going out with other men. "My wife isn't here to speak for herself and I don't want anybody here to take any pity on me. I didn't come here to lie and don't want anyone to lie for me," he said, continuing on with stories of his wife's alleged unfaithfulness and how his oldest daughter had told him she had seen Christine in bed with another man.

Lavine's testimony concluded the defense's case. The prosecution offered the testimony of four witnesses to refute portions of Lavine's story before resting.

Welts subjected Lavine to a grilling cross-examination, asking him how it was that he remembered everything leading up to the shooting with vivid clarity, but nothing thereafter. Over and over, Lavine repeated that he had no recollection of the tragedy. The prosecutor then drew from Lavine an admission to the court that he held a criminal record, was convicted in Wisconsin for auto-theft, had been arrested as a parole violator and had also been arrested for marrying two underage girls.

Defense Counsel John Brisky returned for questioning. Brisky called for Rollins, but he did not appear; he had the record show that Rollins had been subpoenaed, but could not be found. He then introduced a copy of the Lavine's marriage certificate showing that Christine's mother had sworn she was 15 at the time of marriage. The certificate was offered into evidence.

Dick Tasovac was recalled and said that it was true "Rollins caused Lavine a lot of trouble." He had seen Mrs. Lavine and Rollins kissing outside the Nicholson home, but his testimony was stricken when Welts brought out that Tasovac had never told Lavine about it.

Closing

In Prosecutor Richard Welts' first murder case, he gave his summation of the testimony and urged the jury to find Lavine guilty and to inflict upon him the death penalty. In his summation he stated, "Murder is usually committed in a sly manner, but this one is obviously clear in regard to premeditation." He recalled the testimony given about how Lavine had tried to borrow a gun, and the numerous threats he had made to kill his wife as indicators of premeditation.

Welts brought forward the fact that Christine had sought protection from her husband by obtaining a court order, and how "Lavine violated this and took the law into his own hands." The only tangible reason he had for killing her, Welts conferred, was that he had been through a tumultuous divorce and wanted to blacken her name.

Welts scathingly denounced Lavine, stating that he had "sealed the lips of his wife in death, so she could not come here and defend herself when he tried to drag her name through the filth in an effort to clear himself for her murder." Suddenly and startling the court, Lavine rose to his feet and shouted, "Aw, shut up!"

Mrs. Maude Spangenberg took hold of her son's arm to quiet him down as Judge Brickey rapped his gavel for order in the court. The judge shouted, "We'll have no more of this," and ordered Lavine to remain silent. The prosecutor continued, whereupon Lavine started weeping until the conclusion of the prosecutor's address. "Mrs. Lavine spent most of her married life bearing children for her husband, which is silent proof that there was not constant drinking of liquor, as claimed," Welts continued. He pointed out to the jury that:

> "Lavine made a grandstand play when he came out of the house with a child under each arm after the shooting and told an officer that one of the children was not his own. This shows that he knew what he was doing and was not mentally irresponsible at the time as he claims. He's crying now, but the tears are for himself, not for his wife or children."

In his own closing, Defense Attorney Brisky pleaded that Lavine be spared from the gallows, insisting that he had gone to the Nicholson house on August 21st to see his children, not to kill his wife. In an effort to tie up loose ends he said that Christine's mother was to blame for her daughter's marriage at the age of 13, since it was she who had lied so that the marriage license could be obtained.

"Martin tried in every way to help at home; he loved the children, helped take care of them, took them to Sunday school," Brisky declared.

> "Everything was going along nicely until Frank Rollins started coming to the home. The three of them would drink together. The association became noticeable that friends started warning Lavine about it. His wife admitted she'd been unfaithful. He forgave her because of his intense love for the children. They went to Kirkland, but Rollins followed them down there and tried to make trouble. Lavine stood for everything in an effort to preserve his home. I don't know of anything that could drive a man more quickly to insanity than to watch his home breaking up. Rollins

is the man that should be here on trial instead of Martin Lavine. Mr. Welts said murder is the worse crime that can be committed. There is a worse crime and that is breaking up a man's home. It injures more people that way. Frank Rollins committed a worse crime than Lavine ever thought of committing. Lavine's wife got a restraining order preventing Lavine from seeing his children. What more can a woman do to drive a man crazy?"

In rebuttal, Welts recalled that Mrs. Tasovac said Lavine had told her that "he didn't give a darn for his wife," and that county jailer Ted Pierson had heard Lavine say, "I suppose they're burying my old woman today." Welts also reiterated how *Daily Herald* city editor Oliver Noce interviewed Lavine as saying that the shooting was accidental, and how Lavine, at that time, made no mention of mental irresponsibility. Furthermore, Welts charged that Lavine "has come here to trial his divorce case having silenced his wife's lips in death. He knew no court would give him the children. He said on the stand he loved his wife, but Mrs. Tasovac said that he told her that he didn't give a darn about his wife, and you heard the comment he made the day of the Christine's funeral. Does this sound as if he loved her?"

Welts concluded by exposing that no evidence had been submitted to show that there was cause for temporary insanity.

The testimony ended; the state had called twenty-three witnesses and the defense had called fourteen.

The fate of Martin Lavine was placed in the hands of the jury on Friday, October 29, at 11:45 am. In his final instructions, Judge Brickey relayed the possible verdicts:

"The defendant is or is not guilty of first degree murder as charged. If guilty of first degree murder, shall the penalty be death? Did the defendant do the acts he is charged to have done? Do you acquit the defendant of the crime because of mental irresponsibility at the time of the commission of such acts by him? Does such mental irresponsibility continue and exist at this time? If such mental irresponsibility does not continue and exist at this time, is there such likelihood of a relapse or recurrence of such that the defendant is not a safe person to be at large?"

During jury deliberations, Lavine seemed more interested in the newspaper accounts of his trial than in his own fated outcome. He contacted the *Daily Herald* and asked for newspapers to be brought to him.

After the jury had deliberated for two hours and only after four rounds of voting, the verdict was returned at 3:30 pm. Grant Sisson, who had been elected jury foreman, passed the verdict to Bailiff Bob Rowley who passed it on to Judge Brickey. After studying the verdict a moment, the judge declared that it was not complete and instructed the jury to return to its room and complete it. When asked the question, "Shall the death penalty be inflicted?" The jury had voted against with the word "No,"[12] but had failed to decide upon the degree of guilt. A few minutes later the jury returned. They looked to Lavine, who was sitting with his head slightly bowed, staring at the floor. The verdict read, "Guilty in the first degree."

Attached to the verdict was a mandatory life sentence; the jury took pity on Lavine, saving him from the hangman's noose. As Deputy Sheriff Lester Finsen led him back to his cell, Lavine declared, "I'm not through yet. I'm going to get another trial."

---

12   Only two jurors favored the death penalty.

Saved From Death. Anacortes Daily Mercury, October 29, 1937.

A Daily Herald reporter visited Lavine at his cell. "I got a rotten trial," Lavine said. "I never for one minute thought I'd be found guilty of first degree murder. Up until the last minute, I thought I'd be acquitted." He blamed his conviction on not being permitted to bring out everything he wanted to about his wife and he complained that the court was "on the side of the law" during the trial, instead of his. Dogging his defense, Lavine said, "A smart criminal lawyer would have brought about my freedom," but offered that John Brisky had done a good job. "I got a rotten trial," he repeated, "and the public thinks so too."

After the Trial

The county welfare service was given custody of the Lavine children, who were written as having "endured physical and affectional [sic] discomfort in the home of the parents." It was found that they suffered from malnutrition, poor hygiene and a lack of discipline. They appeared to be nervous and underweight. One welfare representative, who had visited the Lavines at their home sometime earlier, reported that Martin and Christine swore at the children and treated them brutally. Relatives expressed an interest in caring for the children, but it was concluded that they were incapable.

The Chief of Police held that both parents were to be blamed, having answered several complaints from neighbors over the years for drunken brawls and domestic abuse. Neighbors complained that Lavine was a petty thief and believed that he had stolen chickens and other goods from their properties. It had been reported several times that the wife was cruel to the eldest, Isabel-Fern, and not a fit mother for the children. Isabel-Fern was given a psychological examination and found to be of "borderline mentality." She was emotionally unstable, partially resulting from her "traumatic and environmental history," and was offered mental services at that time.

Penitentiary Years – The Fun Begins!

Martin Lavine, alias Martin Albert Lavine alias Eddy Ross, was received into the Washington State Penitentiary at Walla Walla on December 1, 1937. He was given the designation, Prisoner No. 17231.

Comments on his prison medical entry record indicated that he was missing his right ring fingernail and that he had a seven-inch open scar on the right side of his stomach, a 4" x 3" surgical scar on his right shin, and another 2.5" scar curved under the back corner of his jaw line.

A hefty 180-page clemency file on Martin Lavine exists at the Washington State Archives in Olympia. The file sheds light on his incarceration. There are gaps in correspondence, where documents were not retained. Reading through what is available, it's obvious that Lavine cleverly used his time behind bars to manipulate others in supporting his cause for early release.

From 1937 to early 1944 Lavine appears to have been a model prisoner. In 1944, Warden Webb reported that Lavine was trustworthy, and he was permitted to work in paid work crews on nearby farms, in kitchens and creameries and was given paint shop duties. A note in his file indicated that he "Shows progress."

By 1945, Lavine figured that although he earned the trust of the prison system, that trust wasn't going to get him an early release. He wrote a barrage of letters to elicit support for early parole to state officials, but was twice denied parole by the Board of Prison Terms and Paroles. One response in his letter writing campaign came from the office of Governor Arthur B. Langlie dated December 18, 1944. In his response, Langlie said that he supported Judge Brickey's sentencing and was unwilling to intercede on the applicants' behalf. "It seems that in view of the defendant's previous record, heavy drinking and economic and social insecurity, plus his low intelligence, that (Lavine) would be a poor risk when on parole," said Langlie.

On April 28, 1945 at 12:30 pm, Lavine, feeling as though he was far from release, escaped from prison. Living a month on the run, he was captured and returned on May 28th. From here, he aimed to entice a larger audience to support his cause, and henceforth found religion. Lavine embraced all forms of religious orders, writing letters to anyone that would listen to his pleas for help. He converted from Protestantism to Judeo-Christianity, and endeavored to learn the bible inside out. He became a member of the Moody Bible Institution[13] and was ordained in 1949 by Reverend Paul Edgar of Auburn, Washington. He started signing all correspondence, "Rev. Martin Lavine" followed by, "Your in Him."

With his new ordained title, Lavine started a letter writing campaign to all the ministries in Washington State, asking them to write the governor and the parole board on his behalf. He claimed that his only meaning in life was to spread the Word of God, and to one day have a small church of his own.

---

13   The Moody Bible Institute (MBI) is a Christian institution of higher education ("training for those who may completely and effectively proclaim the gospel of Jesus Christ.") that was founded by evangelist and businessman Dwight Lyman Moody in 1886.

At one point, he met Governor Langlie while on a prison tour, and attempted to plea his case. The governor backed away, assuring Lavine he would look into the matter, as a means to cease interacting with him.

In a September 4, 1949 letter enlisting the help of Rev. Gilbert of Seattle, St Paul's Parish Episcopal wrote:

"Dear Brother Gilbert, I write this in Jesus' name. I love for you to call Brother Jack Nelson and ask Bro. Nelson to get some one to go over and talk to the Governor. I talked to the Governor here and he said he would keep me in mind. But the way the Governor talked, he has never seen or talked with no one about me and I need to have some one back me up and a man to take me in his care – so some one must go and talk face to face…"

A second letter was sent to Seattle Mayor William F. Devin:

"Dear Christian Bro + all in Christ's Greetings in our Lords dear name [sic]. So many good people think I can be a Paul here in prison. I was told to leave the men alone and not preach. I'm looking forward to being a Paul to the outside world…I caught my wife in bed two times and I was shooting in the dark at her and this man Frank Rollins was run out of Anacortes…The judge was my mother-in-law's lawyer years before and she had a baby by the judge, she too was run out of Skagit County."

A major supporter to Lavine's cause came from Reverend Dr. Armin A. Holzer, General Director of the Palestine Prayer Fellowship of Seattle. A diligent man, Holzer would write tens of letters to the governor and parole board and organized his worshipers to write daily and form petition volunteers to obtain signatures of support. Lavine's parole would be the Order's primary mission. Holzer then whipped up a frenzy of support from colleagues from the state's Lutheran, Episcopal and Baptist ministries.

Dr. Henry H. Ness, presiding chairman at the Board of Prison Terms and Paroles, was inundated with letters, petitions and daily phone calls for months because of Lavine. Holzer informed Ness in one letter "The Lord Jesus forgives us seventy times, seventy a day...Perhaps your honor will take that Divine Compassion into consideration." The campaign infuriated Ness, who had to allocate personnel to answer correspondence.

Lavine's efforts for freedom became compounded by yet another escape on July 22, 1950. While on outside garden crew, he walked off unnoticed; this time he managed to run for two months and twenty-four days before he was apprehended by the LAPD and detained in the Los Angeles County Jail, to be returned to Walla Walla on September 16, 1950. From Los Angeles he started another letter writing campaign stating that he had escaped after he had been brutally attacked by guards, including one in particular, Al Rumboldt, who he claimed made his life miserable. In a letter to Governor Arthur Langlie, he explained that it was officer Al Rumboldt that caused him to run off, telling Langlie to "Make him stop using me as a dog and to lay off me when I do go back." Lavine used the escape to explain to his growing supporters that he was abused and suppressed by the prison from spreading the Word and because he was a Christian-Jew.

Lavine's allegations fueled his supporters to increase their efforts under the pretext that he was being tormented and that his religious beliefs were being suppressed by the state. More letters were sent to Henry Ness wanting to know what was being done to release Lavine. Many letters cited correspondence from the prisoner's own letters, and referred to the governor's failed promise to look into the case. Ness was becoming increasingly perturbed and wrote Governor Langlie regarding the matter:

"I have just answered a letter directed to you from Reverend Armin A. Holzer (General Director Palestine Prayer Fellowship)…This man, Lavine, is nothing but a pest and is writing hundreds of letters and appealing to people everywhere…It seems to me the sensors [sic] at Walla Walla should not allow inmates to send letters out to their friends asking them to appeal to your offices or our office in their behalf. It takes up a lot of our time and as far as I can see, it is absolutely unnecessary."

In reply was a circled note to Ness on his letter: "Gov. did see him. Thought him a screw-ball."

Further petitions and letters streamed in from as far as Idaho and Montana, offering Lavine jobs and homes if released. The Universal Christian Hebrew Fellowship pleaded for the state Board of Prison Terms and Paroles for a pardon or reduction of sentence. As the pleas increased Henry Ness held his ground that Lavine was nothing more than a murderer, manipulating the masses. He wrote the governor that Lavine was just a cause for these religious groups, and once released, they would turn their backs on him and go straight to their next cause.

As time went on, some ardent followers were giving up on Lavine, or had awakened to his charade. A typical letter of Lavine's is provided below, alluding to his religious faith. It runs for pages, intermixed with pleas of support for release. In most cases he gets to the point only after five or six pages in – this one comes early:

"Dear Brother in our Messiah Christ Jesus. As it is Passover time starting last Friday, so my mind and heart has been with you my people. It has been over fourteen years since I have been able to enjoy our Passover and I think how wonderful it would be if Dr. Ness would let me out with you on my own again. I pray for the salvation of Israel and the peace of our people. I am sure we are in the last days, because our people have gone back home to Israel…I am alone with the Messiah's hand in mine. I wish the Messiah would open the way so all the Christian Jews would get together and petition Dr. Ness to let me out."

In response, a seemingly defeated or irritated Holzer answered back. The last correspondence by Holzer in Lavine's clemency file reads:

"Seemingly you have exhausted all the Protestant resources…It has occurred to me…why not turn to the Catholic Chaplain, sometimes they wield more of an influence in police circles than protestants. It may be a last resort…Forget your ordination. As far as I am concerned, it does not add anything to you. I rather think that it is a hindrance than a help and it isn't worth the paper it is written on…Signed, The Rev. Dr Armin A. Holzer, Palestine Prayer Fellowship General Director May 1, 1951."

A psychiatric report dated Jan 21, 1952, administered in Lavine's fifteenth year of incarceration dictates depression and despondency in:

"During the present interview Mr. Lavine was cooperative to the best of his ability which, however, was somewhat limited. He is unstable emotionally as well as retarded intellectually, reasoning power was poor and judgment was impaired. He claims to be very religious and that he has found his goal in life through religion. He is lacking in insight and rationalized on a superficial level. He seems easily led and very suggestible. Nothing in his behavior would suggest any psychotic or neurotic symptoms." Mr. Lavine is at present a case without psychosis, borderline intelligence with psychopathic trends...however because of his poor reasoning power, lack of insight and emotional instability he should be very carefully and strictly supervised, otherwise his ultimate outlook to civilian adjustment is only questionable. (Board of Prison Terms and Paroles – May 22, 1953) Dr. Henry H. Ness, Chairman."

Nothing more was written in Martin Lavine's clemency file that can offer us a picture of how he spent his last years at Walla Walla. It seems reasonable to assume that his supporters drifted away as their efforts failed to release him. Correspondence ceased regarding Lavine's religious crusade, begging us to wonder if it was a clever charade after all.

Despite all that worked against him, Lavine was finally released for good behavior and paroled to Wisconsin by Governor Albert Rosellini on November 27, 1961. He was last known to reside in Hennepin County, Minneapolis, Minnesota where he altered his last name to "Lavigne." Martin Lavine died on November 1, 1982.

Maps

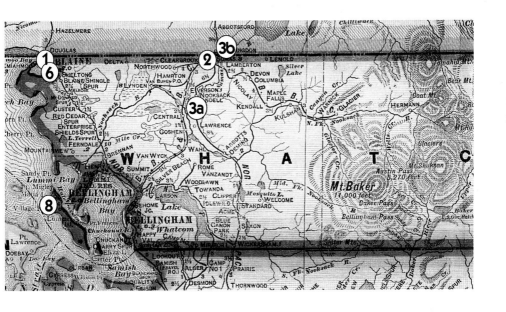

Whatcom County

1 ~ Addie Roper murder   2 ~ Young Shee Wah murder

3a ~ James Bell murder   3b ~ Louie Sam lynching

6 ~ McGuire family murder   8 ~ Double murders

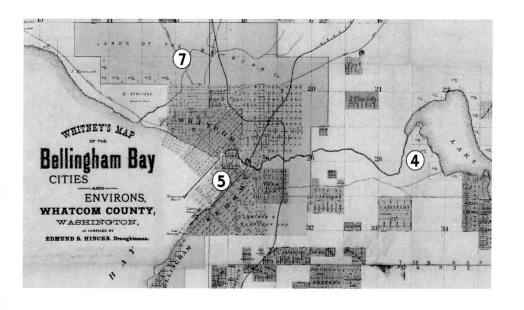

City of Bellingham

4 ~ Wilson murder

5 ~ George Ralph Shoemaker murder

7 ~ John Erickson murder

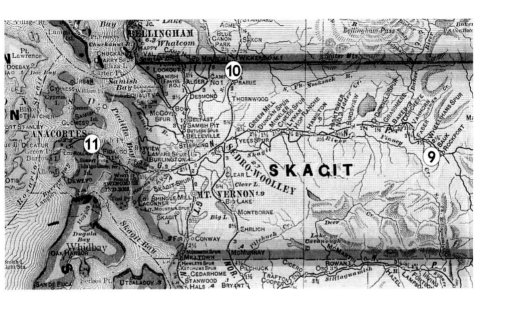

Skagit County

9 ~ Grimm murders
10 ~ Hermit Smith murder
11 ~ Christine Lavine murder

Law Enforcement
Photo Gallery

Bellingham Police Chief Hiram M. Cade

Chief of Police James E. Dorr

Whatcom Police Force standing on the steps of City Hall in 1902. Left to Right: Captain J. L. Parberry, Andrew Williams (later promoted to Chief and then to Sheriff), Patrick W. Jessup, Frank Alvord, Thomas Nugent, and Chief Clarence Logsdon. Photo courtesy of Whatcom Museum.

Bellingham Police Force, 1916

Police Judge Henry C. Beach

Captain of Police Alexander L. Callahan

City Detective Neil Blue

Desk Sergeant Charles Schysler

Desk Sergeant Frank Lock

Desk Sergeant George A. Sybrant

Desk Sergeant Nick Rust

Officer Patrick W. Jessup

Officer Michel Nugent

Officer Olaf E. Qualley

Officer Oliver Belland

Officer Gilbert Belland

Officer Jesse S. Johnston

Officer M. L. Lasse

Officer Benjamin H. Jordan

Officer Thomas Nugent

Officer A. S. Crosslin

Protective Officer Edith Fuller

Whatcom County Sheriff Andrew Williams

Deputy Sheriff Flanagan

Sheriff John Cave

Whatcom County Sheriff Spencer Van Zandt

New Jail 1917, Left to Right: Jailer William Carpentier, Deputy Chris Patterson, Deputy Al Medhurst, Head Deputy Sheriff J. B. Bennet and Sheriff Will D. Wallace. (GenWeb-Marcy Jonson.)

Whatcom Superior Court Judge Jeremiah Neterer   Whatcom Superior Court Judge William Pemberton

Whatcom Prosecutor Baldrey Loomis   Whatcom County Prosecutor Virgil Peringer

Attorney James B. Abrams   Whatcom Prosecuting Attorney George Livesay

Whatcom County Coroner J. Whitney Wear   Whatcom County Coroner Henry Thompson

Whatcom County Courthouse

City Hall. The city jail was in the basement. Bellingham police force, 1919.

Northern State Hospital at Sedro-Woolley, Washington.

Medical Lake (Eastern State) asylum.

Washington State Penitentiary, at Walla Walla, Washington.

BIBLIOGRAPHY

PART I

Chapter 1: Ghastly Dealings in Blaine

Books

Arbuckle, Marie, Lillian Barnes-Hinds, Carol Ann Post, and Marjorie
Reichhardt. "A Symbol of Our Heritage...The Old Fir Tree." *Blaine
Centennial History 1884-1984*. Lynden: Profile Publications, 1984.
Print.

DeHaven, T.H. "Clue of the Red Bandana." *True Detective Mysteries*. No. 2
ed. Vol. 33. 1939. Print.

Heise, Jack. "If Addie Had'a Trusted in Banks." *Official Detective Stories*. No.
8 ed. Vol. XII. 1944. Print.

Documents

Washington vs. William Allen Dell and Harry Watts #731. Justice Docket
Blaine Precinct, John Keen, Justice of the Peace. 13 Apr. 1907.
Print.

Washington v. William Allen Dell, Motion for a New Trial #751.
Washington State Superior Court, Whatcom County. N.d. Print.

Whatcom County Information filed on William Allen Dell. Washington
State Superior Court, Whatcom County. 4 Jan. 1907. Print.

State of Washington v. Harry Watts, Information for Murder in the First
        Degree #775. Washington State Superior Court, Whatcom County.
        N.d. Print.

State of Washington v. William Allen Dell, Affidavit #751. Washington
        State Superior Court, Whatcom County. N.d. Print.

Whatcom County in the Matter of the Application of Harry Watts for
        Writ of Habeas Corpus #723. Washington State Superior Court,
        Whatcom County. N.d. Print.

State of Washington v. Harry Watts Affidavit #775. Washington State
        Superior Court, Whatcom County. N.d. Print.

State of Washington v. Harry Watts Affidavit for Change of Venue #775.
        Washington State Superior Court, Whatcom County. N.d. Print.

State of Washington v. Harry Watts, Witnesses for the State. Washington
        State Superior Court, Whatcom County. N.d. Print.

State of Washington v. Harry Watts, Judgment and Sentence #775.
        Washington State Superior Court, Whatcom County. N.d. Print.

Washington State Penitentiary Inmate Register, #4741, #4897.

Washington State Penitentiary Clemency, #4678.

Whatcom County Criminal Index – Criminal Case Files: No. 716, 1 Apr 1907 Book 3. No. 723, 2 Apr 2007, Book 3. No. 751, 1 Aug 2007, Book 3. No. 775, 8 Oct 2007, Book 3.

Register of Deaths Reported to the Health Officer, Walla Walla, Washington Territory.

Washington State Department of Heath, Bureau of Vital Statistics.

Newspapers

Bellingham Herald [Bellingham] 21-25, 28, 31 Jan 1907: n. pag. Print.

Bellingham Herald [Bellingham] 1-2, 4-5, 14, 16, 18 Feb 1907: n. pag. Print.

Bellingham Herald [Bellingham] 13, 16 Mar 1907: n. pag. Print.

Bellingham Herald [Bellingham] 1 Apr 1907: n. pag. Print.

Bellingham Herald [Bellingham] 5-7, 9-14, 16, 18-21, 27 Sep 1907: n. pag. Print.

Bellingham Herald [Bellingham] 8-9, 22 Oct 1907: n. pag. Print.

Bellingham Herald [Bellingham] 2-3, 6, 10-14, 16-17 Dec 1907: n. pag. Print.

Bellingham Herald [Bellingham] 4, 8, 11 Jan 1908: n. pag. Print.

Bellingham Herald [Bellingham] 10 Feb 1908: n. pag. Print.

Bellingham Herald [Bellingham] 8 Apr 1908: n. pag. Print.

Morning Reveille [Bellingham] 22-23 Jan 1907: n. pag. Print.

Morning Reveille [Bellingham] 14 Apr 1909: n. pag. Print.

"Mystery of the Spinster, Slain for Her Gold." *Seattle Sunday Times, Pacific Parade Magazine* [Seattle] 28 Mar 1948: n. pag. Print.

Seattle Daily Times [Seattle] 18-19 Jan 1907: n. pag. Print.

Websites

www.sanborn.umi.com - Sanborn Map Company, 1907.

Chapter 2: Death on the Border

Documents

Department of Commerce and Labor Immigration Service Correspondence.

Eastern Washington Hospital for the Insane Commitment.

Examination of Lee Wing Wah, No. 825, Office of Chinese Inspection in Charge, Port of Sumas, Washington. 26 Apr1908.

State of Washington v. Lee Wing Wah, Information for Murder in the First Degree, No. 825. Whatcom Superior Court. Print.

State Penitentiary Correspondence, Walla Walla, 9 Mar 1910. Washington
State Archives, Olympia, Washington.

Washington State Penitentiary Order of Commitment.

Washington State Penitentiary Biographical Statement of Convict, #5451.

Washington State Penitentiary Convict Entrance Medical Examination, 17
July 1909.

Washington State Penitentiary Inmate Register, #5451.

Whatcom County Criminal Index – Criminal Case Files: No. 825, 2 May
1908 Book 3.

Newspapers

Bellingham Herald [Bellingham] 27-30 Apr. 1908: n. pag. Print.

Bellingham Herald [Bellingham] 2 May 1908: n. pag. Print.

Bellingham Herald [Bellingham] 5 May 1908: n. pag. Print.

Bellingham Herald [Bellingham] 2 June 1908: n. pag. Print.

Chapter 3: The Lynching of Louie Sam

The story, "The Lynching of Louie Sam," is supported by numerous
documents housed in the Provincial Archives In Victoria, B.C.,
the Vancouver City Archives, the Washington State Archives, from

several newspaper accounts, in addition to personal interviews with those who were there or who had personal knowledge of the events. The author, Jim Berg, has read several published accounts of these events and finds them incomplete in their research and documentation.

Chapter 4: Bulldog

Documents

Ada LeBarron vs. Howard LeBarron, Complaint. Whatcom Superior Court. 17 May 1916. Print.

Ada LeBarron vs. Howard LeBarron, Findings of Fact and Conclusions of Law, No. 12299. Whatcom Superior Court. 17 May 1916. Print.

Ada LeBarron vs. Howard LeBarron No. 12299. Whatcom Superior Court. 17 May 1916. Print.

Newspapers

American Reveille [Bellingham] 9 Jan 1917: n. pag. Print.

Bellingham Herald [Bellingham] 9 Jan 1917: n. pag. Print.

Websites

www.vitalrec.com/wa.html - Washington State Board of Health, Bureau of Vital Statistics Certificate of Marriage.

Chapter 5: Murder at the Turf Saloon

Documents

Bellingham Police Records. Washington State Regional Archives.

Whatcom County Criminal Index – Criminal Case Files: No. 950, 10 Sep 1909 Book 3.

Newspapers

Bellingham Herald [Bellingham] 8 Sep. 1909: n. pag. Print.

Bellingham Herald [Bellingham] 4-6, 8 Nov. 1909: n. pag. Print.

Bellingham Herald [Bellingham] 30 June 1914: n. pag. Print.

Morning Reveille [Bellingham] 8-9 Sep. 1909: n. pag. Print.

Morning Reveille [Bellingham] 4, 6, 9 Nov. 1909: n. pag. Print.

Websites

www.ancestry.com

www.digitalarchives.wa.gov

www.geneologybank.com

www.heritagequest.com

www.wagenweb.org

Chapter 6: Terrible Tragedy in Blaine

Documents

"Whatcom County Superior Court: Petition for Admission, Probate and
    Letters of Administration, Estate of Otis I. McGuire and Orpha –
    Superior Court of the State of Washington for Whatcom County.
    No. 5691." 9 July 1925, 28 Jan 1926, 30 Jan 1926, 8 Mar 1926, 26
    Mar 1926.

Newspapers

Blaine Journal [Blaine] 28 Nov 1919: n. pag. Print.

Seattle Times [Seattle] 25 Nov 1919: n. pag. Print.

Websites

www.ancestry.com

www.digitalarchives.wa.gov - Marriage Return, #2808.

www.geneologybank.com

www.heritagequest.com

www.wagenweb.org

Chapter 7: For a Man's House is His Castle

Documents

Bird v. Holbrook, 4 Bing #628, 130 Eng. Rep. 911. 1825. Print.

Katko v. Briney 183 NW 2d 657. Iowa Supreme Court. 1971. Print.

Superior Court of Whatcom County, at New Whatcom, State of
    Washington Judgment and Sentence.

Washington State Executive Office, Pardon.

Newspapers

Bellingham Bay Express [Bellingham] 12-16 Dec 1893: n. pag. Print.

Daily Reveille [Whatcom-New Whatcom] 13-14 Dec 1893. n. pag. Print.

Daily Reveille [Whatcom-New Whatcom] 13-16 Feb 1894: n. pag. Print.

Daily Reveille [Whatcom-New Whatcom] 1 Mar 1894: n. pag. Print.

Daily Reveille [Whatcom-New Whatcom] 28-29 Mar 1894: n. pag. Print.

Daily Reveille [Whatcom-New Whatcom] 10 May 1895: n. pag. Print.

Weekly World 22 Dec 1893: n. pag. Print.

Websites

www.ancestry.com - U.S. Census. Washington: 1900.

www.digitalarchives.wa.gov - *Certificate of Death: John Erickson.* Filed 12
    Dec 1893. State of Washington, Whatcom County Death Returns,
    1891-1907. Doc. No. 98.

Chapter 8: Double-Murder on Lummi Island

Books

Jeffcott, P.R. "Nooksack Tales and Trails." *Sedro-Woolley Courier-Times.*
    Ferndale, Washington, 1949. Print.

Newspapers

"Capture of the Indian Murderers." *The Northern Light* [Blaine] 4 Sep 1858: n. pag. Print.

"Two White Men Murdered by Indians." *The Northern Light* [Blaine] 28 Aug 1858: n. pag. Print.

PART II

Chapter 9: Grimm Murders in Sauk Valley

Books

Van Clute, Jack, "Washington's Enigma of Missing Men," *True Detective Mysteries*, Vol. 30, No. 4, Nov 1938, p. 66+.

William Sewell, "Murder in the Cascades," *Crime Detective*, Vol. 1, No. 3, Feb 1939, p 76+.

Documents

U.S. Census, Lewis County, Washington: 1930.

U.S. Census, Skagit County, Washington: 1920, 1930, 1940.

Newspapers

Mount Vernon Daily Herald [Mt. Vernon] 13 Nov. 1937: n. pag. Print.

Mount Vernon Daily Herald [Mt. Vernon] 15-17 Nov. 1937: n. pag. Print.

Mount Vernon Daily Herald [Mt. Vernon] 24 Nov. 1937: n. pag. Print.

Mount Vernon Daily Herald [Mt. Vernon] 1 Dec. 1937: n. pag. Print.

Mount Vernon Daily Herald [Mt. Vernon] 7 Dec. 1937: n. pag. Print.

Mount Vernon Daily Herald [Mt. Vernon] 13-18 Dec. 1937: n. pag. Print.

Mount Vernon Daily Herald [Mt. Vernon] 23 Dec. 1937: n. pag. Print.

Mount Vernon Daily Herald [Mt. Vernon] 28 Dec. 1937: n. pag. Print.

Mount Vernon Daily Herald [Mt. Vernon] 19 Feb. 1938: n. pag. Print.

Mount Vernon Daily Herald [Mt. Vernon] 23 Feb. 1938: n. pag. Print.

The Concrete Herald [Concrete] 18 Nov. 1937: n. pag. Print.

The Concrete Herald [Concrete] 25 Nov. 1937: n, pag. Print.

The Concrete Herald [Concrete] 2 Dec. 1937: n. pag. Print.

The Concrete Herald [Concrete] 9 Dec. 1939: n. pag. Print.

The Concrete Herald [Concrete] 16 Dec. 1937: n. pag. Print.

The Concrete Herald [Concrete] 30 Dec. 1937: n. pag. Print.

The Concrete Herald [Concrete] 23 Feb. 1938: n. pag. Print.

The Oregon Statesman [Salem] 14 Nov. 1937: n. pag. Print.

The Oregon Statesman [Salem] 16-18 Dec. 1937: n. pag. Print.

The Oregon Statesman [Salem] 23 Feb. 1938: n. pag. Print.

The Seattle Times [Seattle] 13 Nov. 1937: n. pag. Print.

The Seattle Times [Seattle] 9 Dec. 1937: n. pag. Print.

The Seattle Times [Seattle] 16 Dec. 1937: n. pag. Print.

The Seattle Times [Seattle] 30 Dec. 1937: n. pag. Print.

The Seattle Times [Seattle] 23 Feb. 1938: n. pag. Print.

Walla Walla Union Bulletin [Walla Walla] 23 Feb. 1938: n. pag. Print.

Websites

www.ancestry.com

www.digitalarchives.wa.gov

Chapter 10: The Mysterious Hermit Smith

Books/Magazines

Grover, David H. "The Disappearing Dynamiter." *True West* July 1988: n. pag. Web.

Royer, Marie Hamel. *The Saxon Story: Early Pioneers on the South Fork*. Vol. 2, Bellingham: Whatcom County Historical Society, 1982. Print.

Newspapers

American Reveille [Bellingham] 19 Sep 1909: n. pag. Print.

Bellingham Herald [Bellingham] 11 Sep 1909: n. pag. Print.

Bellingham Herald [Bellingham] 13 Sep 1909: n. pag. Print.

Bellingham Herald [Bellingham] 17 Sep 1909: n. pag. Print.

Morning Reveille [Bellingham] 15 Sep 1909: n. pag. Print.

Chapter 11: The Marineer's Pageant Murder

Documents

Skagit County Directory: 1937.

Washington State Board of Prison Terms and Paroles Correspondence.

Washington State Penitentiary Commitment Record.

Washington Sate Penitentiary Inmate File #17231 Clemency.

Newspapers

Anacortes Daily Mercury [Anacortes] 23 Aug. 1937: n. pag. Print.

Anacortes Daily Mercury [Anacortes] 29 Aug. 1937: n. pag. Print.

Bellingham Herald [Bellingham] 23 Aug. 1937: n. pag. Print.

Bellingham Herald [Bellingham] 25 Aug. 1937: n, pag. Print.

Bellingham Herald [Bellingham] 28 Aug. 1937: n. pag. Print.

Bellingham Herald [Bellingham] 14 Sep. 1937: n. pag. Print.

Bellingham Herald [Bellingham] 26 Oct. 1937: n. pag. Print.

Bellingham Herald [Bellingham] 28-30 Oct. 1937: n. pag. Print.

Mount Vernon Daily Herald [Mt. Vernon] 13 Sep. 1937: n. pag. Print.

Mount Vernon Daily Herald [Mt. Vernon] 16 Sep. 1937: n. pag. Print.

Mount Vernon Daily Herald [Mt. Vernon] 21 Oct. 1937: n. pag. Print.

Mount Vernon Daily Herald [Mt. Vernon] 25-30 Oct. 1937: n. pag. Print.

Mount Vernon Daily Herald [Mt. Vernon] 2 Nov. 1937: n. pag. Print.

Websites

www.ancestry.com - U.S. Census. Wisconsin and Washington: 1890, 1900, 1930, and 1940.

www.digitalarchives.wa.gov

T. A. Warger is an historian and filmmaker based in Bellingham, Washington. Warger is the recipient of the 2009 Washington State Historical Society's David Douglas Award for the documentary film *Shipyard* (2008). His latest documentary, *The Mountain Runners* (2012), is an award-winning and Emmy-nominated film about the 1911-13 Mount Baker Marathon. He is the co-author of *Mount Baker (Images of America)*, and is a contributor to the Whatcom County Historical Society's *Journal* as well as the Journal of the Puget Sound Maritime Historical Society's *Sea Chest*. Warger received his B.A. from the University of Nevada and graduate studies from Western Washington University. Warger is on staff at the Whatcom Museum.